JUDAISM

Monika Grübel

BARRON'S

American text version by: Editorial Office Sulzer-Reichel, Rösrath, Germany
Translated by: Ann Jeffers-Brown, Cambridge, Mass.
Edited by: Bessie Blum, Cambridge, Mass.

First edition for the United States and Canada
published by Barron's Educational Series, Inc., 1997.

First published in the Federal Republic of Germany in 1996 by
DuMont Buchverlag GmbH und Co. Kommanditgesellschaft, Köln.

All inquiries should be addressed to:
Barron's Educational Series, Inc.
250 Wireless Boulevard
Hauppauge, New York 11788

Library of Congress Catalog Card No. 96-78857

ISBN 0-7641-0051-3

Printed in Italy by Editoriale Libraria

Contents

Preface

A crash course in Judaism—is that really possible?

As soon as one attempts to define "Judaism," difficulties arise. Does the term refer to a religion? A culture? A people? The answer is yes, yes, and yes. It refers to all of these, and any introduction to Judaism must address all three.

The history of the people of Israel begins with the revelation on Mount Sinai. From the beginning, tribe and religion formed a unity. For over two thousand years, however, the dispersion of the Diaspora has been a fundamental fact of Jewish existence. Jewish life has evolved in many cultures and places under widely varying circumstances. Thus, Jewish history is characterized by unity and diversity.

This book presents the basics of Jewish history, religion, and culture in graphic and understandable form. It can make no claim to being exhaustive—the breadth of the subject precludes such a claim in so short a space. Its particular aim is to combine a concise textual overview with illustrations that help the reader visualize and understand important aspects of Jewish history.

This crash course in Judaism presents a connected narrative of the important epochs and centers of Jewish history from ancient times to the present. However, since each chapter is essentially autonomous, the book can also be used as a reference.

The Jewish calendar and holidays, the stages of the life cycle, and dietary laws are covered in independent mini-chapters, in which I address aspects of life as practiced by traditional, orthodox Jews. However, Jewish life has always been characterized by great plurality, and the very broad nature of the term itself includes a wide range of outlooks, lifestyles, traditions, and practices. Jewish life today may be seen as following three main paths—Orthodox, Conservative, and Reform Judaism—that differ greatly in their relationship to Jewish tradition in practice and understanding, giving rise to controversies over a number of issues, such as the role of women. Important new impulses for Jewish life are likely to emerge from this ongoing debate.

A detailed glossary, a timeline of Jewish history, a list of Jewish museums around the world, a select bibliography, and an index round out the book.

A technical note: the English form of Hebrew words used here is based on common American English usage, the terms should be accessible and understandable for the layperson. Further, the abbreviations BC and AD have been replaced with BCE (before the common, or Christian, era) and CE (common era).

Monika Grübel, Köln

Anyone who is interested in the early history of Israel should read the bible, for it is the most important—indeed, often the only—source for the origins of the Jewish people. The first great era of Jewish history, the time before the Israelites settled in Canaan, is described in the five books of the Pentateuch (the Torah). The second great era includes the period of settlement and history in the country itself. The capture of Jerusalem, the destruction of the First Temple, and the exile into Babylon end the flow of biblical history as a connected narrative.

Israel before the settling of the land: The age of the patriarchs

The patriarchs Abraham, Isaac, and Jacob lived with their families and flocks in Canaan. They left the country only rarely, for example during famines, and returned again and again. They were not settlers, but tent dwellers. Thus, the memory of nomadic custom became engrained in the patriarchal stories of Israel, but the bible gives no indication of the exact time. Some scientists have unearthed names, law records, and details of life in archaeological finds and nonbiblical texts—many of them names that are also found in the patriarchal stories—and have used such data to try to date the age of the patriarchs. Suggested dates range between 2000 and 1200 BCE. The bible emphasizes the role of the three patriarchs as bearers of a two-pronged divine promise, or covenant: the increase of their progeny, which would

1 Abraham looks to the stars. Lithograph by E.M. Lilien, 1908: "I will make your offspring as numerous as the stars of heaven and as the sand that is on the seashore. And your offspring shall possess the gate of their enemies, and by your offspring shall all the nations of the earth gain blessing for themselves" (Gen. 22:16).

form the people of Israel, and the continuing occupation of the land of Canaan. These two themes recur again and again, for example, in the promise of God to Abraham: "I will make you exceedingly fruitful; and I will make nations of you, and kings shall come from you. I will establish my covenant between me and you, and your offspring after you throughout their generations ... And I will give to you, and to your offspring after you, the land where you are now an alien, all the land of Canaan, for a perpetual holding" (Gen. 17:6–8) (1).

ca. 13th century – 586 BCE

2 The Israelites work as slaves on the buildings of the pharaoh. *Golden Haggadah*, Spain, ca. 1320 CE.

The exodus from Egypt

At the beginning of the book of Exodus, Israel is described for the first time as a people, but is in Egypt. The Egyptians had enslaved the Israelites, whom they considered undesirable aliens, to erect the monumental buildings of Pitom and Ramses (2). After many years of slavery and bitter disputes with the pharaoh, which led to the divine curses of the ten plagues, Moses led his people to freedom. The story of the tenth plague, the killing of the first-born in Egypt, is the source of the Passover holiday (see p. 22) (3).

The overarching theme, however, is the salvation of Israel through Moses, the deliverer sent by God. This tradition fits into the construction of the cities Pitom and Ramses, which also appear in Egyptian texts, during the reign of Pharaoh Ramses II. That means the exodus—if it was an historical event—took place before the end of the 13th century BCE.

3 The tenth plague: Killing of the first born. *Rylands-Haggadah*, Spain, second quarter, 14th century CE. The following text is inscribed next to the picture: "Pharaoh arose in the night, he and all his officials and all the Egyptians; and there was a loud cry in Egypt, for there was not a house without someone dead" (Exod. 13:20).

Israel in the wilderness: Revelation at Sinai

With Exodus 19:1 begins the tradition of Israel's sojourn at Sinai. God's revelation of the Ten Commandments (the Decalogue) forms the central

4 The revelation on Sinai: Moses receives the golden tablets in the midst of a thick cloud; a *shofar* (ram's horn trumpet) resounds in his ear: "On the morning of the third day there was thunder and lightning, as well as a thick cloud on the mountain, and a blast of a trumpet so loud that all the people who were in the camp trembled" (Exod. 19:16). *Sarajevo-Haggadah*, Spain, 14th century CE.

event of the story, accompanied by powerful natural phenomena (thunder, lightning, thick clouds, loud noise). Moses played a key role: Only he was allowed to meet God on the mountain, and God spoke only to him, while the people listened from afar (**4**). Moses also received God's order to share the commandments with the people. It is difficult to create a historical reconstruction of these events. Among students of biblical history, opinions and claims range from complete denial of Moses' historical existence to far-reaching acceptance of the biblical account.

Whatever its factual basis, the biblical account of God's revelation to Moses serves as the foundation of the Jewish religion. The Ten Commandments became the Magna Carta of the Jews who are God's chosen people, governed in their spiritual and daily lives by obedience to the Torah.

With the exception of the story of the Decalogue revelation, the recurring theme in the narrative of the Israelites' wanderings in the wilderness is the people's chafing against the leadership of Moses and his brother Aaron. The Israelites complained of thirst and hunger and reproached Moses for leading them out of Egypt only to land them in a worse predicament. Their protests were ultimately directed against God, who punished them by proclaiming that none of those who fled Egypt would see the promised land, but they would wander in the desert for forty years until the last of the ungrateful exodus generation had died. Joshua and Caleb were the only survivors; even Moses was forbidden entrance into the promised land. In a farewell address, he repeated all the laws proclaimed to the Israelites during their wanderings. He then climbed Mount Nebo, where he died.

Only after Moses' death, the Israelites under Joshua's leadership crossed the Jordan river and began to conquer Canaan. Joshua was Moses' successor, but he was no second Moses. Joshua's instructions were clear: The Torah was completed, he had it before him, and he had to use it as his guide.

Settling the land

The first large-scale turning point in the history of Israel led to the settlement in Canaan. Historians have two hypotheses about how the land was conquered. Most believe that the Israelite tribes acquired the land by a fairly peaceful process, a gradual settling. Some, however, believe that it was a definite immigration and warlike invasion, as described in the biblical account of Joshua.

The time of the Judges

The Israelites who conquered and divided the promised land were still not a nation, but a loose union of tribes who were often attacked by surrounding peoples. Under the influence of their neighbors, they often betrayed their one God (Yahweh) and honored other gods. The bible says that God punished this idolatry by delivering these defectors into their enemies' power: "the anger of the Lord was kindled against Israel, and he gave them over to plunderers who plundered them, and he sold them into the power of their enemies all around" (Judg. 2:14). "But when the Israelites cried out to the Lord, the Lord raised up a deliverer for the Israelites, who delivered them" (Judg. 3:8-9).

This deliverer, a charismatic personality who freed them from their enemies, served as military commander and judge, taught the Torah, and strengthened the feeling of solidarity among the tribes. Under his leadership began a time of

> Then Moses went up from the plains of Moab to Mount Nebo ... and the Lord showed him the whole land. ... The Lord said to him, "This is the land of which I swore to Abraham, to Isaac, and to Jacob, saying, 'I will give it to your descendants'; I have let you see it with your eyes, but you shall not cross over there." Then Moses, the servant of the Lord, died there ... at the Lord's command.
> Deut. 34:1–6

The Anointing of Saul as the First King

5 Samuel is consecrated by his parents to God. *Pesach-Haggadah*, southern Germany, 1470–1500 CE.

prosperity and peace. With the death of the Judge, his influence passed, and the sequence of events—betrayal, crisis, repentance, salvation—repeated itself. The book of Judges looks back upon this period in a negative light. Between the time of Joshua's strengthening leadership and the beginning of the monarchy, the age of Judges was a time of anarchy in which each individual apparently did as he or she wanted. The lack of a stable government over a long period was a serious weakness of the tribal organization. The biblical record seems to reflect the actual character of the age in which Israel was still not unified.

The anointing of Saul as the first king

The book of Samuel records the beginning of the monarchy, starting with the introduction of Samuel (5), who appears to have been the last judge in Israel. The people turned to Samuel and asked him to give them a king. Threatened by the military superiority of the Philistines, the Israelites faced an ongoing danger not limited to the time of a single judge; combatting it required a continuous, strong authority. So Samuel launched a new age in the history of Israel by anointing on God's behalf the one chosen for the new office of king: Saul from the tribe of Benjamin. At first, Saul's successes as king fulfilled all expectations: He defeated the Ammonites in Gilead, the Moabites, the Amalekites, and others, but most importantly his army halted the advance of the Philistines.

His relationship with Samuel, however, was troubled, for Saul repeatedly opposed God's orders as transmitted through Samuel. Ultimately Samuel informed Saul that God had rejected

Now the day before Saul came, the Lord had revealed to Samuel: "Tomorrow about this time I will send to you a man from the land of Benjamin, and you shall anoint him to be ruler over my people Israel. He shall save my people from the hand of the Philistines; for I have seen the suffering of my people, because their outcry has come to me."
1 Sam. 9:15–17

him. Another was chosen to found the first royal dynasty in Israel: David, of the tribe of Judah, from Bethlehem (6).

King David

David, too, was anointed on God's behalf by Samuel. The history of his ascent is essentially a history of the dispute with Saul, from whom David had fled to the archenemies of Israel, the Philistines, whose vassal he had become. This ambivalent position was typical of David, and characterizes his traditional image. A short time later, he mourned the death of Saul in moving words, and began immediately and purposefully to prepare to succeed to the throne. First he became king of Judah. After a civil war that lasted more than seven years, the agents of the northern tribes also offered him the crown, and David became king of both Judah and Israel. The tenuousness of this union became clear after Solomon's death, at the latest.

David conquered Jerusalem, which was at the time occupied by the Jebusites, and made it his capital. He had several practical reasons for doing so: The city's location was strategically favorable and relatively easy to defend. It lay near the boundary of Judah and Israel and did not belong to any of the twelve tribes.

By bringing the Ark of the Covenant to Jerusalem, David established the city as the religious and cultural center of the Jewish people. (Israel celebrated David's founding of the state of Israel from September 1995 to January 1997 under the motto "Jerusalem 3000.")

David's political successes are described only briefly in the bible. He conquered the Philistines,

O Lord, how many are my foes!/Many are rising against me;/many are saying to me,/ "There is no help for you in God." Selah/ But you, O Lord, are a shield around me,/my glory, and the one who lifts up my head./ I cry aloud to the Lord, /and he answers me from his holy hill. Selah
Ps. 3:1–4

ca. 13th century – 586 BCE

6 King Saul with his army, and David slaying Goliath the Philistine. Folk painting, oil on glass, Jerusalem, 20th century.

ca. 13th century – 586 BCE

7 David's great kingdom, from the Euphrates to the boundary of Egypt.

subjugated the Moabites, Ammonites, and Edomites, and extended his power to the north by conquering the Aramaic states of Zoba and Damascus. Thus, Israel's influence extended from the Euphrates to the boundary of Egypt (7).

David is remembered not only as a great king and commander, but also as a gifted artist. He was known for his singing, dancing, and harp playing, and is traditionally considered the author of the book of Psalms (8). Before the bible relates the second significant part of David's history, the problem of the succession to the throne, the prophet Nathan transmitted the word of God: David's descendant will build the Temple, and his kingdom will stand forever.

King Solomon

The history of Solomon, the son of David and Bathseba, begins with the end of the reign of David. After the abolition of his final adversaries, Solomon had the dominion firmly in his hand. Thus began a long period of peace, for Solomon preferred gathering wealth to waging war.

8 "King David as Harpist." Marc Chagall (1887– 1985), cover illustration for the VERVE Bible I. Gouache, 1956.

His politics did not take place on the battlefield, but in the diplomatic arena, with a clear emphasis on trade relations. The many foreign women in his harem (see 1 Kings 11:1) suggest close connections to the lands from which they originated: Moab, Ammon, Edom, Sidon, and Hatti.

14

The story of King Solomon is characterized by three outstanding qualities: Solomon's proverbial wisdom (9), his royal power and pageantry, and his ambitious construction activity.

Solomon's Temple

The bible describes Solomon's buildings in Jerusalem, a Temple and a royal palace, at length. David had already bought the property for the Temple, the threshing floor of the Jebusite Arawna, to erect an altar. Reconstructions of the Temple are based solely on the description in I Kings 6–8 and II Chronicles 2–4. The Temple complex consisted of the Temple itself and several courts: the women were housed in a forecourt; the men participated in ceremonies in the interior court, separate from the inner court (*azarah*), which only the priests were allowed to enter. In this inner court stood the large sacrificial altar, the Bronze Sea—a powerful cast-metal basin standing on the backs of twelve oxen—as well as other implements required for ceremonial sacrifices (10). The Temple itself was an elongated building, divided into three rooms: the entrance hall (*ulam*), before which stood the two huge cast-metal columns of Jachin and Boas; the main chamber (*hekhal*), with the smoking altar, the table for the shewbread (twelve loaves brought there each week for the priests), and ten lamps; and the inner sanctum (*devir*), where the Ark of the Covenant was kept, with the tablets of the law and the two Cherubim, and which

ca. 13th century – 586 BCE

9 The Judgment of Solomon. Anonymous, northeastern France, 13th century. The bible repeatedly emphasizes Solomon's wisdom. This figure illustrates the famous story of two women who came to Solomon to resolve their dispute: each had borne a child, only one of which survived, and both claimed to be the mother of the living child. Solomon decided to cut the child in half to satisfy both and declared the woman who withdrew her claim the true mother, and awarded her the child (1 Kings 3:16–28).

10 The Bronze Sea. Altar of Nicolas of Verdun in Klosterneuburg. Enamel, 12th century. "Then he made the molten sea; .... It stood on twelve oxen, three facing north, three facing west, three facing south, and three facing east; the sea was set on them. The hindquarters of each were toward the inside" (1 Kings 7:23–26).

15

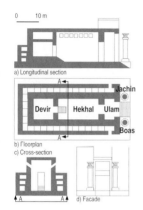

a) Longitudinal section

b) Floorplan

Jachin

Devir | Hekhal | Ulam

Boas

c) Cross-section

d) Facade

A A

11   Solomon's Temple, floor plan.

could be entered only once a year (at Yom Kippur) by the high priests (11, 12). With the building of the Temple, Solomon became the founder and patron of the Temple cult. The end of the story of Solomon tells of his loss of power. He was not a great military leader like David, especially since he behaved passively. Edomite and Aramaic opponents threatened his power, and Jerobeam emerged as a dangerous domestic adversary.

The collapse of the kingdom

The unified kingdom did not survive the death of Solomon. When his son Rehoboam succeeded to the throne, the kingdom was split into two parts: Judah, with Jerusalem as its capital, in the south; and Israel, with Shechem (later Samaria) as its capital, in the north. The bible blames Rehoboam's refusal to reduce forced labor and high taxes paid by the northern tribes for the split. The ten northern tribes made Jeroboam their king. To attract people to worship outside Jerusalem, Jeroboam set up golden calves in central sanctuaries at Beth-el and Dan. Thus began the decline of the legitimate cult in Jerusalem, and for his role in instigating others to sin (by enticing them away from the Temple), idolatry was stereotyped as "Jeroboam's sin."

From that point, biblical history focuses on each king as an individual, laying great importance on each king's religious judgment. The writers of the bible measured the kings by how well they fulfilled the demand. Israelite kings, who perpetuated Jeroboam's sin, were invariably condemned, while some of the kings of Judah (such as Hezekiah and Josiah) were judged in a more positive light.

The Fall of the Northern Kingdom

A merciless civil war raged throughout the two centuries in which both kingdoms co-existed. The north and south fought over territorial questions as well as over religious issues. Taking advantage of the ongoing warfare, the neighboring tribes freed themselves and set up and enlarged their own territories at the expense of Israel and Judah. Although development was similar in both kingdoms, there was an essential difference: Judah was governed throughout by a single dynasty, the house of David, while Israel was subjected to the rise and fall of a total of nine dynasties, leading to military weakness and political instability.

The fall of the Northern Kingdom

In the 9th century BCE, the Assyrians had secured their power in Mesopotamia and were poised to conquer the Near East. Thus ended an era in which the states in Syria and Palestine were largely able to determine the balance of power in their region themselves. In this time, Duvid's monarchy had emerged and fallen again; but no force from outside the region thus far had appeared with any claim to authority. The Assyrians were the first in a long series of great foreign powers (including Asshur, Babylon, Media, Persia, Greece, and Rome) that sought to absorb the area within their sphere of influence (13).

After Hosea, the last king of Israel, had participated in an alliance against Assyria, the Assyrian king Sahalmaneser V attacked Samaria. In 722 BCE, after a three-year siege, his successor Sargon II finally conquered the city. He deported

12 Solomon's Temple, facade with the great columns Jachin and Boas. Reconstruction by T. A. Busink, 1967.

segments of the Israelite population to other areas of his empire and settled people from other conquered areas so that a heterogeneous population emerged, making it impossible for the religious and cultural traditions of Israel to be continued. The end of the Northern Kingdom therefore not only changed the political map, but also deeply affected national and religious identity: a large portion of the people of Israel were lost forever. Since then, the memory of the ten lost tribes is anchored in the consciousness of the Jewish people. Judah, the Southern Kingdom, preserved its existence as a nation by acquiescing to Assyrian rule. Years later, as Assyria's power waned, King Josiah effected a remarkable political and religious renaissance (ca. 622 BCE). His religious reforms—such as cleansing the religion of heathen influences—were triggered, according to the biblical report, when the book of the Torah was found during renovations of the Temple. (The book found was unquestionably the fifth book of Moses, known as Deuteronomy.) After Josiah's death, Judah entered a period of decline, which soon led to its destruction.

13 The end of the kingdom of Israel, 734–722 BCE.

The Babylonian exile

The political vacuum left by the Assyrians was soon filled by the growing power of the Babylonians. Nebuchadnezzar, the Babylonian king, undertook an expedition to Syria and Palestine and in 597 BCE stood outside Jerusalem. King Joachim surrendered the city apparently without resistance; he and the upper echelons of Judah were led into exile in Babylon. In Joachim's place, Nebuchadnezzar crowned his uncle Mattaniah king and changed his name to Zedekiah. Zedekiah, however, rebelled against the king of Babylonia, who wasted no time in responding to the revolt: A Babylonian army advanced against Jerusalem and besieged the city. In 586 BCE, Jerusalem fell, the king's palace and Solomon's Temple were destroyed, and the city wall was demolished. Before burning down the Temple, the Babylonians managed to carry away its contents, including the Ark of the Covenant, which has been missing ever since. A segment of the population fled from the Babylonians into Egypt, but most of the people were carried off to Babylon.

The fall of Jerusalem marks a sharp break in the history of Israel: it brought an end to the four hundred years of King David's dynasty, as well as to the Israelites' national independence. A new era began for the people of Israel—life in the Diaspora (**14**).

The exiles who arrived in Babylonia joined the group who had been displaced ten years earlier. Unlike the Assyrians, the Babylonians settled the Jews close together, which enabled them to protect their traditions and their belief in one God. The group of exiles returned to their religious beliefs. Their life centered on the Torah and on learning. Prayers took the place of ritual sacrifices. In fact, worship without offerings, which led to the founding of the synagogue, may well have had its origin in the period of exile.

Thus, the exiles in Babylon and the fugitives in Egypt survived the collapse of the kingdom. And when, after fifty years of exile, the possibility arose to return, several thousand Jews set out from Babylon toward Jerusalem to build once again a religious and national life.

14 The mourning Jews in exile. Eduard Bendemann (1811–1889), painting, 1832.

The Jewish calendar begins with the creation of the world, set by rabbinical tradition at 3761 BCE. Thus, in the fall of 1996, on the first day of Tishri (the first month of the civil year), the year 5757 began. The Jewish year is a lunar and solar calendar, based on the phases of the moon (months) as well as cycles of the sun (years). The year normally has twelve months. The months begin with the new moon and have 29 or 30 days. Almost every month includes festivals, fasts, or days of remembrance:

Tishri (Sept./Oct., 30 days): *Rosh Hashannah* (New Year), *Yom Kippur* (Day of Atonement), *Sukkot* (Feast of the Tabernacle).

Heshvan (Oct./Nov., 29 days).

Kislev (Nov./Dec., 30 days): *Hanukkah* (Festival of Lights).

Tebet (Dec./Jan., 29 days): Day of fasting in memory of the beginning of the siege of Jerusalem.

Shebat (Jan./Feb., 30 days): *Tu Bishevat* (New Year for Trees).

Adar (Feb./March, 29 days): *Purim* (celebration in memory of Queen Esther saving the Persian Jews).

Nisan (March/April, 30 days): *Pesach* (Passover) commemorates the Exodus from Egypt; *Yom Ha-Shoah* is a day of remembrance of the victims of the Holocaust.

Iyar (April/May, 29 days): *Yom Ha-Atzmaut* (Israeli Independence Day).

Sivan (May/June, 30 days): *Shavuot* (the Feast of Weeks, Pentecost).

Tammuz (June/July, 29 days): Day of fasting to commemorate the breaching of Jerusalem's wall before the destruction of the First and Second Temples.

Ab (July/Aug., 30 days): Day of fasting in remembrance of the destruction of the Temples and other catastrophes, such as the defeat of Bar Kochba and the expulsion of the Spanish Jews (*Tisha be-Ab*).

Elul (Aug./Sept., 29 days): Sounding of the *shofar* (ram's horn) to prepare for the festivals in Tishri.

A regular year, based strictly on the lunar months, has 354 days. To make up the difference of about eleven days with the solar year (365.25 days), seven times in every 19 years (years 3, 6, 8, 11, 14, 17, and 19) a thirteenth month is inserted between Adar and Nisan, called *Adar Sheni* (or Adar II). The Hebrew term for such a leap year is *Shana me'ubberet*, which means "pregnant year."

The day begins at sundown one evening and ends the next, when three stars can be seen in the sky. Thus, the Sabbath (*Shabbat*) begins on Friday evening at sunset and ends on Saturday at nightfall. A week has seven days, echoing the biblical seven days of creation. The first is Sunday, the seventh Shabbat.

The Sabbath

Shabbat (from the Hebrew word, *shavat*, "to rest") commemorates both God's rest after the creation of

Jewish Calendar: Festivals and Days of Mourning

the world, and the Exodus from Egypt. It is the high point of each week. The faithful are supposed to rest on the Sabbath, as the Creator did on the seventh day, and perform no work, including building fires, carrying loads, or traveling (even on foot). Because of this absolute break, all preparations must be made on Friday, the day before the Sabbath: the meals cooked, the house cleaned, the table covered, and the whole family bathed and well dressed. At home, the Sabbath ritual begins with the lighting of candles. That (as well as all the preparatory work, we might note) is traditionally the woman's duty (15). After the candle lighting, some families go to the synagogue for the *Kabbalat Shabbat* (Sabbath reception). Thereafter the parents bless their children. Then the *Kiddush* ("sanctification"), a particular blessing over a cup of wine, is recited, praising God and offering thanks for the Sabbath. After the Kiddush, celebrants wash their hands and say the

16 Challah, the two braided Shabbat breads.

blessing over the *challah*, two loaves of braided bread (16). The head of the family (traditionally the father) sprinkles salt on a piece of challah and eats it, then divides the rest among everyone present. Thus begins the first meal of the Sabbath.

One of the most important Sabbath rituals is the weekly reading of an excerpt from the Torah in the synagogue on Saturday morning. Seven people, or *aliyot*, are called upon to read (or chant) a portion of the Torah, and the excerpts are long enough to allow the entire Torah to be read within one year.

The Sabbath begins with the Kiddush and ends with another ceremony, the *Havdalah* ("division"), which marks the transition from the Sabbath to the ordinary work day. The Havdalah is recited first over wine, like the Kiddush, and then a second blessing is spoken over

15 *Shabbat.* Isidor Kaufmann, ca. 1920. After making preparations, the woman has lighted the candles and waits for her family. On the table stands the Kiddush goblets, and under a white cloth lies the challah.

sweetly aromatic spices, and a third over a braided candle customarily with more than one wick, to thank God for the gifts of light and fire. The spices are kept in a special spice-box, often silver, called a "Bessamim Box."

The High Holy Days: Rosh Hashannah and Yom Kippur

The Jewish New Year holiday, Tishri 1 and 2, is a time of judgment. It is said that three books are opened on the New Year: The names of the just are inscribed in the Book of Life, the godless sinners' in the Book of Death. The third book is for the mediocre, who have both sins and good deeds to be weighed. The final judgment of a person's year remains open from New Year's Day to the Day of Atonement (Rosh Hashannah through Yom Kippur). In these "Ten Days of Penitence," the balance can be tipped by remorse and penance. Thus, the traditional greeting at Rosh Hashannah: "May a good year be inscribed for you [in the Book of Life]."

The blowing of the *shofar* (ram's horn) at New Year's is a traditional call for serious self-examination. The day also brings with it certain traditional foods, such as the apple dipped in honey, accompanied by the wish for a "good and sweet year."

Yom Kippur (the Day of Atonement, Tishri 10) is the peak of the Ten Days of Penitence. The highest and most sacred holiday of the year, it is a day of strict fasting, spent in the synagogue praying for forgiveness of sins committed against God, against others, and against oneself. Important prayers are the confession of sins and the *Kol Nidre* ("declaration"). Yom Kippur ends with the *Neila*, a "closing" service in which prayers signify the "sealing" of the Book of Life, followed by the Havdalah rite of transition observed at the end of the Sabbath, and a final, single blast of the shofar.

The Holidays of Pilgrimages: Passover, Shavuot, and Sukkot

The three pilgrimage festivals were observed by the Israelites at the time of both Temples with a pilgrimage to Jerusalem, bearing sacrifices. All three holidays coincide with important phases in the agricultural cycle (the beginning and end of the growing season, as well as the first harvest), and events in the Exodus from Egypt (see p. 9). During the Diaspora (the dispersion of the Israelites outside Palestine), another day was added to these holidays because of uncertainty concerning the calendar.

Passover derives from the word *Pesach*: God "passed over"—that is, he spared the houses of the Israelites when he killed all the first-born in Egypt. Passover commemorates the flight from Egypt and the end of the Israelites' slavery; it is celebrated from the 14th to the 21st day of Nisan (or the 22nd in Diaspora).

The celebration begins with the *seder* (meaning "order"), a festive meal at home, so called because this evening follows a meticulously prescribed order (17). The *Haggadah*, which tells the story of the Israelites' flight from Egypt, is read and the foods eaten have particular symbolic significance: *seroa* (a roasted bone in remembrance of the Passover offering—the Paschal lamb), *beiza* (a hard-boiled egg in remembrance of the offerings brought on each pilgrimage to Jerusalem—the egg also symbolizes mourning for the destruction of the Temple); *maror* (bitter herbs—usually horseradish—to symbolize the bitterness of slavery in Egypt); parsley or celery (reminiscent of the hyssop used to coat the doors of the Israelites with the blood of the Paschal lamb) dipped into a bowl of salt water (to symbolize the tears and sweat in Egyptian servitude); and *haroset* (a paste of apples and nuts, whose clayish color and consistency are reminiscent of the sun-baked bricks and mortar with which the Israelites were forced to build for the pharaoh). All this, along with three *matzohs* (unleavened bread), is laid on the seder table. Observant Jews eat only unleavened bread during Passover as a reminder of the Israelites' hasty departure from Egypt, which allowed no time for dough to rise. No trace of leavening is allowed in the house during Passover. Thus, before Passover, Jews (usually the women) must clean the house thoroughly. During Passover, they must eat on special dishes. Those who cannot afford an extra set must make their dishes and utensils "kosher for Passover" by heating or boiling. Wine is also placed on the seder table, for in the course of the seder ritual, each person must drink four glasses. Usually the head of the household (traditionally the father) tells the Exodus story, recalling what many consider the central event in Jewish history. This recounting invites both the narrator and listeners to identify with the generation who were enslaved and then freed.

The name "Pentecost" (*Shavuot*) comes from the seven weeks from Passover to Shavuot. Shavuot is

17　Seder. Folk art watercolor and India ink, western Ukraine, 19th century.

celebrated on the sixth day of Sivan. It commemorates the divine revelation on Sinai when God gave Moses the Torah (see p. 9f.). Thus, it is traditional to spend the whole night studying the Torah and, in the morning worship ritual, to place the Ten Commandments at the center of the Torah reading. But Shavuot is also a celebration of the first harvest. The synagogue and houses are decorated with flowers and fresh greens to symbolize the "first fruits". It is also customary to read the book of Ruth at Shavuot because it describes harvest scenes and because King David, who was descended from Ruth, died on Shavuot.

Sukkot, or Tabernacles, takes its name from the tabernacle (the "booth"), the most important symbol

18 Collapsible *sukkah*, first half of the 19th century. In building a ceremonial tabernacle, certain rules must be followed: It must have at least three walls, must stand outdoors, and may only have a provisional roof, covered with foliage and branches, so that sunlight and stars remain visible. Construction of the sukkah begins on the day after Yom Kippur.

of the holiday. This goes back to an order from the Torah: "You shall live in booths for seven days; all that are citizens in Israel shall live in booths, so that your generations may know that I made the people of Israel live in booths when I brought them out of the land of Egypt" (Lev. 23:42–43). Dwelling in the tabernacle (from Tishri 15–22/23) (**18**), like the symbolic foods at Passover, reminds each Jewish person that for forty years on the journey to freedom, his or her ancestors lived in makeshift huts.

The second symbol, a palm branch (*lulav*), reminds us that Sukkot also was originally an agricultural festival. The plants represent the entire flora, for which one thanks God. Before prayer, especially before the psalms at the morning worship, the lulav is shaken in the four directions. The last day of Sukkot celebrates the Torah with a closing festival, *Simhat Torah*. The Torah is divided into fifty-four weekly excerpts. On each Sabbath, a section is read, so that in the course of a year observers read the entire Pentateuch. This cycle ends on the last day of the Tabernacle festival: the last paragraph of the Torah—Deut. 34—is read, and immediately a new cycle begins with Gen. 1. Afterward, all the Torah scrolls in the synagogue are carried seven times around the lectern in a procession. With singing and dancing, Jews celebrate their ongoing delight in the Torah.

19 A burning Hanukkiya, silver, 1817. The candelabra used at Hanukkah always has nine candle holders: eight for the eight days of celebration and a ninth (the shamash, "the servant") used to light the others.

Hanukkah and Purim

In contrast to the pilgrimage festivals, Hanukkah and Purim are not ordained by biblical command, but are based on historical events from the time of the Second Temple.

Hanukkah is a week-long Festival of Lights commemorating the rededication of the Temple by Judas Maccabeus in Jerusalem after its desecration by the hellenistic Seleucids in 164 BCE (see p. 30 ff.). According to Talmudic legend, the Maccabees found only one bottle of pure oil in the Temple, enough to give light for just one day. Miraculously, however, the Temple lamps burned for a full eight days. In remembrance of this miracle, observant Jews light a special nine-branched candelabra called the *Hanukkiya* (a menorah used especially on Hanukkah) on each of the eight days of Hanukkah, beginning on Kislev 25. On the first night one candle is lit, on the second two, until on the eighth night all the lights are burning (19). Hanukkah customs include children playing the dreidl game, gift giving (a more recently developed custom with little or no historical or religious basis), and eating potato latkes (pancakes) and doughnuts, perhaps because they are fried in oil and remind the faithful of the oil lamps in the Temple.

Purim is celebrated on the 14th and 15th days of Adar. This celebration commemorates the salvation of the Persian Jews from the attack by Haman, a protégé of the Persian king Ahasuerus (probably Xerxes I). As recounted in the book of Esther, the anti-Semite Haman planned to hold a lottery to determine the date on which all Jews in the empire, from India to Ethiopia, would be killed. The Jewess Esther, a favorite of the Persian sovereign, with her kinsman Mordechai frustrated this plan and saved their people. It is customary on Purim to read the book of Esther while the children rattle noisemakers at the mention of the name of the villainous Haman.

Purim is probably the most boisterous festival in the Jewish year. Work is allowed, as is the drinking of liquor, even inebriation to the point where the merrymaker can hardly distinguish between the sayings "Cursed be Haman" and "Blessed be Mordechai." Costume and certain foods are also traditional, the most popular of which is hamantaschen, a three-cornered pastry filled with poppyseeds or jam.

The books of Ezra and Nehemiah provide the only narrative account of the time after the Babylonian exile. They relate two chapters in the history of the Israelites after the exile: the time leading up to the completion of the reconstruction of the Temple (538–515 BCE) and the reforms under Ezra and Nehemiah (458 and/or 445 BCE). The texts say nothing about the decades in between.

In the middle of the sixth century BCE, the Persian king Cyrus took power over large parts of the Near East; in 539 he conquered Babylon. A year later, in a written edict, he granted the exiled Israelites the right to return to Jerusalem and to rebuild the Temple (Ezra 1:2f.). This account is completely consistent with what is known of Cyrus's politics concerning subjected peoples, as well as with an archaeological discovery, the Cyrus Cylinder (**20**), which reports on the repatriation of exiles and religious artifacts, and the restoration of sanctuaries in different areas of his empire. Biblical and extrabiblical sources are therefore in close agreement. Cyrus appointed Sheshbazzar and, after him, Zerubbabel as commissioners to oversee the implementation of his edicts.

In the spring of 515 BCE, after many delays, the Second Temple was dedicated. It followed the basic plan of Solomon's Temple, but was somewhat simpler. Also, some important elements were missing, namely, the Ark of the Cov-

20 The Cyrus Cylinder. Terra cotta, 5th century BCE.

enant, the Bronze Sea, and the two columns Jachin and Boas.

Not all exiles, however, took advantage of the decree and returned to Jerusalem. Many remained in the foreign lands, which had become their homes and offered better economic prospects than Judah. This created a demographic situation that became a permanent characteristic of Jewish life: Israel formed a center for the widely dispersed nation.

While there is little doubt that the return to Jerusalem is of great significance in Jewish history, at the same time two large, thriving Jewish communities were developing within the existing civilizations of Egypt and Babylon (**21**).

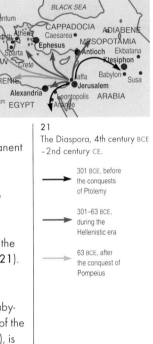

21
The Diaspora, 4th century BCE – 2nd century CE.

301 BCE, before the conquests of Ptolemy

301–63 BCE, during the Hellenistic era

63 BCE, after the conquest of Pompeius

538 BCE – 70 CE

The time of Ezra and Nehemiah

Ezra and Nehemiah both came out of the Babylonian-Persian Diaspora. Ezra's title, "Scribe of the Law of God of the Heavens" (Ezra 7:12, 21), is understood to be something of a Persian honorific: "Law of the God of the Heavens" was an official Aramaic designation for the Jewish religion, whose God was honored as creator of the world and as "God of the Heavens." Ezra was therefore the official for affairs of the Jewish religion.

Diaspora: Literally, "dispersion." This Greek designation is a collective word for the Jewish community outside of Israel.
Menorah: Literally, "small candelabra." The seven-branched candelabra (the Hanukkiyah is a special nine-branched menorah used for Hanukkah) was among the cultic objects of the earliest Israelites and is described exactly in the bible (Exod. 25:31–40; 37:17 ff.). The menorah also stood in the Second Temple. It was the most widespread Jewish symbol even in ancient times.
Qumran: Ruin site on the northwest bank of the Dead Sea. Qumran became famous in 1947 when the Dead Sea Scrolls were found in caves there. These scrolls constitute the only large block of literature in Hebrew/Aramaic from the 2nd century BCE to the 1st century CE that is preserved in the original.

Nehemiah held a leading position at the Persian court: "I was cupbearer to the king" (Neh. 1:11). With the full authority of the Persian king, both men returned to Judah to engage in local affairs. Ezra was commanded: "you are sent by the king and his seven counselors to make inquiries about Judah and Jerusalem according to the law of your God, which is in your hand" (Ezra 7:14). He was to be the judge and legal interpreter to those who knew "the Law" and to teach others (Ezra 25). It seems that Ezra went to Israel to oversee the observance of Jewish law among the Persian king's Jewish subjects there. And, according to biblical account, this was quite necessary.

The Israelites who had remained had lived for years in a "wayward" manner: without the Temple and religious authorities, and among foreign populations such as Babylonian soldiers and neighboring peoples who had filled the cultural vacuum created by the exile. This resulted in mixed marriages between Jews and gentiles. The bible reports comprehensively on the reform work of Ezra and Nehemiah, who opposed these mixed marriages and finally decreed the dissolution of all marriages with non-Jews. This is a clear instance of the effort to maintain the purity of the Jewish community, which required a separation from the "peoples of the lands."

Another of Ezra's important deeds is related in the book of Nehemiah. During a major religious ceremony, Ezra for the first time read aloud from the book of the Torah and began a tradition that is key to this day (**22**). This act is also a manifestation of the Israelites' independent religious development in the period following the Babylonian exile. Besides the Temple, with its ritual of burnt offering, the reading and interpretation of the Torah formed a new center around which the

22 Ezra reading from the Torah. Mural from the synagogue in Dura Europus on the Euphrates, 3rd century CE. Today in the National Museum at Damascus. The Babylonian Jews were proud that a sage from their ranks after the exile had brought back order in Judah through Jewish religious law. Thus, it is understandable that Ezra's picture stood in a prominent place near the Torah shrine in a Babylonian synagogue.

Jewish community and all of Judah rallied.

In 445 BCE, Nehemiah returned to Jerusalem, where he was governor of Judah for twelve years. Despite much resistance, he successfully reconstructed the city wall around Jerusalem (**23**). He also managed to resettle a tenth of the inhabitants from other areas of Judah in Jerusalem. With these measures, he again gave the Jewish province a political (as well as a spiritual) center. Through a general forgiveness of debt, he not only defused social tensions between the impoverished rural population and the upper class, but also made the Jewish community viable. With the recounting of Nehemiah's deeds, the historical narrative of the bible ends.

23 Nehemiah and his comrades at the gates of Jerusalem (Neh. 2:13). Woodblock print after a drawing by Gustave Doré, 1865.

538 BCE – 70 CE

Alexander the Great, the Ptolemies, and the Seleucids

In 332 BCE, Alexander of Macedonia conquered Syria and Palestine (**24**). The Jews, represented by the high priests, resisted submission so that no Macedonian governor was installed, and Judah remained an autonomous "Temple State." Since political power did not interfere in religious practice, there was no occasion for conflict in the religious sphere.

After Alexander's death, Judah fell to the dominion of the Ptolemies, the Macedonian kings of Egypt (**25**), who continued to allow the Temple State to maintain its autonomy under the high priests. Each of the high priests was responsible for the tax revenue of his own area. Judaism now began to wrestle with Greek, or Hellenistic, culture in the country of Israel itself, while the Jews in Diaspora were already long familiar with Hellenistic civilization and most spoke Greek. The "Letter of Aristeas" (ca. 100 BCE)—a letter

24 Alexander the Great (356–323). Mosaic from Pompeii. Copy of a Greek painting from the 4th century BCE, attributed to Philoxenos of Eritrea.

25 Ptolemy I Soter (ca. 366–283), friend and field commander of Alexander the Great, conquered Palestine in 301. Coin, ca. 300 BCE.

26 The Seleucid king Antiochus IV Epiphanes advocated active Hellenistic politics, which triggered the revolt of the Maccabees. In Jewish history, he is seen as the prototype of the persecutor of the Jews.

There was an extreme of Hellenization and increase in the adoption of foreign ways because of the surpassing wickedness of Jason, who was ungodly and no true high priest.   *2 Macc. 4:13*

supposedly written by a Jewish writer in Greek telling the story of Ptolemy II (283–246 BCE) commissioning a Greek translation of the Torah in Alexandria—might well be accurate. According to legend, the translation was made by seventy-two learned Jews in seventy-two days, and the translation was therefore called the Septuagint ("seventy"). Now Gentiles could also read the Torah, and the Greek translation would later be adopted as the Old Testament by the Christian church.

After the Fifth Syrian War, Judah fell to the Seleucids (198 BCE). Antiochus III sought to reconcile the Jews with the new foreign rule by lowering taxes and by allowing Jewish laws, as well as Judah's status as an independent Temple State, to remain in place. The departure from these policies under Antiochus IV Epiphanes ushered in the end of Seleucid dominion in this region.

The revolt of the Maccabees and the establishment of Hanukkah

In traditional Jewish history, Antiochus IV (175–164 BCE) (**26**) is the archetypical villain: he doubled taxes, plundered the Temple, stationed troops in Samaria and Judah, and built the Acra, a fortress manned by Syrians, in the heart of Jerusalem. In 174 BCE, he sold the official duties of the high priests to Jason, a devoted Hellenist, who erected a Greek gymnasium, or sports ground, on the Temple site.

In the summer of 167 BCE, Antiochus commanded the Jews to give up their religion under threat of death. Circumcision and observance of the Sabbath were outlawed; the Temple was used for the sacrifice of "impure" animals, and the Temple itself was dedicated to the Greek god Zeus of Olympus. These actions angered even the moderate Hellenistic priests, and in

December of the same year the Jewish sacrifical rites were discontinued. The Jews were subjected to a sacrificial test: refusal to sacrifice to the Greek gods was a sign of active, willful resistance against the official syncretic religion.

The Seleucid officials and the king recognized too late that, to devout Jews, this situation represented nothing more than a choice between martyrdom and active resistance. They chose the latter. All, even those who held a more moderate position, were united in the belief that the Torah must be installed again at any price.

According to I Maccabees, the revolt began with the act of the priest Mattathias, whom royal officials wanted to perform a sacrifice as a model for the rest of the people. Mattathias not only refused the king's officers' command but even "gave vent to righteous anger" when he killed a Jew who was prepared for sacrifice to the heathen Gods. The flight of Mattathias with his five sons and followers signaled the start of the Jews' active resistance. The biblical account claims that the revolt was also directed at those Jews who had voluntarily submitted to Greek customs. Mattathias's sons became the real heroes of the resistance, which was successful by all measures. The oldest son, Judas Maccabeus ("hammer"), alongside the Hasidim (the "pious"), conquered Jerusalem and the Temple (**27**, **28**). The name "Maccabee" at this point was adjoined to the House of Hasmon, with which it ultimately became synonymous.

By the end of 164 BCE, the Temple was purified of all traces of idolatry, rededicated, and was again the site of sacrificial offerings; Hanukkah commemorates this rededication (consecration; see p. 25). The decree of Antiochus was also revoked. This had been the goal of the Hasidim, and they were satisfied.

27 Judas Maccabeus. Enameled buckle cover, France, 16th century.

538 BCE – 70 CE

28 The attack of Judas Maccabeus on the Acra in Jerusalem. Alba Bible, 15th century.

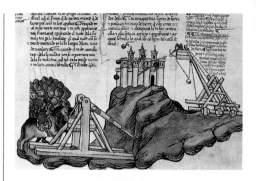

538 BCE – 70 CE

Then Judas and his brothers said, "See, our enemies are crushed; let us go up to cleanse the sanctuary and dedicate it." ... they took unhewn stones ... and built a new altar like the former one. ... they offered incense on the altar and lit the lamps on the lamp-stand, and these gave light in the temple. ... they rose and offered sacrifice ... So they celebrated the de-dication of the altar for eight days, and joyfully offered burnt offerings ... Then Judas and his brothers and all the assembly of Israel determined that every year at that season the days of dedica-tion of the altar should be observed with joy and gladness for eight days, begin-ning with the twenty-fifth day of the month of Kislev."

1 Macc. 4:36–59.

The same cannot be said of the politically ambitious Maccabees who were not satisfied with what they had achieved.

What started as a religious conflict developed more and more into a battle over power and family politics, fueled by internal conflicts in the Seleucid dynasty. With the throne up for grabs, the two Seleucid competitors each sought to win the favor of Jonathan, Judah's successor. Through skillful tactics, Jonathan exploited the changing power structures and was finally confirmed as high priest and Seleucid governor (161–142 BCE).

Jonathan's arrangement with hostile "worldly powers" sent a shock wave through two camps in particular: the Zaddikim (see p. 40), whose hereditary right to the high priesthood had been usurped; and the pious circles, who saw the fight against the Seleucids as the final test before reaching the eschatological Kingdom of God.

Khirbet Qumran on the Dead Sea

At this time, Zaddikim-led groups with great eschatological expectations founded a com-munity under the "Teacher of Righteousness" and settled at the present Khirbet Qumran on the Dead Sea. For them, the Temple of Jerusalem was ritually polluted and Jonathan Maccabeus was deemed in their scrolls as a "sacreligious priest." It is possible, though controversy persists among modern scholars— that they belonged to the sects that the Roman historian Flavius Josephus called the Essenes (see p. 40 f.) (**29**).

538 BCE – 70 CE

29 Qumran: the caves in which the famous Dead Sea Scrolls were found.

The rise and fall of the Hasmoneans

Jonathan's decision to negotiate with the enemy force rather than fight it launched an expansionist phase of the Seleucid feudal state. In 140 BCE, Jonathan's successor Simon became "Prince of the People" (*ethnarch*), commander (*strategos*), and high priest, and made this position hereditary. With it began the dynastic phase of Hasmonean history.

The Hasmonean expansion was territorial and military, but also had a religious/political aspect. As the Hasmoneans annexed territories, they converted Gentile populations to Judaism. John Hyrcanus I (134 – 104 BCE) conquered the areas of the Samaritans in the north and the Idumaeans in the south, whom he subjugated completely and forcibly converted to Judaism (**30**). Herod the Great's origin in Idumaea later became one of the factors behind the tensions between him and the population of Judah. John Hyrcanus was also the first Hasmonean to mint his own coins (**31**).

The Hasmonean state became more and more Hellenistic in its military and civil structures, architecture, and language even in the history of succession squabbles. So it was that during the rule of Alexander Janneus (103 – 76 BCE), despite the

30 The ascent of the Hasmonean state, 2nd – 1st century BCE.

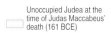
Unoccupied Judea at the time of Judas Maccabeus' death (161 BCE)

Territorial expansion under:

Jonathan (161–142 BCE)

Simeon (142–134 BCE)

John Hyrcanus (134–104 BCE)

Aristobulus I (104–103 BCE)

Alexander Janneus (103–76 BCE)

31 Bronze coins of John Hyrcanus. The inscription on the reverse, "John the High Priest," shows how important the office of high priest was for the preservation of Hasmonean authority.

state's foreign policy successes, rebellion against the sovereign grew. The Pharisees (see p. 40) openly questioned Janneus's priestly qualities and were cruelly punished for it by his mercenaries. Near the end of his reign, he recognized how questionable his mercenary-based power was and supposedly advised his widow, Salome Alexandra (76–67 BCE), to compromise with the Pharisees. Her regency appears to have restored internal peace, at least to some extent, though shortly after her death a quarrel arose between her sons Aristobulus II and Hyrcanus II. Their implacability invited external intervention: hence, Rome appeared as a governing power in Judea. Pompeius (**32**) conquered the country and, in 63 BCE, penetrated into the Temple held by Aristobulus's followers, where he unleashed a bloodbath.

Thus began the 700-year dominion of the Romans over Judea. To the Jews, Pompeius's intrusion into the inner sanctum was an act of utter arrogance. Rome, which had often been party to treaties with the Hasmoneans, was now suddenly a hostile power. Aristobulus II and his sons, Alexander and Antigonus, had publicly ridden in Pompeius's triumphal procession in Rome. Hyrcanus II, on the other hand, was confirmed as a high priest, but was subject to the Roman governor of Syria. Antipater, an Idumaean, won the real power in Judea and enjoyed the trust of Rome. Under Caesar, he expanded his power further and entrusted his sons with high posts: Phasael became *strategos* in Jerusalem; Herod in Galilee.

The invasion of Parthia in 40 BCE led to one more Hasmonean interlude. After Hyrcanus II and Phasael were ousted, the Hasmoneans were able to establish Antigonus for a scant three years as king and high priest in Judea (40–37 BCE). Herod, who fled to Rome, had himself

32 Gnaeus Pompeius Magnus, commander of the Roman armies in the east, used the conflict among the heirs of Alexander Janneus to bring Judah under his control, beginning 700 years of Roman dominion.

appointed king of Judea by the senate there and reigned for thirty-seven years. The beheading of Antigonus finally brought the era of the Hasmoneans to a close. Still, the Hasmoneans were honored in folk legend as heroes in the fight against foreign domination. Herod, aware of this, tried to garner Hasmonean prestige for himself during the siege of Jerusalem by marrying the Hasmonean princess Mariamme, granddaughter of Hyrcanus II.

33 Greek inscription on the outer wall of the Temple of Jerusalem: "Gentiles are forbidden to enter the sanctuary." Herodean era, Istanbul Archaeological Museum.

538 BCE – 70 CE

Herod the Great

The Jews again had a king, albeit by the grace of Rome. Herod came from an Idumaean family that had converted to Judaism only two generations before. While Herod (37–4 BCE) strove mightily to be king of the Jews, he was little inclined to dispense with the governing style of a Hellenistic monarch. While he tried to avoid violations against the Torah, he still conducted his personal and family politics according to his own will and discretion. All attempts at opposition, even within his own family, were nipped in the bud—leading ultimately to the murder of his beloved wife Mariamme and their sons Alexander and Aristobulus.

In the New Testament, Herod's reputation is typified by the story of the murder of all the

34 Caesarea. Aqueduct from the time of Herod.

538 BCE – 70 CE

35 The fort of Masada on a rock plateau over 100 feet high above the Dead Sea and the desert. Herod built the fort at the northern edge of the rocks where, even on the hottest days, a cool breeze fans his palace on three sides.

young children in Bethlehem. In Gentile areas, he discontinued the Hasmonean policy of Jewish conversion and built heathen temples.

Dependent on Rome, Herod, as king of Judea, was not able to institute independent foreign policy. This limitation to his arena of action could help explain the tremendous amounts of energy and money he spent on grandiose and costly building projects. He founded the cities of Caesarea and Sebaste (**34**). Throughout the country he ordered the construction of royal forts and palaces, often on foundations left from Hasmonean times, including Masada at the Dead Sea, Herodeon on a mountain in Bethlehem, and Jericho (**35–37**). Jerusalem was not neglected either.

Perhaps Herod wanted to prove his loyalty to Judaism when he surprised his subjects with a plan to renew the dilapidated Temple building of Zerubbabel. Construction began around 20 BCE. The Temple's grounds were almost doubled and surrounded by a new wall of gigantic square stones; the proportions of Solomon's Temple had to be observed. Herod built the fort Antonia at the northwest corner of the Temple grounds,

36 Herodeon, near Bethlehem. According to Flavius Josephus, Herod was buried here.

37 The north wing of Herod's winter palace in Jericho.

538 BCE – 70 CE

38 The facade of the Herodean Temple. Model in the park of the Holy Land Hotel in Jerusalem.

affording him direct access to the Temple plateau.

Despite its magnificent renewal, the Herodean Temple is still known as the Second Temple (38). Today only the Wailing Wall—or West Wall—remains. This fragment of wall was not part of the Temple itself, but of the wall erected by Herod surrounding the Temple grounds to support the Temple mountain (39). In the last two decades of Herod's reign, his subjects' lives were relatively secure and economically stable. Religious persons in particular (the priesthood and Levites), whose earnings climbed constantly, profited under Herod's rule. But in devout circles, it was precisely the magnificent rebuilding of the Temple and the burgeoning religious industry that stirred resentments against the Temple sect and intensified the longing for a wholly different dominion—the messianic Kingdom of God.

The death of Herod in the year 4 BCE marked the end of an era. Rome abolished the monarchy and in the course of time assumed all power itself, to be administered through its governors, called Proxies. Often cruel and corrupt, the Proxies defied the Jews' religious sensibilities by erecting portraits of Caesar in synagogues or provoked the people by staging public military parades with the Roman eagle—to the Jews a

39 The Wailing Wall. The best-known part of the wall, with which Herod edged the plateau on the Temple mountain. As the last relic of the Temple, the Wailing Wall is today the most important sanctuary of the Jews.

"carved idol" and thus an abomination—prominently displayed. The Proxies' disregard and disdain for the Jews' system of beliefs only engendered increasing enmity among the Jews toward Rome. Religious fanatics, the so-called Zealots (see p. 41), organized themselves into a new religious political party. For wider and wider circles of Palestinians, zealous attacks on the Roman occupiers seemed justified by the Proxies' arbitrary displays of their dominion. Most Jews were now united in the belief that the Roman empire must fall to make room for the Kingdom of God.

The first Jewish-Roman war

In the spring of 66 CE the rebellion against Rome broke out. After the initial successes of the insurgents, Titus Flavius Vespasianus was charged with suppression of the revolt. In the summer of the same year, he marched into Galilee and took Jotapata. This fort was defended under the leadership of Joseph ben Mattathias, the scion of a noble priestly family. After Joseph was forced to surrender, he prophesied that High Commander Vespasian would become emperor, for which his life was spared. Later, as Flavius Josephus, he became the greatest Jewish historian of his time and wrote about the Jewish War among other things. In his literary works, he tried to reconcile Rome's worldwide power with Judaism.

In June 69 CE, Josephus's prophecy was fulfilled: Vespasian was elevated to the position of emperor and founded the Flavian dynasty (**40**). His son Titus was charged with leading an expedition to end the Jewish War, which he fulfilled in the year 70 with the conquest and destruction of Jerusalem. The Second Temple burned on the ninth day of Ab, the same day on

40 Bronze coin of the emperor Vespasian. A Roman soldier in victorious pose guards a mourning woman under a palm tree (a symbol of Judea). The inscription on the border of the coin reads "Judaea Capta" (Judea is conquered); under the display, it reads "SC" (Senatus Consulto).

which, according to Jewish tradition, the First Temple was destroyed by Nebuchadnezzar. Even today, the ninth of Ab (Tisha be-Ab) is a day of supreme mourning and fasting for observant Jews.

With the destruction of the Temple, the Jews lost their central holy place. The Temple was plundered and its effects were taken to Rome where they were displayed in a triumphal procession. Later, they were immortalized in a relief in a passageway of the Titus Arch in the Roman Forum (**41**). In the fort of Masada, the resistance of the Zealots continued for three more years. When the situation of the besieged became hopeless, approximately 960 men, women, and children committed mass suicide to escape the humiliation of capture by the Romans. In 1963–65, under the direction of Yigael Yadin, Masada was completely unearthed. Among other things, the archaeological team discovered one of the three oldest known synagogues of Palestine (**42, 43**). The others are at Gamla and Herodeon. Today Masada is a symbol of resistance and freedom for the State of Israel, a fitting site for the swearing in of its military recruits.

41 The menorah, the seven-branched candelabra. The relief on the Titus Arch in the Roman Forum shows the Temple implements that Titus brought to Rome as booty after the destruction of the Temple.

42, 43 The synagogue at Masada. It was erected in Herod's time and rebuilt by the Zealots during the rebellion against the Romans in 66–73 CE.

538 BCE – 70 CE

In the centuries before the destruction of the Second Temple, Judaism was anything but monolithic. Flavius Josephus mentioned four different groups in his time: the Pharisees, the Sadducees, the Essenes, and the Zealots. Because very little is known from original sources, people often forget the variety of which he spoke. The discovery of the Dead Sea Scrolls awoke new consciousness of the diversity of Judaism prior to 70 CE. Early Christianity also belongs to the many strands within the Judaism of this time.

The Sadducees: The Sadducees were a tribe of priests and aristocrats; their traditional adversaries were the Pharisees. The name Sadducees is probably derived from the priestly lineage of Zadok. They believed that the world consisted only of what our senses can perceive. Hence, they denied the existence of angels and spirits. They did not believe in the immortality of the soul or in divine intervention in human affairs. Since the Sadducees were bound narrowly to the existence of the Temple and the Jewish state, and enjoyed no broad support among the people, they lost their political and religious power with the destruction of the Temple.

The Pharisees: The Pharisees emerged probably after the Maccabean uprising. They were adversaries of the Sadducean Temple aristocracy and the ruling Hasmonean dynasty. Their doctrines included

44 *Mikveh* (ritual baths) of the Qumran community, 1st century CE

belief in the immortality of the soul, the existence of angels, the resurrection of the dead, punishment in the afterlife, and the free will of individual humans in connection with divine providence. After the destruction of the Temple, a moderate segment of the Pharisees appears to have been the only political and religious group to survive, and this group played an important role in the reorganization of Jewish life after the year 70 CE. Christianity was heavily influenced by the doctrines of the Pharisees.

The Qumran community (the Essenes?): Descriptions of the Essenes by Josephus and other ancient authors agree in many details with what we know today about the Qumran community. Many scholars assume that the Qumran community should be identified with the Essenes, though there is also evidence to contradict this assumption. The community evidently settled itself in the middle of the second century BCE (the time of Jonathan Maccabeus) in an uninhabited area on the north-western shore of the Dead Sea near the present-day Khirbet Qumran. The Essenes were convinced that God had a special covenant with their particular group, and so withdrew themselves from contact with any other Jews. Sect members had a center with common rooms (dining room, workshops, *mikveh* [ritual baths]) (**44**), but apparently lived in nearby caves in the mountainside. Exploration of these caves began in 1947. In eleven of them, archaeologists have found writings of inestimable value: the Dead Sea Scrolls: biblical texts, parabiblical Jewish literature, and texts of the sect (including a delineation of sect rules). They represent the only large trove of literature in the Hebrew-Aramaic language preserved in the original from this time (second century BCE through the first century CE). Their value as original sources for the study of early Judaism and especially for the eschatologically oriented Essenes is unique. Most of the texts have been published, and the seven most important scrolls reside in the "Shrine of the Book" in the Israel Museum in Jerusalem (**45**). The Qumran community was tightly organized; members led an ascetic life of priestly ritual and considered themselves the last generation before the coming of the Messiah, or before a universal apocalypse that would destroy all the "Sons of Darkness" (faithless Jews and heathens). In their view, the Temple sect in Jerusalem was profaned by the ruling elite and also followed an erroneous ritual calendar.

How the texts got into the caves is still unclear. Perhaps the members of the community simply dumped their library there before the Romans destroyed the community center on their way to Jerusalem (68 CE).

Zealots: The Zealots (from the Greek for "fanatic") were radical resisters against Roman dominion from the beginning of the first century CE. The mass suicide of the final 1,000 Zealots to avoid conquest by 15,000 Roman troops at the fort of Masada brought their movement to an end.

45 The "Shrine of the Book" containing the famous Dead Sea Scrolls. In the background is the Knesset (the Israeli parliament). The dome covered with white porcelain suggests the covers of the jars in which the scrolls were found.

The new order in Yavneh

The consolidation of Judaism after the first Jewish-Roman war is closely associated with the personage of Johanan ben Zakkai, a moderate Pharisee. According to legend, he was smuggled out of besieged Jerusalem in a coffin, outwitting the fanatical Zealots who had prohibited residents from leaving the city alive. Johanan successfully petitioned the Romans for permission to establish a center of learning (*Bet Midrash*) in Yavneh (south of present-day Tel Aviv). He wanted to convince his fellow believers that the destruction of the Temple and the end of the state's autonomy did not mean the end of the Jewish people or Jewish tradition. Though not of noble birth, Johanan was given the title Rabban ("Our master"), which was usually reserved for the *Nasi* ("prince," or "patriarch"). After him, Rabban Gamaliel from the house of Hillel took over leadership of the "collective" at Yavneh. He and his successors, as Nasi, represented the Jewish people in Palestine until 425 CE.

During the Yavneh period, measures were introduced to consolidate Judaism under certain altered conditions. The *Halakhah*, the body of Jewish law governing daily life (see p. 44), was simplified and rendered more specific, new ritual forms were developed for the holidays, which had included a pilgrimage to the Jerusalem Temple (now destroyed), and the Rabbis managed to bring the divergent currents in the population under their control. Sects such as the Sadducees and the Essenes no longer created dissension or unrest.

The Bar Kochba uprising

Once more the Jews tried to extricate themselves from the Roman yoke, and, in 132 CE, several factors converged to create a propitious opportunity. Emperor Hadrian, without regard for Jerusalem's history or its meaning for the Jews, decided to turn it into a heathen-Roman city called Aelia Capitolina, including plans to erect a temple to Jupiter on the ruins of the Second Temple. Other sources blame the riot on Hadrian's prohibition of circumcision. It is also possible that many Jews expected some dramatic event because seventy years had passed since the destruction of the Second Temple, exactly the time between the destruction of the First and the rebuilding of the Second Temple.

The rebellion broke out in 132 CE and lasted three and a half years. The insurgents were led by Simon Bar Kosiba. The messianic twist on his name, Bar Kochba ("son of the stars"), is attributed to Rabbi Akiba Ben Joseph, who supposedly suggested that the prophecy in Numbers (see below) refers to Bar Kosiba. The Roman occupation was taken completely by surprise, and Bar Kochba initially succeeded in occupying Judea, including Jerusalem. He even went so far as to have coins minted, dated with the year of the "Deliverance of Israel" or the "Freedom of Jerusalem" (46). Hadrian entrusted the proven governor of Britain, Julius Severus, to wage the war. With overwhelming force, Severus took back Judea piece by piece, and finally also Jerusalem. Bar Kochba fell, and numerous famous scribes, including Rabbi Akiba, were tortured and executed.

The consequences of the rebellion were even more severe than after the first Jewish-Roman

70 – 700 CE

46 Coins from the time of the Bar Kochba uprising (132–135 CE). In the second Jewish-Roman war, political ambition and religious strife were utterly enmeshed. The coins therefore bear Jewish religious symbols. The front shows the Temple facade with the Ark of the Covenant. The reverse shows the *lulav* and *etrog*, symbols of the festival of the Tabernacles.

> I see him, but not now; I behold him, but not near— a star shall come out of Jacob, and a scepter shall rise out of Israel.
> Num. 24:17

Cohen, pl. **Cohanim**: Priests. The Cohanim were responsible for the religious practice in the time of the Temples. When the Second Temple was destroyed in 70 CE, the priests lost their primary function; however, in memory of the Temple, they retained some rights and responsibilities.

Halakhah (literally, "go, change"): the body of Jewish religious law—the binding legal, moral, and ritual norms of Judaism that comrise the "path" that law-abiding Jews strive to follow.

47 The five Rabbis of Bnai Brakh. *Ashkenazi Haggadah*, North Italy and Germany, 1460–70. This medieval miniature shows five rabbis engaged in furious debate. The text explains that the rabbis are Eliezer, Joshua, Eleazar ben Asaria, Akiba, and Tarfan discussing the Exodus from Egypt.

war: Jerusalem was reconstructed as the Roman city Aelia Capitolina and Jews were forbidden to live in the city. Hadrian changed the name of the province from Judea to Syria-Palaestina—an obvious attempt to eradicate all memory of the connection between the Jewish people and the country. Jewish prisoners of war were sold as slaves throughout the empire.

With Judea totally devastated, the Jewish center was displaced to Galilee, where numerous synagogues sprang up after the 3rd century. The failed rebellion also destroyed the delicate balance between Palestine and the Diaspora. The strong community in Babylonia gradually assumed leadership of the Jewish people in religious, cultural, and social matters.

Rabbinical literature

The era from 70 CE to the Arabic conquest of Palestine in the 7th century is known as the rabbinical or Talmudic time, shaped as it was by the rabbis' teachings. The literature of this time, including the Mishnah and the Talmud, is called rabbinical literature and formed the foundations of Jewish culture for generations to come.

The Mishnah

According to Jewish tradition, Moses received on Sinai not only the "written teachings" (the Torah), but also the "oral teachings," which were passed on from generation to generation. There are two elements of Jewish oral doctrine: the *Halakhah* and the *Aggadah*. The Halakhah (*halakh*, "to go") relays the religious laws that govern the legal, moral, and ritual norms of Jewish life, delineating the path a law-abiding Jew should follow. The Aggadah (*haggid*, "to say, tell") has no normative authority. Its stories, legends, and metaphors reflect Jewish ethics, as well as recounting history, folklore, medicine, and science.

It is also replete with exaggeration, imagination, and satire, and a strong didactic tone is evident throughout.

According to Jewish tradition, the Halakhah was organized, edited, and committed to writing by the patriarch Rabbi Judah ha-Nasi (often called only "Rabbi") around the year 200. Thus, the *Mishnah* ("repetition," "teachings") emerged, producing for the first time a clear and verifiable record of the binding norms to which religious practice and righteous life should conform. The Mishnah is divided into six orders: (1) *Zeraim* ("seeds") governing agriculture; (2) *Moed* ("appointed time") appointing the Sabbath and festivals and fast days; (3) *Nashim* ("women") delineating marriage and family law; (4) *Nezikin* ("damages") covering civil and criminal law; (5) *Kodashim* ("sanctities") governing sacrifices in the Temple; and (6) *Tohorot* ("impurities") explaining the laws of ritual contamination and purification. These six orders encompass a total of sixty-three treatises. In a largely hostile environment, without a Jewish state and without a central holy place, the writing down of oral doctrine was essential to Judaism's very survival. It is not for nothing that Rabbi Judah ha-Nasi was given the surname "the holy one" and is considered the supreme Rabbi.

70 – 700 CE

The Talmud

In the ensuing centuries, the Mishnah was studied, discussed, and commentated in the learning centers of Palestine and Babylonia. The records of these discussions were collected in the *Gemara* ("completion"); the Mishnah and the Gemara together constitute the *Talmud* ("learn, study"). From the two centers of erudition emerged two Talmudim: the Palestinian or Jerusalem Talmud (ca. 425 CE) and the more

48 Study scene. *Coburger Pentateuch*, 1396. The hourglass in the background measures the lesson time, the teacher holds a rod, symbol of school authority, in his hand, and the child follows the letters with a small staff. The text the child should read is the golden rule of Hillel, one of the greatest rabbinical authorities before the destruction of the Second Temple: "What to you is hateful, that also, do not do to your neighbor. That is the whole Torah, everything else is interpretation. Go out and learn!" (Babylonian Talmud, Tract Shabbat 31a).

45

extensive Babylonian Talmud (6th century CE). The material collected in the two Talmudim is very different, but as in almost all areas of Jewish literature the Babylonian version attained canonical position and almost completely displaced the older Palestinian Talmud.

As commentary on the Mishnah, the Talmud is also divided into sections and tracts. Later, it too required explanation, which led to the addition of further commentaries. The Babylonian Talmud was printed for the first time in 1520–23 by Daniel Bomberg in Venice. The layout of this printing is still binding today (**49**).

70 – 700 CE

49 The first page of the Babylonian Talmud. The text, which is read from right to left, begins at the framed initial word over the middle column.

Rashi's commentary was enhanced in the late Middle Ages by further additions called the Tosafot. They appear on the outside of the page and were made by the pupils of Rashi (12th–14th century).

The text starts with 13.5 of the Mishnah.

The middle of the 14th line is marked with the letters "GM," the beginning of Gemara after the asterisk. This ongoing discussion then extends over several pages.

The commentary of Rashi (1040–1105, see p. 63) is always printed on the inside of the page and, of course, in "Rashi-writing," which deviates from normal Hebrew print.

The commentaries, or glosses, in the smallest writing completely outside and/or below the width of the page have different forms and authors, varying from tract to tract.

The synagogue: Origin and function

The word synagogue—used exclusively in European languages—comes from the Greek. It encompasses the community itself as well as its meeting place, thus corresponding to the Hebrew *bet ha-Keneset* ("house of assembly"). The origins of the synagogue are still shrouded in mystery, though literary sources and archaeological finds attest to the existence of synagogues not only in the Diaspora, but also in Palestine and even in Jerusalem as early as the time of the Second Temple (**50**). This suggests that the synagogue was never a substitute for the Temple, but a concurrent center, possibly established for secular purposes.

In contrast to the Temples, synagogues were never home to sacrifical rites with incense, burnt offerings, or animal sacrifice, which took place only in the Temple. Synagogues did not contain an altar, but from the beginning served as the site for worship services, with readings from the Torah and the prophets, study of the scriptures, and prayers. While the Temple served as the central holy place for all Jews, the synagogue was and is the gathering place of a smaller community, usually the population of a given place. Synagogues are still multipurpose centers used for prayer, study, and instruction, occasionally as a courthouse, and as a social and cultural center. The synagogue is not a sacred building or hallowed place like a Catholic church. It derives its meaning through the Torah which is read there and contains God's word.

While the cult practice in the Temple was overseen by a hereditary priest caste, the *Cohanim*, the service of God's word in the synagogue is carried out by the laity. A rabbi is not necessary for the direction of the service. Ten male Jews over the age of thirteen constitute a *minyan*, the quorum, in essence, of members necessary to

50 The Theodotos inscription. This Greek inscription, found in 1914 in a cistern on the southeast hill of Jerusalem, describes a synagogue in that location which existed before the destruction of the Second Temple (70 CE): "Theodotos, the son of Vettenos, priest and synagogue leader, grandson of a synagogue leader, constructed the synagogue for reading and instruction in the orders, furthermore the guest house and the chambers and the water provide for the stranger who requires a lodging. His father and Simonides had laid the cornerstone."

70 – 700 CE

form a community and to perform a complete service. Despite these distinctions between the ritual practice of the Temple and the more common service of the synagogue, there are reciprocal relationships between the two. The times of prayer are derived from Temple practice, and since ancient times prayers have been spoken while facing Jerusalem. This practice has shaped synagogue architecture up to modern times.

51 The synagogue of Capernaum (4th century).

Ancient synagogues

The oldest synagogues unearthed in Israel are Gamla, Masada, and Herodeon, which date back to the 1st century CE. From the 3rd to 7th century, archaeologists have found widely scattered structural synagogue ruins, which generally fall into three categories: the early Galilean (2nd–4th century), the transitional (end of the 3rd–5th century), and the late (5th–7th century) periods. The early Galilean synagogues did not yet have a fixed place for the Torah shrine and the *bimah* (the platform from which the Torah is read). It is assumed that the Torah shrine was a moveable object, a kind of cart that could be pushed into the room when it was required for the service. The bimah was probably a wooden stand, since no stone bases have been found. Synagogues were originally simple buildings, the floors were tiled with stones, and decorative embellishment was limited to the trimming of stone friezes and capitals. The largest and most important synagogue of this type is Capernaum on Lake Genesaret (**51, 52**).

The portable Torah shrine of the early synagogues was apparently unsatisfactory. Thus, in the

52 The synagogue of Capernaum (4th century). Reconstruction of the entire building.

transitional synagogues, designers began to look for a suitable location for a permanent Torah shrine. The artistic design of the buildings also changed in this period of experimentation. In place of carved decoration, synagogues were now tiled with splendid floor mosaics and even adorned with elaborate murals (**53**, **54**).

The 6th-century Beth-Alpha synagogue is a good example of the late style buildings: a niche in the wall facing Jerusalem became the permanent resting place for the Torah shrine. The building has three arks and elaborate geometric floor mosaics in the nave aisles as well as scenes with figures of people and animals. These mosaics caused a sensation when they were found in 1928, for they contradicted the prevailing thesis that there was no pictorial art in the synagogues because of the biblical prohibition against images (Exod. 20:4). Since the discovery of the Beth-Alpha synagogue many ancient synagogues containing figurative art have been excavated. Fine art was apparently tolerated (despite rabbinical denunciations of ostentation) if it was intended solely for decoration and there was no danger of idolatry. The synagogue mosaics illustrated biblical stories or had symbolic qualities; they were not objects of adoration and therefore were permitted.

70 – 700 CE

53, 54 The synagogue of Dura Europus (3rd century) is the only known synagogue building to have a fresco cycle. The cycle illustrates biblical themes that are distributed on several areas tiled onto the walls of the

assembly hall. View of the Torah niche (above) and on the west wall (below).

55 The synagogue of Beth-Alpha (6th century). Detail of the mosaic of the sacrifice of Isaac (Gen. 22). In the left background are Abraham's servants. The center shows the ram bound to a tree as a replacement offering. On the right, Abraham stands ready, knife in hand, to place his chained son Isaac on the burning altar. The hand that descends from the heavens symbolizes divine intervention. A text underneath reads: "Do not lay your hand on [the boy]."

There is evidence of Jewish settlements in Spain as early as the 1st century CE. By the 4th century, there were already sizeable communities, large enough that the Christian church found it necessary to forbid personal relationships between Christians and Jews. In 474, the Aryan Visigoths (West Goths) invaded and conquered the Iberian peninsula. At first they treated the Jews like Roman citizens, but in 589, when King Reccared I was converted to Catholicism, the situation of the Jews became considerably more difficult. In the 7th century, the Council of Toledo instituted forced baptism, dispossession, and enslavement. How consistently these anti-Jewish decisions were enforced remains unknown.

Jewish life under the Muslims

In 711, the Berber Tarik Ibn-Ziyad landed in Gibraltar and quickly conquered the Iberian peninsula. The triumphant Islamic armies were greeted as deliverers from the Visigoths. The Muslims treated both Jews and Christians in the conquered areas as members of a "book religion" (*ahl al-kitab*, "people of the book"), and better than other non-Muslims, who were seen merely as heathens and idolators. The rights and responsibilities of the Jewish and Christian minorities were determined by the so-called Treaty of Omar, which guaranteed the *Dhimmi* ("protected ones") the safety of their person and property and freedom of religious belief and practice, as well as far-reaching autonomy in their community affairs. For this protection, they had to pay per-capita and property taxes. The state also decreed that Jewish Dhimmi had to wear some article of yellow clothing to distinguish them from Muslims. They could build no new places of worship, hold no Muslim slaves, carry no arms, and ride no horses, and they were supposed to practice their religion as inconspicuously as possible. However,

56 Toledo, originally a synagogue and later the Church of Santa Maria la Blanca, ca. 1200, the earliest preserved synagogue on Spanish soil. The prayer room on a trapezoidal floor plan is subdivided by wide horseshoe-shaped arches into five naves. The synagogue is an architectural mixture of both Christian (basilica, capitals) and Islamic (horseshoe arches, stucco) elements. Today, the building is a national monument.

these regulations were not consistently enforced.

Although the Jewish subjects could live anywhere, they usually lived together, in areas called *Juderias*, in order to practice their religion. The ghettoes of later Christian Europe were unheard of under Islamic dominion. Jews were not limited to certain professions, but were especially successful at manufacture and trade in textiles, medicines, and spices. Some were state tax collectors.

The leaders of the communities were often scholars who had achieved some degree of fame in the arts or sciences and thus came to the attention of the *caliph* (Islamic ruler). One such person was Hisdai (or Hasdai) Ibn-Shaprut (**58**). He

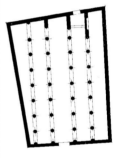

57 Toledo, floor plan.

Sephardim: Sepharad was the name of a land in the bible (Obadiah 20), but the name had long been familiarly applied as a Hebrew designation for the Iberian peninsula. The term "Sephardic" refers to the culture and tradition of Spanish and Portuguese Judaism (in contrast to the Ashkenazim; see p. 61). The descendants of the expelled Spanish Jews are still known all over the world as the Sephardim.

Marranos: The Spanish epithet Marrano ("pig") was common through the sixteenth century for the Jews who were forced, or at least pressured, to convert to Christianity in the thirteenth century, many of whom remained secretly faithful to Judaism. In official documents, the designation is *converso* ("convert") or *nuevo christiano* ("new Christian"). Many Marranos later emigrated to other countries, where the practice of Judaism was not a punishable offense, and returned there to their original religion.

58 An audience with Abd ar-Rahman III in the palace of Medina Azahara. Painting by Domingo Baixeras, 1885. The greatest scholars of the time, among them Hisdai Ibn-Shaprut, gathered at the court of this caliph of Cordoba.

59 Cordoba, synagogue 1315. After 1492, the building was transformed into a hospital and is today a national monument. The principle of the wall partitions—a base zone (originally covered with colored tiling), a main zone with rich stucco works, and finally the window zone—follows the Mudejar style of the 14th century. The Arabic inscription banners typical of Islamic-Spanish art are replaced here by Hebrew. This view shows the south wall with the entry portal and the elevated women's area, the oldest preserved in Spain. The middle of the west wall, facing the Torah shrine, contains another niche that counterbalanced well with the *bimah* (lectern).

served the caliph in Cordoba between 940 and 975 as physician, translator, diplomat, and minister of foreign trade. He was a patron to the Spanish yeshivas as well as to many scholars. With his support, the study of the Hebrew language blossomed.

With the end of the Umayyad dynasty (756–1030), the caliphate in Cordoba disintegrated into a number of fragmented kingdoms, each with its own center—Seville, Granada, Malaga, Saragossa, among others—which offered the Jews new possibilities. Sephardic Judaism experienced its first cultural peak in these small Muslim principalities. Samuel ha-Nagid was typical of the Jewish upper class of this time. From 1030 until his death in 1056, he was commander-in-chief of the army of Granada; he also wrote poems in both Arabic and Hebrew, taught the Halakhah and was well versed in the bible and Talmud, as well as in the works of the old and contemporary philosophers.

Near the end of the 11th century, King Alfonso VI conquered Toledo. The *Reconquista*, the Christian recapture of Spain, reached central Spain, threatening the weakened Muslim sovereignties. In 1082, the King of Seville sought help from the fanatical North African sect of the

Almoravids who soon took control of southern Spain. Though Almoravid rule was short-lived, it marked a major turning point in the treatment of the Jewish population, causing first groups to emigrate.

The Almoravids were displaced in 1146 by the even more extreme Almohads. Synagogues and yeshivas were destroyed; Jews were forced to accept Islam. This period of oppression sparked a massive migration to the areas conquered by the Christian Reconquista in northern Spain and to North Africa. A contemporary chronicler, Rabbi Abraham Ibn Daud, reports that the Jews turned to the Christians, "and sold themselves, so that they helped them, to flee from the country of Ismael, while others fled, naked and barefoot."

The golden age of the Spanish Jews

Through the Reconquista and the immigration from the Islamic south, the center of Jewish life shifted to Christian Spain in the early 12th century. At first, the Reconquista worked out in the Jews' favor. The Christian conquerors took an interest in the Jews for economic and cultural reasons: the Jews settled cities deserted by the Arabs and, because of their knowledge of Islamic culture and governing practice, assumed important political and administrative positions.

Their legal relationship with the king involved direct service in exchange for the king's protection, as established in a contract called the *Fuero*. In exchange for taxes the Jews paid the king, they were allowed to practice all professions, from urban trade to agriculture, own a house and property, and conduct their community life with little interference from the Christian government. Under these conditions, Jewish culture attained what is called the golden age of Spanish-Jewish history. In this golden age, Jewish scholars translated many important texts which introduced Greek and Islamic scholarship and cultures to the Christian Occident. Aristotle was often translated, first from Greek into Arabic and then from Arabic into Hebrew and Latin. Besides works of philo-

60 Tapestry page from a bible, Burgos 1260. The bible was copied by the clerk Menachem ben Abraham Malik and is one of the oldest preserved examples of Spanish illumination. These tapestry pages are set before or after the main parts of the bible. The page pictured here is found before the books of the Prophets. Typically, the border around the script is a heavy line, edged by two lines in very tiny script. This "micrography" is an art developed by Jewish scribes and is still practiced today. The basic plan of a richly ornamented tapestry page can be traced back to Islamic wall decoration.

711 – 1492

The Jews belong to the king; even if they live on the territory of a nobleman, or their knights, or others, or on monastic territory; they must always be subordinate to the king, in his protection and in his service.
  From a *Fuero* (Spanish law governing the Sephardim)

61   An astrolabe. Spain or northern Africa, ca. 1300. The astrolabe is one the most common astronomical instruments of the Middle Ages. It was used to determine and observe the positions of the stars and to measure the earth. Jews played a critical role in the further development of the ancient astrolabe by translating the essays of the Islamic astronomer Azarchiel (ca. 1029–87), which describe his improved instrument, into Castilian at the court of Alfonso the Wise (Alfonso X, 1252–84). At the court of Aragon, Jews were authorized to produce astrolabes. This example is the only known astrolabe with a Judeo-Arabic inscription.

sophy, Jewish scholars translated works of mathematics, geometry, astronomy (**61**), and medicine, bringing the ancient classics of medicine by Galen and Hippocrates to Christian Europe for the first time.

Deep-seated changes took place in the late 13th century, both in Christian-Jewish relations and within Judaism itself. In reaction to the rationalism of the philosophically trained elite, a Jewish mysticism called *Kabbalah* ("tradition") emerged in the southern French Provence and especially in the northern Spanish province of Gerona, and rapidly spread. The chief work of the Kabbalah was the *Zohar* ("illumination" or "brightness"), probably written by Moses de Leon in Guadalajara, Spain. The kabbalists yearned for a mystical union with God, while Maimonides (see p. 58 f.) and his followers sought a rational knowledge of God. The latter taught a studied approach to the Torah, while the kabbalists saw it as a revelation full of mysteries.

Meanwhile, the relationship between Christians and Jews began to deteriorate: The prosperity of many Jews and their proximity to the rulers provoked envy and resentment. An amplifying mood of anti-Semitism was fueled by anti-Jewish propaganda issued by the church, launching an age of religious disputation. Jewish scholars were forced to debate with Christian theologians over the truth of their beliefs; in such contests, biased in their design and structure, the "victory" of the Christians was a foregone conclusion. These unfair debates were supposed to prompt Jews to convert. Thus, in the controversy of Barcelona in 1263, the famous doctor, biblical commentator, and Kabbalah member Rabbi Moses ben-Nachman (known as RaMBaN, or Nachmanides) debated the baptized Jew Pablo Christiani. Nachmanides represented Judaism

aggressively and confidently, then recorded the debate in an effort to counter-
act the church's distorted propaganda.
When he published his notes, he was
expelled from Spain by order of the pope,
and emigrated in 1267 to Jerusalem.

At the end of the 14th century, the
tensions in Spain exploded into violence:
due to economic depression and a weak
young king, the latent anti-Semitism was
inflamed under the influence of the Arch-
deacon Fernando Martinez de Ecija and
the Dominican Vinzenz Ferrer. A wave of
persecution began in June 1391 in the
Juderia of Seville (**62**) and spread over
the whole country. A contemporary, Rabbi
Chasdai Crescas, wrote: "At the New
Moon of the fateful month of Tammus of
the year 5151 [1391], the Lord stretched
the bows of the enemies against the community of Seville, which was numerous in
people, for there were there 6,000–
7,000 fathers of families, and the enemies
destroyed their gates through fires and
killed a large number of people. The
greatest number, however, changed their
belief ... after many of them, blessing
God's name, suffered death, though also
many who had broken the holy bond then
embraced the fire ... in the holy city of the
community Cordoba. Here, too, many went over
[converted], and the community was
devastated."

62 An alley in the Juderia of
Seville.

This description suggests that only some Jews
were prepared to become martyrs (to "sanctify
the divine name"). The majority converted to
Christianity under this duress and were baptized.
From this time, then, Spain was burdened with
the problem of the converts (*conversos*), also
called "New Christians" (*nuevo Christianos*) or

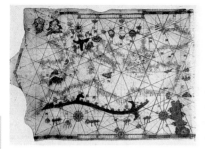

63 Nautical chart of the Mediterranean and the surrounding areas. Judah Ibn Zarah, Alexandria, 1500. Medieval Spain boasted numerous Jewish cartographers. The island of Majorca, then part of the kingdom of Aragon, was a center of cartography. Judah Ibn Zarah was among the most important cartographers of Majorca; he emigrated first to Alexandria, then to Zafed. These sea charts, drawn over a grid of interlocking squares, rectangles, and triangles, were very exact and indispensable for navigation. Columbus, who started on his first famous expedition west in the year of the expulsion of the Spanish Jews, had no scruples about using the work of Jewish cartographers and astronomers.

Marranos ("pigs"). After their baptism, New Christians were granted the same rights accorded "Old Christians." They could marry into the high nobility and assume positions previously closed to them. Their success, however, fed the envy of the Old Christians. Moreover, the church and the Christian populace questioned the sincerity of the conversos' professed beliefs and suspected that many, despite the guise of Christianity, still clung to their old beliefs. This fundamentally anti-Semitic mistrust gave rise to the Spanish Inquisition. A body of informers now took it upon themselves to spy on the conversos, to see if they avoided pork or kept unleavened bread at home at Easter time (i.e., for Passover). In the face of these informants, no one was secure.

In 1413–14, at the instigation of Vinzenzo Ferrer in Tortosa, the "truth" of the Jews' religious belief was once more pitted publicly in debate against the tenets of Christianity. The Rabbis were forced into a defensive stance from the outset, faced with a fanatical convert, Geronimo de Santa Fé. After a year and nine months of grueling "discussion," the Jews gave up. The church appeared to triumph—it fulfilled its purpose: over 50,000 Jews supposedly converted, but this "victory" only exacerbated the "converso problem". The Jews who did not convert became noticeably more isolated by an onslaught of discriminatory laws.

Events of the late 15th century led to the final expulsion of the Sephardic Jews. The Catholic monarchs Ferdinand of Aragon and Isabella of Castile, who through their marriage in 1469 had united their kingdoms, renewed the Reconquista. In that same year, the first conversos accused of

"Jewishizing" were burned in Seville. Two years later, the Dominican and father confessor of the kings, Tomás de Torquemada, was summoned to be Grand Inquisitor. With fanatical zeal he sought out the hidden Jews among the conversos, to deliver them to the Auto da fé, "act of belief"—mostly, death on the pyre.

In January 1492, the Reconquista came to an end with the conquest of Granada and the expulsion of the last Muslims from Spain. The Iberian peninsula was again Christian—except for the Jews. The Edict of March 31, 1492, ordering the expulsion of all Jews within four months, served two ends: complete the political and religious unity and withdrawing the support of existing Jewish communities from the conversos. About 150,000 Jews emigrated in the summer of 1492. Many turned to Portugal, from which they were in turn expelled in 1496–97. The majority fled to North Africa and to the Ottoman empire, while some made their way to northwestern Europe (see pp. 115 and 126). The downfall of Spanish Judaism, at that time the largest and most important community in the Diaspora, was perceived in the Jewish world as a disaster. Many saw it as a sign of the end of the world, giving rise to a surge of messianic hopes.

64 An Aragonian Jew in the costume of the Jewish elite, detail from a Haggadah. Spain, 3rd quarter, 14th century. The *cotte* (a robe) is long, usually an overcoat or, as in this case, a *houce* (a hood) is worn over it. The *cotte* has wide, funnel-shaped sleeves with noticeably deep-cut armholes that allow the wearer to withdraw his arms. The neck hole has a double flap. The *houce* is attached with the *chaperon* (a cowl collar), whose small mantle is pushed inside the robe.

65 "Auto da fé" (public execution by burning) in Portugal. Engraving by Bernard Picart, 1722. Joods History Museum, Amsterdam.

66 Bronze monument to Moses ben Maimon, called Maimonides, in his native town of Cordoba in the Calle Judios.

Although Maimonides was one of the most important scholars of the Middle Ages, relatively few gentiles know his name. Jews, on the other hand, praise this rationalist, scholar, and physician even today with the common aphorism: "From Moses [who received the Torah] to Moses [Maimonides] there were none like Moses."

Maimonides (Rabbi Moses ben Maimon, often referred to in Jewish literature by the abbreviation RaMBaM) was born in 1135 in Cordoba. His father, Rabbi Maimon ben Josef, saw that he received a thorough education. Arabic teachers taught him Greek and Arabic philosophy and the sciences. In 1148, when he was thirteen years old, the extremist Almohads overran Maimonides's home town and forced all "nonbelievers" to accept Islam or to emigrate. Maimonides's family fled first to Christian northern Spain and eventually settled in Fez, Morocco. There was at the time an animated public discussion of the judgment of the Jews who had converted to Islam under religious persecution. In 1165 Maimonides published his "Letter on Disloyalty" in which he defended the forced converts and rebutted those who self-righteously and without corresponding experience condemned the converts as heretics and defectors.

When, in 1165, the situation for the Jews in Fez worsened, the family moved on again: to Akko, Jerusalem, and finally Fostat near Cairo. From here, Maimonides's fame spread—as a philosopher, an expert on law, and a physician (he was personal physician to the sultan Saladin's vizier, and published several medical treatises). He died at the age of seventy in Fostat and was buried, according to his own wishes, in Tiberias.

Two works are especially associated with the name of Maimonides: written in Hebrew, the *Mishneh Torah* (1180), deals with the entire Talmud. In fourteen books that treat all important areas of human life, Maimonides distilled the important teachings from the tangled cornucopia of rabbinical literature and presented the Talmud in a systematic codex, leaving out apparently contradictory opinions or issues unresolved in the Torah.

Through the *Mishneh Torah*, Maimonides considerably simplified Talmudic study, but his codex soon provoked criticism on exactly these grounds. Many Rabbis feared that this bare, systematic registration of the laws would undermine the traditional method of teaching and truth-seeking by discussion. It was also criticized because it omitted the names of the rabbinical authorities and sources. The criticism of the *Mishneh Torah* may well have been motivated by other, more practical reasons, for Maimonides's edition of the Talmud allowed practicing judges more independence from rabbinical learning and eroded their prestige. Thus, a flood of literature debating the pros and cons of Maimonides's work emerged, and the *Mishneh Torah* itself became known as *Yad Ha-Hazakah* ("Strong Hand")–from Deut. 34:12–because an individual had exercised a "strong hand" and systematically organized the material on religious law.

His primary work on religious philosophy was the *Guide to the Perplexed*, written around 1190 in Arabic and directed toward the elite Arabic "perplexed." They considered themselves devout, but were confused by apparent contradictions between their religious faith and the teachings of rational philosophy.

Maimonides tried to ease their conflict by means of a manual in which he philosophically debated the unsolved, controversial problems. He attempted to prove that belief and divine revelation, on one hand, and Aristotelian philosophy and reason, on the other, can indeed be reconciled, that students need not see the differing views as an either/or proposition. The *Guide* was quickly disseminated. It was translated into Hebrew during Maimonides's lifetime and a later Latin translation (before 1240) brought the work to Christian scholars as well.

The widespread popularity of Maimonides's ideas led soon after his death to an ongoing quarrel between his pupils and traditionalist and kabbalistic adversaries, the intensity of which waxed and waned repeatedly over the centuries. In the late Middle Ages and in modern times, Maimonides was despised by the majority of Jews, while in the 18th and 19th centuries, during the so-called Age of Enlightenment and beyond, he became the idol of Jewish Rationalists and reformers. Thus, reading the *Guide* was an early turning point for the young German Jewish philosopher Moses Mendelssohn (see p. 139ff.). He read it day and night; he even attributed his humpback to his intense study, though he averred that "it has repaid me the damage seven-fold, as it refreshed my soul."

321 – 16th cent.

Exactly when Jews first settled in Germany is not known, though it is reasonable to assume that they followed on the heels of the Romans marching to the Rhine, as was the case in other countries of the Roman empire. The earliest historical evidence of Jews in Germany comes from Cologne. In 321 CE, Emperor Constantine wrote: "To the council of the city of Cologne. By general law We allow all officials to call the Jews to the city council. To maintain a certain compensation for the previous regulation, We allow that two or three should always enjoy this privilege without being called into any office." (**67**).

The call to the city council was a dubious honor as civil service carried a hefty price. The councilors had to make up any discrepancies between the taxes collected and the sum demanded by Rome out of their own pockets , and they could neither move nor sell their property. Thus, this decree revoked a privilege that the Jews had enjoyed until now, namely, exemption from costly honorary offices. Since these offices could only be held by wealthy landowners, and wealth and influence were not accumulated overnight, this proclamation appears to be evidence that Jews had been living in Cologne for some time before 321.

In a second decree of 331, the emperor ordered that "Rabbis, Archsynagogues, Synagogue Fathers" and other community officials be relieved of service in the council. This

67 Letter of Emperor Constantine from December 321 to the *decurios* ("councilmen") of Cologne; with this document, the Jews were summoned to service in the council. Excerpt from the Codex Theodosianus, 5th century.

suggests further that the Jews of Cologne already lived in an organized community. Under Roman dominion, they were citizens with full rights. It is also reasonable to infer that decrees made in Cologne applied to other cities on the Rhine, the Maas, and the Danube, including Mainz, Speyer, Worms, Metz, Trier (**68**), Augsburg, Regensburg, and Vienna.

Traces of Jewish settlements were lost in the turmoil of the next few centuries, as the Romans retreated from German soil and mass migrations took place. We will probably never know whether Jews remained in the cities and formed the core of medieval Jewish communities, or if they were founded by new groups of Jewish immigrants, particularly from France and Italy.

68   Clay lamp with a seven-branched candlestick (menorah) between palm leaves. The lamp was found in Trier and dates from the 4th century.

321 – 16th cent.

The protection of the Carolingians

In the Carolingian era, evidence of Jewish residents reappears in northern France and surrounding the capital Aachen. The politics of the Carolingians were essentially friendly toward the Jews. The Jews were free, they could own land, and they could bear arms. Still, they were considered foreigners, and as such were unprotected unless the emperor chose to extend protection and privileges to them, as did Charlemagne (747– 814) and Ludwig the Pious (778–840). At the time, Jews were active as

Ashkenaz, Ashkenazi, Ashkenazim: Ashkenaz is originally the name of a people mentioned in Genesis 10:3. In the Middle Ages, Ashkenaz became the familiar Hebrew designation for Germany and northeastern France. By the time of the crusades, the Ashkenazim also included the Jews who had fled to Russia and Poland and their descendants (as distinct from the Sephardim; see p. 50ff.).
Yeshiva: Literally, "sitting, meeting." The yeshivas were Talmud academies of higher education for Talmudic scholars and rabbis.
Takkanot: Literally, "improvement, reform, order." The Takkanot was a legally binding ordinance of individual Talmud scholars or synods as an expansion or circumscription of religious law as understood at the time.

OBEN MARSPFORTEN

69 The medieval community center of Cologne, based on the work of Professor Doppelfeld, 1958. Sketch by G. Grosch, 1980.
The public and private buildings of the community were found on the site of the present-day city hall.
1 Synagogue
2 Women's synagogue
3 Mikveh (baths for ritual purification)
4 Warm baths for hygienic purposes
5 Bakery
6 Wedding house and theater
7 Family hostel for traveling Jews

70 View from the glass pyramid over the mikveh. In the background is the historic city hall of Cologne.

importers and purveyors to the court, and were also recruited for diplomatic missions. From Europe they exported slaves, weapons, animal pelts, and silk goods. From the Orient they brought back luxury goods—spices, expensive fabrics, precious metals, and medicines.

The protection conferred upon the Jews by the emperors extended beyond life and property: They were also guaranteed unfettered trade and some relief from tariffs, and were allowed to employ Christian workers. In return for these rights, the Jews owed the emperor one-tenth of their profits and were expected to provide faithful service to the imperial court. Since these privileges were extended only to individual Jews or small communities rather than to all Jews, no specific body of Jewish rights existed as such.

The Jewish communities on the Rhine

In the 10th and 11th centuries, the old Roman settlements on the Rhine—Mainz, Cologne, Worms, and Speyer—rapidly developed into centers of economic and cultural life for Ashkenazi Judaism. The communities of Mainz and Cologne had emerged in the late 9th century. Jewish life in Mainz blossomed with the immigration of the Kalonymus family from Lucca in northern Italy. Around 980, Moses Kalonymus the Elder introduced the Palestinian-Italian tradition of liturgical poetry (*pijut*) into Germany. Under the influence of this family, which spawned many learned rabbis, liturgical poets and philosophical authors, Mainz became a center of Jewish learning.

Gershom ben-Judah (960–1028) was undoubtedly the first widely renowned teacher in Ashkenazi Judaism; he was so revered that succeeding generations granted him the title *Meor ha-Golah* ("Light of the Exile"). Among other things, the Takkanot (see p. 61) forbidding polygamy and divorce without the wife's consent are ascribed to him. His ethical and legal decisions helped establish the legitimacy of European Jewish academies and their independence from the Babylonian scholars who had dominated academia until that point.

There is evidence of a Jewish quarter in Cologne from the time of the Archbishop Anno (1056–75), including reports that the Cologne Jews mourned the archbishop's death in their synagogue. The community must have been quite affluent in the 11th century judging by the substantial loans they made to the archbishop. In 1956–57, archaeological digs unearthed the medieval community center in the heart of Cologne complete with a synagogue, *mikveh* (ritual bath), bakery, theater, and hostel. In contemporary Cologne, these structures are outlined on the pavement. The mikveh has been restored and is open to the public (**69**, **70**).

The Jewish communities of Worms and Speyer date back to the late 10th and the 11th centuries. Gershom ben-Judah already reported on the financial transactions of the Jews of Worms (and Mainz) at the Cologne Fair. The most famous student of the Worms academy was Rabbi Shlomo Yitzhaki (or ben-Isaac), called Rashi, who was born in 1040 in Troyes. After his student days in Worms and Mainz (around 1060), Rashi returned to Troyes and there founded the highly respected *yeshiva* (Talmudic school). Through his biblical and Talmudic commentaries, distinctive in their clarity, intelligibility, and vividness, he attained a degree of authority that continues today. His commentary is printed in every edition of the Babylonian Talmud (see

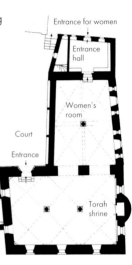

321 – 16th cent.

71 Floor plan of the synagogue of Worms. The synagogue was built in 1174–75 with the women's room added in 1212–13; the study center labeled "Rashi Chapel" and entrance hall to the women's room were added ca. 1623.

72 Worms. Synagogue court with sitting niches in the women's synagogue. Near the Romanesque entryway of the men's synagogue is the founders' inscription marking the beginning of construction in 1034.

73 Worms. Interior view of the men's synagogue with a view of the bimah (lectern) and the Torah shrine.

p. 46). Until it was destroyed by the Nazis, the synagogue in Worms was the oldest synagogue in continuous use in Europe. It was reconstructed after the Second World War and rededicated in 1961 (**71–73**).

The Speyer community in southwestern Germany (**74**) was founded on the initiative of Bishop Rüdiger Hutzmann, who in 1084 settled the Jews in order to "increase the standing of the city a thousandfold." He assured them of "laws … that are better than the Jews enjoy in any city of the German empire." The economic importance of the Jews of Speyer and Worms was soon recognized by the German emperors. In 1090, Henry IV followed the Carolingian model and conferred upon the Jews of both cities extensive privileges, guaranteeing freedom of trade and of worship in the city. For the first time, the Jews here were identified as "belonging to the imperial chamber." This reference had no possessory implications, but simply emphasized their legal relationship to the emperor.

A Cologne document of 1301 provides clues about the internal structure of the communities: "We, the [Jewish]-bishop, the administrative authorities, and all the Jews," the document reads. The Jewish-bishop, later also called the *Judenmeister* ("Jewish Master"), represented the Jews to gentile authorities. The Judenmeister is not to be confused with the rabbi, who was responsible for matters internal to the Jewish community. The "administrative authorities" supported the Judenmeister in running the community's affairs.

74 Speyer. From the medieval synagogue, only the east wall remains today. The women's synagogue is on the left, the men's on the right.

The four Jewish settlements discussed above—Mainz, Cologne, Worms, and Speyer—were by no means the only ones in the Carolingian regions north of the

Alps. Important communities in northern France include Limoges, Orléans, Rouen, Reims, and Troyes. Communities emerged in Magdeburg, Merseburg, Regensburg, and Prague (**75**) in the 10th century and in Trier, Bonn, Xanten, and Neuss in the 11th, to name only the most important.

The crusades

In 1095, only five years after Henry IV granted privileges to the Jews, Pope Urban II exhorted all Christendom to war at the Council of Clermont, bringing about unforeseeable catastrophies for the Jewish communities. Wild, fanatical hordes joined armies of knights and set off to free the holy sites in Jerusalem from Muslim control, overrunning Jewish settlements along their way. In 1095–96, the communities in Metz and Rouen were attacked and many Jews were killed. In the spring and summer of 1096, the plundering and murdering masses reached the Rhineland and destroyed the burgeoning communities of Speyer, Worms, Mainz, Trier, Cologne, Neuss, and Xanten. As the crusaders drove through Bohemia, the Jews of Prague suffered a similar fate. The Protective Order of Henry IV proved useless, and the varyingly sincere attempts of some bishops to seek protection for the Jews uniformly failed.

After the massacres, the surviving Jews returned to the cities, set up their houses and synagogues again, and carried on outwardly as before. Nevertheless, the crusades would have far-reaching consequences.

The Hasidei Ashkenaz

The grief felt throughout the Jewish community spawned a new consciousness of a shared destiny. The inwardly directed spirituality that the Ashkenazi Jews had already displayed during

75 The *Altneuschul* ("Old-New School") in Prague, ca. 1300. This is the oldest original synagogue in the Ashkenazi region.

321 – 16th cent.

As [the crusaders] now came on their march through the cities in which Jews lived, they spoke among themselves: "See, we travel afar, to locate the burial sites and to avenge ourselves on the Ismaelites, and see, here Jews live among us [the Christians] whose forefathers have unjustly killed and crucified him [Jesus]! Let us therefore first take revenge on them and obliterate them from among the people, so that the name Israel may be mentioned no more; or they shall become like us and convert to our beliefs."
    Shlomo bar Simeon

> The enemies hurled stones and arrows against them, and they did not think of escape. ... As those gathered in the chambers and saw such righteous deeds and how the enemies attacked them, they all cried: "It is best to sacrifice our lives!" And the women there girt their loins with power and slaughtered their sons and daughters and then themselves; many men fortified themselves and slaughtered their women, their children and their servants; the delicate and soft mother slaughtered her dear child; all arose, man like woman, and slaughtered one the other ... and called out with loud voice: "Look and see, our God, what we do for the sanctification of your great name, to avoid replacing you with the crucified one."
>
> Shlomo bar Simeon on the "Sanctification of the Holy Name"
> (*Kiddush ha-Shem*) by suicide in Mainz

76 A young German Jew wearing the *tallit katan* (small prayer shawl). *Ashkenazi Haggadah*, northern Italy and Germany, 1460–70. The small prayer shawl is a rectangular, sleeveless garment with a neck opening for the head. Because it has fringes (*tzitzit*) on the four corners, like the large prayer shawl, it is also called *arba kanfot* ("four ends").

persecution and martyrdom developed into the medieval German movement of the Hasidei Ashkenaz ("Pious of Ashkenaz"). Their most prominent member was Judah ben Samuel HeHasid (ca. 1150–1217), author of the *Book of the Pious*. The originally elitist Hasidei Ashkenaz held themselves to very high standards but taught indulgence and gentleness toward others. The Hasid was supposed to recite his prayer with great spiritual and emotional concentration to a melody that corresponded to the theme of the prayer. Prayers of the common, uneducated people, however, were held to a different standard: "If someone comes to you who understands no Hebrew, or a woman, but fears God, then tell them, that they should make the prayers their own in a language they understand. For prayer stems from the capacity of the heart, and if the heart does not understand what comes out of the mouth, what value has that? Thus, it is better to pray in the language one understands."

Aside from the Torah, the Hasidim followed a "heavenly law"; for them, the law of the Torah was the lowest standard given a Jew, and the Hasid strived for his deeds to conform with the highest standard, the heavenly law. Thus, for example, according to the Torah a robber must replace the full value of goods he has stolen; for the Hasidim, this compensation does not suffice: "The robber should consider the suffering he has caused [the robbed] and all his dependants, and also the hardships which he caused; and he should pay them for both the full damage and its consequences, and also according to the position of the robbed."

The writings of the Hasidei Ashkenaz are very interesting, for they give us a glimpse of the real life of Jewish communities of the time: the Hasidim criticized the existing social order and asked why prosperity is not distributed more justly in the world, and strove to make material changes. For example, they found it inappropriate that poor and rich had to pay equal sums in taxes, and pleaded for a taxation system that takes into account an individual's financial resources. They were interested in issues of sexuality, marriage, and family life, and idealized martyrdom. This particular pious vein of German Judaism soon encompassed the majority of Ashkenazi Jews, even among the theologically unschooled, and survived in the traditions of those who fled to eastern Europe.

Crisis in the thirteenth century

Apart from the atrocities committed during the crusades, pointed anti-Semitism in the general population first arose in the 13th century. Up to this time Jews had played a major role in trade with the Middle East, but were now forced out by the crusaders, who erected their own trading posts. Their displacement from international commerce, exclusion from the Christian guilds, and stricter

77 Moses accepts the Tablets of the Law. From a *mahzor* (prayer book for the holidays), 1st quarter, 14th century. Shown here are Moses, Aaron, and the men and women of Israel. Aaron carries a miter, the men carry the "Jew's hat," the women are represented with animal heads. While the yellow spot/ring was seen as a blemish and almost never represented in Jewish illumination, and in Christian art only rarely, the Jew's hat was widespread in both Jewish illumination by the early 13th century and in Christian art by the beginning of the 15th century. The German Jews had long worn a pointed hat, even before it was required of them. From the beginning of the 15th century, as this headgear increasingly became a tool of discrimination, it disappeared from the pictures.

78 Moses presents the Tablets of the Law to the Israelites. Fresco in the middle vault of St. Mary's in Lyskirchen, Cologne, mid-13th century. Biblical Jews are identified by the pointed Jew's hat in Christian art as well.

79 Pope Innocence III, at the fourth Lateran Council, ordered the identification of the Jews on the following grounds: "It occurs occasionally that erroneously Christians mix with Jewish or Saracens and Jews or Saracens mix with Christian women. To prevent this in future, we establish that Jews and Saracens of both sexes should publicly distinguish themselves through the style of their robe from the remaining population."

enforcement of the 12th century prohibition of Christians charging interest forced the Jews into the disparaged trades of making loans and running pawnshops. This association with money handling clung to the Jews, who were soon known as "usurers," for centuries.

This altered their position in German and French society irrevocably. Respected foreign traders—albeit considered foreigners themselves—until the 12th century, in the course of the 13th century they became a scorned minority exploited by the imposition of special taxes and ever higher charges for flimsy protection.

The fourth Lateran Council of 1215

Pressure from the Christian church also increased in the early 13th century. The fourth Lateran Council under Pope Innocence III renewed, and even intensified, anti-Jewish legislation by the Church. In four articles, the Jews' living conditions were severely restricted: The measures included a new duty on interest income, identification by marker (**79**), exclusion from public offices, and a ban on proselytizing.

These regulations, initially directed at both the Jews and the Saracens, were soon applied only to Jews. Exactly how the Jews should be identified was not specified, and varied from country to country. In Germany, the pointed Jew's hat (**77**, **78**) was common from the 13th century on, and the yellow patch or ring (**80**) from the 15th century.

Accusations of ritual murder in Fulda

In 1235, accusations of Jews performing ritual murder surfaced for the first time in the German empire. Such charges had already appeared in Norwich, England, in 1144 and in Blois, France, in 1171, both times resulting in bloody riots against Jewish communities.

In Fulda, a city in central Germany, a miller's house burned down on Christmas Eve, killing his five children. Immediately, rumors spread that the Jews had killed the children because they needed Christian blood for medicinal purposes. Thirty-two Jews were arrested and killed, and murder charges were brought against all Jews in the empire. The events were recited before Frederick II, who

> Neither in the Old nor in the New Testament is it to be found that the Jews would hunger after human blood. On the contrary: they guard themselves against defilement by any blood. This emerges from the book, which is called in Hebrew *Berakhot* [Torah] ... It is also highly probable that those for whom even the blood of permitted animals is forbidden, can have no thirst for human blood. It speaks against this slander, its hideousness, its unnaturalness and the natural human feeling which the Jews extend even to the Christians.
>
> Frederick II

ordered an investigation that ended in acquittal.

The "servants of the chamber"

Frederick issued the acquittal in 1236, along with a renewal of the old privileges granted by Henry IV in 1090. In this document the term *Kammerknechte* (*servi nostri et servi camerae nostrae*, "our servants and the servants of our chamber") is found for the first time. The Jews of the entire empire would henceforth be under the exclusive protection and exclusive authority of the emperor. No doubt Frederick's proclamation also reinstated the Jew's financial obligations, for they had slipped out of the king's (or emperor's) grasp as source of tax revenue. The Jews had to pay various masters—the emperor, the bishop, the city—often all simultaneously in the never-ending pursuit of rights and protection.

After the decline of the Staufer dynasty, the notion of "Kammerknechtschaft"—the right to offer and receive payment for protection of the

80 Dress of 16th century Jews in Worms: coat with a yellow ring. The purse implies financial transactions, the garlic (*shum*) suggests this man comes from one of the "Shum-cities" of Speyer, Worms, and Mainz.

81 The Esslingen Mahzor, 1290. "The Mighty King," a hymn from the weekly excerpt.

82 The "Jewish Sow" of Frankfurt. Leaflet etching, 18th century. In Trient, there was a much-sensationalized accusation of ritual murder in the year 1475. The Jews were accused of murdering the two-year-old Simon. Illustrated books or pamphlets quickly fueled these rumors. In Frankfurt the horror story so captured the imagination of the city fathers that they commissioned a representation of Simon's martyrdom along with a slandererous caricature of the Jews.

Jews as servants of the ruler's chamber—dissolved into the sovereign's financial right, which at the emperor's discretion could be given away, leased, or pawned. With each change of hands the "protection" became more expensive. The extent to which the protection rights were commercialized and exploited in the next century is expressed in the Golden Edict of Charles IV in 1356: "We establish ... that all electors legally may hold rights to all gold and silver mines, also tin, copper, iron and other mines as well as all salt mines, including all Jewish rights." The implication here is that the rights of the Jews (or the rights to the Jews), like mineral rights are a commodity to be exchanged without thought to their political or social significance. The Jews had no more intrinsic value than a grain of salt or a nugget of tin.

Talmud burning in Paris

In response to denunciation from the convert Nikolaus Donin from La Rochelle, Pope Gregory IX ordered in 1239 that the Talmud be confiscated and examined. The Talmud was then debated publicly in June 1240 at the royal court in Paris, with Donin arguing against four rabbinical scholars. Despite the success of the Jewish scholars' defense of the Talmud, the adept refutation of the convert's accusations, and the fact that the record of the debate noted that the Jews had "withstood" this test, the judgment came down to burn all copies of the Talmud. In the summer of 1242, twenty-four carts loaded with volumes of the Talmud and other Hebrew writings were towed to a plaza in Paris and burnt in a public spectacle. This action launched the fateful history of the defamation of the Talmud, which continues even today and has served repeatedly as a justification for discrimination against Jews.

The book burning also explains why so few Hebrew manuscripts from before the 13th century have survived. The oldest dated Ashkenazi text is a *mahzor* (prayer book for the holidays), written in Esslingen, Germany, in 1290 (81).

Defiling of the host

From accusations of ritual murder, it was a small step in the late 13th century to rumors that they were also defiling the host (the sanctified bread that symbolizes Christ's body in the Christian sacrament of Holy Communion). Supposedly, Jews, in their implacable hate for Christ, would pierce the host with knives and awls in order to torture the body of Christ anew. In Paris in 1290, the Jews who were so accused were sentenced to death.

In 1298, the Franconian nobleman Rindfleisch spent six months tramping through Franconia, Bavaria, and Austria wreaking havoc in over 140 Jewish communities to avenge the alleged desecration of the host by Jews in Röttlingen. In reality, the accusations of ritual murder and host defilement were not the reason for the persecutions. In a context of social and economic disparity, the agrarian crisis of the 14th century was exacerbated by famines and plagues, as well as intensifying conflict between city and country; this crisis became a crisis for Judaism itself. Farmers, forced by feudal landlords to borrow money, saw Jews as *the* agents of the urban economy and were ready to strike out on any imagined provocation.

The Jews' tenuous position in the city made them the obvious scapegoats. It is no wonder that in the following period anti-Semitic riots

83 Unique to Germany in the second half of the 13th century is this particularly insulting caricature: the Jew together with the pig. Its special perversity derives from the fact that, for Jews, the pig is an impure animal and the consumption of pork is forbidden. The motif of the "Jewish Sow" became more extreme and more obscene in the course of the centuries. Lampoons showed the Jew being nursed by a pig, drinking its urine, or, often in the company of the devil, riding on its back. Side piece of the choir stool in the Cologne cathedral, oak, ca. 1322. Two Jews empty a trough, from which a dead pig and its suckling fall.

321 – 16th cent.

broke out again and again. In 1336–38, discontented farmers organized under the banner "Jew beaters" (*Judenschläger*). They were led by a seedy nobleman who allowed himself to be called "King Armleder." Once again, countless Jews in Franconia, Swabia, Austria, and Styria were murdered. Another army of farmers followed the innkeeper Johann Zimberli and murdered and plundered their way through Alsace and the Rhine district. Nonetheless, this unrest and violence pales into a mere prologue to the events of the mid-14th century, when the plague spread through Europe.

The black death and poisoned wells

Between 1348 and 1350, over one-third of the population of Europe died of the plague. Since nobody understood what caused the black death, rumors and speculations abounded. Once more, the Jews were a convenient scapegoat: this time they were accused of causing the plague by poisoning the public wells. In the wake of this rumor came the pogroms, from France through the Swiss Alps to Germany. Even in towns spared from the plague, Jews were persecuted. The *Nuremberg Memorbuch* reports 300 communities where Jews were "killed, drowned, burnt, broken on the wheel, hung, exterminated ... and tortured with every means of death, all to sanctify the name of God." These were the worst persecutions since the first crusade.

Like the crusades, the plague pogroms also brought about decisive change. Some cities allowed expelled Jews to return, but only a limited number and for a limited time. Those who returned were sequestered in undesirable areas and had to obey petty clothing regulations (**84**). Meanwhile, the economic situation continued to deteriorate. Near the end of the Middle Ages,

84 The Cologne Jewish Ordinance of July 8, 1404. In 24 regulations, the clothes and the conduct of the Jews are specified in minute detail: For example, "the collars of the skirts and wraps may not be more than one finger wide. On workdays Jewish women may wear rings of at most three guilders' value and on each hand only one. In Holy week and on Easter, the Jews should remain in their houses. They may not walk, stand or sit under the portico in front of the city hall, except when the council has summoned them."

the Christian prohibition on charging interest was ignored, and Christian banking was established. In comparison with large trading firms (for example Fugger and Welser), Jewish lenders had shrunk to insignificance. Forced into the small-loan and pawn business, the Jews became economically unnecessary, especially in the cities. Thus, in the 15th and 16th centuries, the Jews were expelled from almost all the major cities of the German empire and from other major nations of Europe: England had expelled them in 1290, France between 1306 and 1394, Spain in 1492, and Portugal in 1496–97.

Most of those driven away fled to Poland, which, since the crusades, had been the gathering place for expelled Jews from all of Europe. The fact that Yiddish—originally a German dialect—became the language of the Jews in eastern Europe demonstrates the numerical and cultural significance of the immigrants (see p. 76 ff.). Others emigrated to Italy, where communities of Sephardim exiled from Spain were already established. The fragmented German empire, in which princes and cities constantly squabbled over unclear jurisdictions, never expelled the Jews entirely, as was the case in other countries with central governments (see above). Thus, a portion of the Jews expelled from the cities remained in Germany, living in the country where they were taken in by other worldly or spiritual princes who believed the Jews could be of use to them. But their days as part of the urban population were over. Jewish communities survived in a few cities, such as Frankfurt and Worms. Most Jews lived in the country, and as late as the 18th century, the picture of the *Landjuden* ("country Jews") was representative of German Judaism.

85 Living cross. Tablet painting, oil on wood, 2nd half of the 16th century. The Christian art of past ages clearly tells us how the Christians viewed their Jewish neighbors. Thus, we can see that each age had its own caricature of the Jew. Portal sculptures as well as paintings from the 13th century frequently display the triumphant Ecclesia and the blind Synagoga in female form (here, on the left and right of the cross). Synagoga is shown with closed eyes, blindly facing the new religion of Christianity. She is stripped of the symbols of her earlier majesty: the crown is pushed from her head. The inscription on the banner of the triumphant Ecclesia reads: "The church glorious through the blood of Christ." Synagoga's banner reads: "Synagoga banished with the blood of the bull and the buck."

Literally translated, the Hebrew word mikveh means "water gathering." In the rabbinical writings, however, it is described as a ritual immersion bath that transforms persons or objects from cultic impurity to purity. Along with the synagogue and the cemetery, the mikveh is still one of the essential structures of a Jewish community. Scholarly interest in the mikveh is a more recent development, however. For example, research for a 1992 exhibit in the Jewish Museum in Frankfurt, Germany, yielded an unexpected result: despite all the persecutions of the Jews in Germany, from the crusades to the Holocaust, many mikvehs have survived—almost 400 were documented in the 1992 exhibit alone.

The mikveh and its use

Instructions for the use of the mikveh are found in the Mishnah tract, the Mikvaot, which prescribes complete submersion in undrawn, "living" water, such as groundwater, collected rainwater, a spring, a river, or the sea.

Most medieval mikvehs were groundwater mikvehs. To reach groundwater level, a shaft was sunk deep into the earth; at the same time, the bath was equipped with steps to reach the seasonally variable water level. At least 40 Sea (an ancient measure of volume) must fill the bath. Exact conversions to modern measurement are problematic, ranging from 500 to 1,000 liters.

Who goes to the mikveh?

Many mikveh regulations relate to service in the Temple, but with its destruction, their importance faded. Since then, men are recommended to take a submersion bath before the Sabbath and the holidays. The regulations for women are much more comprehensive. Jewish religious law ordains an initial immersion bath before the wedding, and thereafter, at the end of the seven-day "clean" period following menstruation, and after giving birth. Marital relations are forbidden from the onset of the menstrual period until after the mikveh bath. Anything that could form a barrier between the woman's body and the water, such as nail polish, lipstick, jewelry, or hair clips must be removed.

86 Friedberg. Mikveh, 1260.
Bath shaft with a view of the immersion basin.

The Mikveh—The Ritual Bath

87 Goblets and decanters are purified in the mikveh. Illustration from a Haggadah, Spain, 1st quarter of the 14th century.

When she submerges herself, not even her hair may project from the water. This serves the ritual cleansing. Bodily cleansing is an explicit prerequisite for the mikveh, but ritual cleansing is only possible in "living" water. Converts to Judaism must take a ritual immersion bath before their conversion. The mikveh is also used for the submersion of new cooking and eating containers and utensils (**87**).

Monumental and cellar mikvehs

The best-known mikvehs are deeply excavated medieval monuments, such as the one in Friedberg, Hesse (**86**). 72 graduated steps descend 83 feet (25 meters) into the earth, past niches where oil lamps once cast their sparse light. Similar mikvehs have been uncovered throughout Germany, in Offenburg, Speyer, Andernach, Cologne, and Worms. With the demise of the cultural and economic blossoming of the Jewish communities after the plague pogroms of the 14th century, the Jews had to reestablish themselves in designated quarters or in the country, where they built hidden mikvehs in the cellars of apartment buildings and houses. The Jews dug narrow stairways to reach groundwater level, where a bath-tub sized immersion basin was excavated.

The use of heated water in the mikveh, which was always allowed but seldom practicable, was introduced about 150 years ago. Modern mikvehs, while not terribly common, are modern bathing facilities with every amenity.

88 A modern mikveh in the community center in Mannheim, Germany, 1987.

1264 – 19th cent.

89 The "Statute of Kalish." Illuminated title page, Arthur Szyk (1894–1951), 1926–28. The Jewish artist, native of Poland, set the text of the medieval privileges on 45 pages in different languages and illustrated them with scenes from Polish-Jewish history. For centuries, these privileges formed the legal basis for the status of Jews in Poland.

For many centuries, until its decimation in the Holocaust, eastern European Judaism was the most important Jewish society in the world. Even at the time of the crusades, Poland had become the land of refuge and opportunities for the Ashkenazim. The king of Poland and the grand duke of Lithuania granted the immigrant Jews in their countries extensive privileges. In 1264, King Boleslav V of Greater Poland granted a privilege, called the "Statute of Kalish," explicitly designed to encourage Jewish immigration (**89**). This statute formed the basis of laws concerning the Jews for centuries to come. It guaranteed freedom of trade, far-reaching autonomy, and protection for Jewish establishments such as synagogues and cemeteries.

The Jews were assigned to noble courts—that is, they were exempted from municipal jurisdiction where anti-Semitic bias was to be expected. It was also explicitly forbidden to accuse Jews of kidnapping and murdering Christian children to obtain blood for ritual purposes.

In 1364, under King Kasimir III, these privileges were not only confirmed but expanded and extended to all of Poland. Kasimir, it was explicitly stated, endeavored to increase the prosperity of his cabinet. His goal was obviously to attract Jewish settlers who would become pioneers in trading, business, and finance in the still underdeveloped kingdom.

The same was true of Lithuania. The grand duke extended broad privileges to Jews, even going so far as to offer exemption from taxation for Jewish cemeteries and synagogues. It is not surprising, therefore, that the Ashkenazi Jews immigrated to Poland and Lithuania en masse after the plague pogroms in the 14th century and the expulsion of Jews from the German cities in the 15th and 16th centuries. From medieval Germany they brought with them not only their customs and trades, but also their language, Yiddish, and they maintained it over the course of centuries (see p. 96 ff.). The Sephardic immigrants who had been expelled from Spain and Portugal assimilated themselves quickly into the much larger group of the Ashkenazim.

90 Page from an illuminated prayerbook of the Rabbi of Rushin, probably Polish, 15th century.

1264 – 19th cent.

New sources of income in the country
Legislative generosity was accompanied by professional freedom. In addition to the trades and money lending, unlike in their native countries, Jewish people were also active in handcrafts and, from the 16th century, in agriculture. The eastern expansion of Poland after the Lublin Union of 1569, in which the united Polish-Lithuanian state established its own empire, proved

Cheder: Literally, "room." The religious instruction of boys began in the cheder, the elementary school, with reading and study of the Torah and the Rashi commentary. The Talmud was taught in the yeshiva.
Melammed: Literally, "teacher." Children's teacher in the cheder.
Mitnagged, pl. **Mitnaggedim**: Literally, "adversaries." The designation given their rabbinical adversaries by followers of Hasidism.
Zaddik, pl. **Zaddikim**: Literally, "judge." Designation for a charismatic personality in east European Hasidism, who takes over the role of mediator between God and the pious.

(We surrender to) the worthy Master Abraham son of Samuel and his wife ... and to their offspring our estates as specified below, namely the town ... and therewith (certain estates and villages) ... and the following monetary payments that come from them, from their mills, lodging places and inns (for the sale of all) liquors, and mead; likewise the ... duty on the city together with the Boyars and all the persons whether required or not required to provide labour therein ... on their plough-fields, their labours and their waggons, the tax on grain, on beehives ... on fish ponds, mills and the payments for them, whether these are already in existence or shall be built in the future, together with the lakes, places for beaver hunting, with the fields, the meadows, the forests, the woods, the threshing floors ... and in general with all the various sources of livelihood, for five full and consecutive years ... for five thousand Polish zloty.

Typical lease document of 1595

favorable to them. The Polish nobility colonized the newly won land but did not want to manage the difficult estates in the east personally. And so for a number of years they leased fiefs including the people living there to trusted Jews in exchange for a prespecified compensation.

The Jewish tenants managed the estates with the help of Jewish servants. They sold agricultural products through Jewish dealers, and so the Jewish merchants in the cities also profited from the *Arrenda* ("leased business") system. That led not only to a period of general prosperity under the Jews' management but also to an astonishing rise in the Jewish population in the colonized areas. Ukraine's Jewish population, according to an official census, grew from 24 settlements with approximately 4,000 inhabitants before the Lublin Union of 1569 to 115 communities with 51,325 inhabitants by 1648.

The *Arrenda* system and the close ties with the Polish and Lithuanian nobility brought certain inherent dangers, as evidenced by the cruel Cossack massacres under Chmielnicki (see p. 81).

Jewish autonomy in Poland and Lithuania

Another outgrowth of the favorable conditions in the Polish-Lithuanian empire was the development of a statewide organization of Polish and Lithuanian Jews. Since the 15th century, the elders of the Polish countries and the most important rabbis had met during trade fairs in Lublin and Yaroslavl. These ad hoc councils developed into a more formal organization. In 1533, King Sigismund I approved the convening of an intraregional court during the Lublin Fair. This became the basis of the Council of the Four Lands, on record since 1580, in which the regional assemblies of Greater and Lesser Poland, Rotreussia, and Volhynia were combined to form an overarching organization. In 1623, the

Lithuanian Jews seceded and founded their own national synod.

The Council of the Four Lands met once or twice a year. It was responsible for the payment of the fixed general taxes and organized their disbursement to the individual provinces and communities. It cultivated relations with the crown and the government court. An advocate called a *shtadlen* was specifically employed to represent Jewish interests at all meetings of the Polish Sejm (parliament). The Council of the Four Lands also protected the Polish Jews' business interests and regulated administrative questions (e.g., delegations for parish councils), religious affairs (posting of pronouncements, accomodation of religious instructions to the needs of modern life, etc.), and social affairs.

The state legislatures in Poland and Lithuania lasted almost through the end of the Polish empire; in 1764, they were dissolved by the Sejm. Their reputation eventually reached central Europe, where similar Jewish regional assemblies developed starting in the 17th century.

91, 92 A Lithuanian Jewish couple with their daughter (above) and a Hasidic couple (below). Colored copper engravings, 1846.

1264 – 19th cent.

Polish-Jewish scholarship

These favorable legal and economic conditions led to intellectual and cultural achievements, particularly in the 16th century.

One noteworthy figure is Jakob Polak, who was born in Prague and came to Cracow as a youth. He is known as the founder of *Pilpul* (from *pilpel*, "pepper"), a tradition

of shrewd, subtle discussion of religious law. *Pilpul* was pursued as much for its inherent wittiness as for binding decision making. Once a sign of high status and scholarly accomplishment, *Pilpul* later degenerated into an end in itself, argument for argument's sake, in which the content mattered less than exercising one's powers of subtle reasoning, like flexing one's intellectual muscles. Today the term often denotes hair-splitting.

Moses ben-Israel Isserles (ca. 1525–72), considered the Maimonides of Polish Judaism, also came from Cracow. A widely respected authority on Talmudic law, he enhanced the *Shulchan Aruch* ("Prepared Table"), the codex of Joseph Caro, a Sephardic scholar from Palestine whose work had neglected the

customs and practices of the Ashkenazim. Isserles added commentaries incorporating German-Polish customs. By 1578, Caro's *Shulchan Aruch* appeared with Isserles's commentaries, which were appropriately designated the *Mapah*

93　Model of the Rema synagogue of the Rabbi Moses Isserles, 1553, Cracow. Jewish Diaspora Museum, Tel Aviv. The Rabbi is buried in the cemetery of this synagogue.

("Tablecloth"). This combination of "table" and "tablecloth" in Isserles's version of the *Shulchan Aruch* remains the definitive codex of the Halakhah.

Talmud commentator Shlomo ben Jechiel Luria (ca. 1510–73) distinguished himself through his independent and critical spirit. He opposed not only Jakob Polak's *Pilpul* but also Caro and Isserles's codification of Jewish law. With Luria, east European Judaism assumed a leading position in the spiritual and cultural arenas.

The Chmielnicki pogroms

The tensions growing out of the *Arrenda* exploded in 1648, when the death of King Vladislav IV created a power vacuum. Violent confrontations were strengthened by religious and social conflicts: between the Catholic Polish nobility and the rural Russian Orthodox population stood the Jews as tenants. Most of the Ukrainian farmers and Cossacks did not know their real landlords—who lived in the cities or at the royal court—but only their representatives, the Jews, whom they targeted as the "real" exploiters. Under the leadership of Bogdan Chmielnicki (**94**), the Cossacks, supported by local farmers, overran the Jews and Poles. In Ukraine, White Russia (Belorus), Podolia, and Volhynia, they perpetrated vicious massacres. According to Jewish sources, 300 communities were destroyed and 100,000 Jews were killed in the pogroms, which continued for years. The centuries of eastward migration by European Jews were now over; descendants of the earlier immigrants returned west. The economic and social expansion—another so-called golden age—came to a dead halt.

The pogroms also brought about some fundamental changes in the religious life of the east European Jews. From persecution and poverty emerged new spiritual currents that took hold across social strata and helped maintain hope despite the miserable living conditions.

94 Bogdan Chmielnicki, copper engraving by Hondius, Danzig 1651.

1264 – 19th cent.

East European Hasidism

Hasidism emerged amidst a climate of persecution, impoverishment, and faltering rabbinical scholarship after 1648. But it also arose from the Jewish communities' profound disappointment over the conversion (to Islam) of the pseudo-messiah Shabbetai Zevi (see p. 118 ff.).

95 The synagogue of Baal Shem Tov in Medshibosh.

96 Hasidim in America. Today Hasidim are scattered over the world. Most still wear their traditional clothes—the dark caftan and hat.

The founder of east European Hasidism was the charismatic faith healer Israel ben-Eliezer (ca. 1700–60) who acquired the surname Baal Shem Tov ("Master of the Divine Name") because it was believed that he could work miracles, write effective amulets, and set curses through his knowledge of the mysterious divine name. Baal Shem Tov rejected the rabbinical art of argument as well as the convoluted teachings of purely theoretical mysticism and advocated a popular, spiritualized piety in which prayer plays an especially important role. For the Hasidim, prayer is the primary connection to the higher spheres and should be spoken with conscious "intention" (*kavvanah*), which could be expressed in the service as cries and ecstatic movements. The emphasis on the supremacy of prayer represented a departure from the traditional view in which Talmudic study, the study of the word of God, is the most sublime of religious activities. Thus, the Hasidim soon came into conflict with traditional rabbis, who saw their authority threatened and/or saw the Hasidic perspective as heretical. The Hasidim likewise rejected the grim asceticism, mourning, and fasting spread by the Kabbalists, and instead emphasized the delight that comes from divine worship. For the Hasid, any activity performed joyfully and for God's sake was a fulfillment of divine law. The simple activities of ordinary life—eating, drinking, bathing, dancing, singing, and sexual intercourse—could be considered acts in the service of God.

This view led to the emergence of a new type of religious leader personality, the *Zaddik* ("righteous one"). A *Zaddik* was not supposed to raise his own spiritual level through self-castigation and withdrawal from the world, but should live among the people and guide his community.

> But when Israel [Baal Shem Tov] in the lonely nights took account over his existence and that of the Jewish community in Okop and at other places, then he came to the conclusion, that the Rabbis themselves ... had fallen into error. ... They put forward an exaggerated casuistry, their commentaries were only games of the intellect and about scholarly ambition; the simple and fair Jews, who longed to serve the Almighty with total sincerity and enthusiasm and without hairsplitting, they had neglected fully. The Rabbis themselves were isolated from each other, each sunk into his own finicky work. There were many pious Jews who fasted each Monday and Thursday and observed still other days of fasting. There were also penitents, who were already in exile because of a bad thought ... and there were some who covered their eyes, so that they could not see a woman and therefore possibly desire her. However everything was joined with the fear of punishment, and Israel found, that the true service at God should bring delight and elevation, not dejection and fear of Gehenna [hell].
>
> Isaac Bashevis Singer,
> *The Fields of Heaven*

If he keeps his distance from the people, his attention to his own spiritual development could even have negative repercussions—his people could be punished because they cannot match the *Zaddik*'s standards. As mediator between God and the people, the *Zaddik* must therefore descend from his exalted spiritual position and raise his people up with him. After the death of Baal Shem Tov in 1760, Dov Baer of Mezhirech, the great *Maggid* ("preacher"), became head of the movement. After his death in 1772, several strands developed among his students. Leadership later became hereditary, giving rise to the large dynasties of Zaddikim from which today's Hasidic leaders are descended.

The Mitnaggedim

Hasidism found particular resonance among the poorer Jews in Galicia and Ukraine, while the fewer followers in Lithuania faced strong opposition (**97**). The resistance of the rabbinical *Mitnaggedim* ("adversaries") was organized under Elijah, Goan of Vilna (**98**) (Goan, or "excellency," was an honorary title for a religious scholar and teacher). Elijah was convinced that

97 The expansion of Hasidism after 1770.

the emphasis on inward piety and abdication of clearly determined law led the Hasidim astray, to offend against the Torah. The idea of the *Zaddik* as mediator between God and the people struck him as idolatrous, especially since he considered many of the great Hasidic personalities, among them Baal Shem Tov, fools. He also criticized the Hasidim for using a specially sharpened knife for butchering and for incorporating prayers from the Sephardic rite into their service. The Hasidim's ecstatic singing and dancing appeared to him to undermine the dignity of prayer. The Gaon declared: "All who follow this way, turn to it no more—it is heresy."

In 1772 and 1782, at Gaon Elijah's instigation, bans against Hasidim were issued and soon backed by all the Lithuanian Jewish communities. Both camps brought fervor and vehemence to the dispute. Beside bans and denunciations of the gentile authorities, the Hasidim and the Mitnaggedim both disseminated polemical writings in which they expressed mutual scorn. The Gaon Elijah of Vilna did not achieve a decisive victory, but he did manage to stabilize Lithuanian Judaism and to stimulate the establishment of new centers of intellectual and cultural activity, namely, the large yeshivas.

In one matter, however, Mitnaggedim and Hasidim were united: rejection of the "Enlightenment," or, in Hebrew, *Haskalah* (see p. 141 f.). For both sides, modernization of Jewish customs and religion, which they considered an indivisible whole, was out of the question. The Hasidim communities and the Lithuanian yeshivas created a blockade against the invasion of the educa-

98 The country of Israel divided into tribes. Map attributed to the Gaon of Vilna, ca. 1802.

tional and assimilatory efforts of western Europe. The east European Jews' adamant adherence to tradition and old customs was not mere backwardness. For the Jewish history of the following period, perhaps for the very survival of Judaism, the spiritual resources lay in the east.

The Pale of Settlement and life in the shtetl

With the divisions of Poland in 1772, 1793, and 1795, and at the Congress of Vienna in 1815, a large portion of Poland and Lithuania fell under Russian control. In the space of a few short years, the majority of the world's Jewish population came under the dominion of a country that had refused Jews permission to settle since the Middle Ages. To prevent the Jews from spreading throughout the Russian empire, Catherine II (99) ordered the so-called Pale of Settlement (100), which limited the area where Jews could live to a specified region in the west of Russia. This included the area from the Baltic Sea in the north to the Black Sea in the south, from Kalish in the west to Minsk and Kiev in the east. This regulation remained in force, with few changes, until the First World War. The Jews, once driven out of the cities to the country, were now forced back to the cities and were once again torn from their occupations and sources of income. They were allowed to conduct business and trade only with one another. The policies of the czarina Catherine (the Great) helped promote the emergence of the east European *shtetls*, places of poverty that developed a Jewish culture and religious style all their own (101).

Schools, culture, and Torah study in the shtetl

Since the religious upbringing of children was traditionally a father's duty,

99　Catherine the Great of Russia (1729–96).

1264 – 19th cent.

100　Ukrainian lumberjacks in a Jewish inn. Color print by F. Lewicki, Podolia, 1870.

101 A street in a Polish shtetl. Photograph by Vladimir Volynsk, 1914. This is a typical shtetl, with lopsided wooden houses, unpaved streets, and lots of children. Jewish actor Alexander Granach describes the shtetl of his childhood: "The small wooden houses stood strung together. One house pressed itself, supported itself, leaned itself on the other like fragile, sickly beings, which are weak and frozen and afraid to be alone."

1264 – 19th cent.

those with rabbinical education instructed their children themselves, while the rich hired private tutors. For the poor majority, a kind of elementary school called a *cheder* (102) was established. Each cheder was headed by a teacher, the *melammed*, and was privately financed. The often mediocre quality of their instruction corresponded to the meager pay and public disregard for the melammed. In a rather unsystematic fashion, the children learned paragraphs from the Torah in the original Hebrew and in Yiddish translation, along with easier Talmud lessons. Young boys (only boys attended the cheder until their *bar mitzvah*) started at the cheder between the ages of three and five years and the schoolday was longer than it is in most places today—as long as eight to twelve hours.

The upbringing and education of girls was quite different. In keeping with accepted domestic roles, their religious education focused on keeping a ritually correct household. There were special prayer books and devotional literature for girls and women, mostly in Yiddish. In addition, they enjoyed a certain degree of freedom

The city has 18,000 inhabitants, of which 15,000 are Jews. ... Of the 15,000 Jews, 8,000 live from trade. They are small shopkeepers, medium shopkeepers, and large shopkeepers. The other 7,000 are artisans, laborers, water carriers, scholars, religious officials, synagogue workers, teachers, clerks, writers, Torah scribes, weavers, doctors, lawyers, officials, beggars and the shamed poor, who live on public charity, gravediggers, undertakers and gravestone carvers. The city has two churches, a synagogue and about 40 small prayer houses. The Jews pray three times daily. They would have to make six trips to the synagogue and back to their homes or shops, if they did not have so many prayer houses, in which one not only prays but also pursues Jewish studies. There are Jewish scholars, who study from five in the morning to twelve at night in the prayer house. Only on the Sabbath and the holidays do they come home for meals. ... Their families and the house are cared for by the women, who do a small trade in maize in the summer, with naphtha in the winter.

Joseph Roth, *Jews in Migration*

to read secular material (where it was available in a language they could understand), in sharp contrast with the men, whose study time was dedicated exclusively to holy writings. Thus, it is possible that the women's horizons were wider those visible to their "only" rabbinically schooled husbands.

After a boy was finished at the cheder, he and his family faced a decisive question: Does the boy have the aptitude for lifelong study, or should he interrupt his education and learn a trade? If he did appear to have a knack for study, he went to the yeshiva, a kind of theological university, and became a *yeshiva-bocher* ("yeshiva-boy") (**103**). Since only a few of the boys who attended the yeshiva came from families that could afford to pay for their education, the community assumed responsibility not only for the support of the yeshiva but also for that of the poorer students, vividly demonstrating the importance of religious study in the shtetl.

Yeshiva education was almost exclusively limited to study of traditional texts, that is, the Talmud and rabbinical compendia of laws. Secular subjects were prohibited, as were the writings of the Jewish scholar Maimonides (see p. 58 f.): Since Maimonides believed that modern science and rationality were essential elements in education, traditionalists considered him a heretic. Students who were not satisfied with the traditional material took to reading Maimonides under their desks.

Due to the support of gifted students from poor families and the opportunity for social mobility, yeshiva graduates enjoyed high prestige in the Jewish communities. Rich families were always ready to marry their daughters to poor but learned men and to finance their son-in-law's lifelong study. Since learning topped the scale of Jewish values, scholars in the shtetl were among

102 In the cheder. Slonim, 1938. Photo by Roman Vishniac.

1264 – 19th cent.

103 Yeshiva students discuss the Talmud. Warsaw, 1936. Photo by Roman Vishniac.

104 Jewish married couple. Warsaw, ca. 1846. The man wears a black caftan with a belt and a spodek on his head. The woman wears a *sterntichel* in the form of a diadem, and an apron. They both wear the slipper-like shoes with no heels that were common in the 19th century.

the elite, the *sheyne yidin*. An ideal sheyne was both learned and affluent; he was charitable, of noble descent, and his social conduct corresponded to the norms of eastern Jewish culture.

The lower strata of shtetl society, the *proste yidin*, were equally capable of drawing subtle distinctions in their social hierarchy. The order ranged from the tradesmen, retailers, peddlers, and publicans, to the poorest members of the community—the load and water carriers, musicians, gravediggers, beggars, and the oft-described *Luftmenschen*—a Yiddish term for an impractical contemplative person who has no visible means of support—he draws his living, as it were, out of the air.

Learning was just as highly valued by the working class people in the shtetl as by the upper classes. The uneducated also tried to show off by sprinkling their conversation with quotations, allusions, and proverbs from the holy writings, although in their relative ignorance, the scripture was often skewed or invoked in an

The well-known *luftmensch*, "the man of air," is the one who literally lives on hope and miracles. He has no fixed business, no regular means of support. He is a small-scale "commissionaire," darting about, seizing on almost anything, making a customer materialize almost out of thin air, selling to him almost by hypnotism, and collecting a fee that is almost invisible. Into each effort the luftmensch puts all the fervor and conviction of the artist shaping a masterpiece, although for the most part, his efforts miscarry and his hopes of reward vanish into the air, his element.

Mark Zborowski and Elizabeth Herzog,
Life is with People. The Jewish Little Town of Eastern Europe

inappropriate context. Tevya, the dairyman, a recurring character in the stories of the popular Yiddish writer Sholom Aleichem (Shalom Rabinovitz), is a famous example of this type.

Clothing in the shtetl
The Jews in the shtetls of Poland, Russia, and Galicia wore certain clothing, with minor local

variations, a costume for men and a costume for women that evolved through custom and tradition.

The men wore a caftan, a long, narrow, buttoned coat, often tied with a cloth belt (**104**). Because it was so often worn by the Jewish minority, the caftan was thought of as the typical Jewish garment. In the 19th century, it was worn mainly by orthodox Jews.

The Jewish custom of always covering the head led to a large number of hats and hoods worn by different classes and on different occasions: Men wore their *yarmulke*, a small skullcap usually made of black silk or cotton, wherever they went. On the street, they wore another hat over the *yarmulke*. Members of the upper classes often wore *yarmulkes* intricately embroidered with gold and silver (**105**). The *streimel*, a pointed velvet cap trimmed with fox, marten, or sable, was worn by wealthy Jews and Hasidim on holidays outside the house (**106**). The *spodek*, a taller version of the *streimel*, was mainly a headgear for weekdays, though on holidays a man might wear a spodek trimmed with sable (**107**). These kinds of headgear are still worn today in traditional orthodox and/or Hassidic circles. A beard and earlocks gave the mature man dignity (**106**); both had been visible marks of Judaism since the Middle Ages. The beard, however, was also thought to be a characteristic created by God to distinguish men from women. The wearing of earlocks can be traced back to a biblical order: "You shall not round off the hair on your temples or mar the edges of your beard" (Lev. 19:27).

105 Two silk yarmulkes trimmed with Spanish brocade. Volhynia/Podolia, 19th century.

1264 – 19th cent.

106 Portrait of a bearded Jew. Isidor Kaufmann (1854–1921). The man with full beard and earlocks wears a streimel as head covering. The light prayer shawl is embroidered at the neck opening. These decorative borders are called *atara* ("crown").

107 A spodek of velvet and sable pelt, date unknown.

108 A forge in Polonnoye, 1914–16. Since the middle of the 19th century, Jewish workers and artisans have worn the visored cap, the *kashket* or *kartus*.

109 *Sterntichel* in the form of a diadem. Russia, 19th/20th century. The diadem has a silver fastener and is studded with pearls and garnets. It was worn over the forehead on a close-fitting hood called a *kupke*. Sometimes a Star of David was worked into the middle as a jeweled motif.

Cutting off the beard or the earlocks was considered humiliating and humbling. If forced upon a man—for example, by gentiles during a pogrom or by German stormtroopers in Polish towns during the Holocaust—the Jewish community tacitly accepted it so as not to shame the victim. If a man voluntarily shaved his beard or cut his earlocks, however, he was likely to be suspected of being tinged by the heresy of the Enlightenment.

From the mid-19th century, Jewish workers and artisans have worn the *kashket*, a peaked cap made of black cloth. A *kashket* with a visor made of leather or lacquer was called a *kartus* (**108**).

As the Enlightenment spread to eastern Europe, a middle-class style of clothing cropped up. Three garments of Jewish women, however, proved resistant to the winds of changing fashions and were worn until the First World War: headgear of all kinds, a *brusttichel*, or bodice covering, and aprons.

Married women, divorcees, and widows always wore some sort of headdress. The practice of cutting the hair short before or after a woman's wedding was common only among the Jews or Jewish women of eastern Europe in the 18th and 19th centuries, though it is still observed today among some orthodox Ashkenazi women. The Sephardic Jews do not have this custom. Women could choose from a large selection of head coverings: scarves, hairbands, hoods, veils, turbans, and a kind of tiara (**109**). Many 19th-century Jewish women wore wigs. The oldest wigs were made of fabric draped to appear curly, or from silk fringe to imitate long hair (**110**). Wigs of artificial or genuine hair, usually called by the Yiddish word *sheitl*, were first produced in the late 19th century. It was always possible to wear a combination of head coverings—a wig with a veil or scarf, a hairband with a hood or strips of fabric (111).

The *brusttichel*, a long, rectangular strip of cloth that concealed the buttoned closure of the blouse, was once believed to have magical protective powers. It was tied around the neck with strings, and the bottom was tucked into the skirt or apron (112). Women who wore the *brusttichel* frequently stood in a stereotypical pose: they held their hands in it as in a muff (111).

The apron was a particularly persistent element in women's dress, partly due to the widespread superstition that it protected the wearer from the *dybbuk*, a spirit that could enter and possess the body.

110   Velvet cap with side fringes, imitating long hair. Volhynia/Podolia, 19th century.

It was also worn for practical or decorative reasons. Even at the turn of the century, when the *brusttichel* was no longer in style, many conservative Jewish women continued to wear the apron under their dresses.

112   Three festive brusttichels. Volhynia/Podolia, 19th century.

111   Jewish woman from Poland. Etching taken from J.P. Norblin, 1817. The *kupke*, adorned with lace, has a broad band of cloth. The woman wears an embroidered *brusttichel*, a light, patterned apron, and shoes with high heels. She holds her hand inside the *brusttichel*— a common pose.

1264 – 19th cent.

Music in the shtetl—The klezmer band

The word klezmer comes from the Hebrew "kle zemer," which means musical instruments. In common usage, it denotes the ensemble as a whole, as well as each individual in the group.

Jewish weddings or religious festivities such as Simhat Torah and Purim were inconceivable in the shtetl without a klezmer band (113, 114). The klezmorim not only played their own songs, but also adapted well-known melodies and texts

113 Klezmer band from Rohatyn (Galicia). 1912.

for a Yiddish-speaking public. The typical klezmer band included a violin, contrabass, cymbals, clarinet, flute, and dulcimer.

Most of the klezmorim were well-trained, professional musicians who were also in demand with their gentile neighbors, and were known to play at the weddings and parties of wealthy Christians. There were regular klezmorim families in which the profession was handed down from generation to generation.

Today klezmer music is enjoying a renaissance throughout the world, particularly in the United States, where "old-time" musicians have expanded their repertoire to include the traditional Jewish music. This renaissance, however, is no mere revival of old material, but a diverse explosion of creative forays into contemporary and traditional works, by such groups as the Klezmatics and the Klezmer Conservatory Band, among many others. A contemporary popularizer of klezmer music is world-famous violinist Itzhak Perlman, who re-explored the klezmer music of his childhood and has recorded with some of the prominent klezmorim of our day.

The synagogues of eastern Europe
After the Middle Ages, very few synagogues were erected in eastern Europe. In the 16th and 17th centuries in Poland, only one building project was undertaken. The documented syna-

114 Klezmer band. Ca. 1910–14.

gogues can be classified into two broad groups according to their building material: stone buildings, erected in the larger cities, and wooden structures, in smaller localities. Within these two groups different building types developed.

The older stone synagogues of the 16th and 17th centuries were long, narrow rooms in the Renaissance style with an entrance in the west and a women's area on an upper level (where the men could not see them). The 17th- and 18th-century buildings were more nearly square with four central supports—a style found only in Poland and, in Poland, only in synagogue architecture. In all buildings of this type, a square podium for the *bimah* (lectern), which was mounted via two stairways on the sides, stood in the middle of the room. At the four corners of the podium stood columns connected by arches over the capitals. The painted or windowed *bimah* construction was topped by a horizontal ledge that supported the arches (**115**). Thus, the *bimah* was not freestanding, but was directly attached to the vault.

Around the same time, a new kind of synagogue developed in eastern Europe: the defense, or fortress, synagogue (**116**). These synagogues, with their massive, closed exterior and ramparts, were the equal of many a European fortress, and were meant to be just that. During

115 Luzk synagogue, 1st half 17th century. The four-columned bimah construction is ornately painted.

1264 – 19th cent.

116 Vilna. Fortress synagogue, 1st half 17th century. Model. The synagogue had a watchtower accessed through a protected passage. The interior followed the design with four central columns.

117 Grodno. Wooden synagogue, 2nd half 18th century. The *bimah* (on the left) and the three-tiered Torah shrine (on the right) are covered with rich carvings. The arched parts of the ceiling were joined with a balustrade behind which there is a gangway.

the Cossack uprising or in other dire times, Jews could find shelter there and defend themselves from above. Not surprisingly, most of the fortress synagogues were built during the century of the Chmielnicki pogroms. The interiors of most fortress synagogues followed the *bimah* schema, with four central supports

In villages and small towns, where wood-frame construction was more common, wooden synagogues were erected especially in the 18th century. While their exterior—apart from the high arched roofs—was quite plain, the interior of these synagogues was often dazzling. The many-tiered Torah shrine, the *bimah*, and the balustrades were decorated with artistic wood carvings (**117, 118**). Most striking are the rich, colorful paintings that adorn the walls and ceilings. Banners with Hebrew text divided the walls into panels filled with Jewish symbols (animals, signs of the zodiac, temple accessories) and elements of domestic folk art (**119**). Some of the murals were signed, thus identifying the artists.

Many of the wooden synagogues were dilapidated and their paintings faded by the time interest in them was piqued in the early 20th century. What remained was destroyed by the Germans in the Second World War. All that remains are reconstructions based on old black-and-white photographs and colored drawings, most of which were collected by the St. Petersburg Jewish Historical-Ethnographic Organization, founded in 1908. This

118 Skillfully carved and colorfully stained wooden door of a Torah shrine. Poland, 18th century. The text in the ribbon reads: "Be bold like a leopard, swift like an eagle, fleet like a deer and strong like a lion" (Sayings of the Fathers, 5:23). The four scenes illustrate the text.

organization arranged expeditions to the villages of Volhynia and Podolia to collect evidence of Jewish culture. On one of these expeditions, the Russian painters Issachar Ryback and El Lissitzky copied paintings from around 200 wooden synagogues.

Until recently it was assumed that all the wooden synagogues had collapsed or been destroyed. But the recent dramatic political changes in eastern Europe finally made it possible to search unfettered for signs of Jewish culture. In 1993, a group of young researchers from the Center for Jewish Art of the University of Jerusalem in cooperation with members of the Jewish University of St. Petersburg visited 32 shtetls in Lithuania and discovered several stone synagogues, as well as six wooden synagogues that currently serve as warehouses, movie theaters, or concert halls.

1264 – 19th cent.

119 Chodorow, mid-17th-century style. The synagogue in Chodorow was a simple building with barrel vaults. In the middle of the vault there is a double eagle with two hares symboling God's salvation of the people Israel, surrounded by 12 medallions with the signs of the zodiac.

120 Tarnow, Poland. The four central supports of the *bimah* are all that remain of the stone synagogue. Photo 1991.

אידיש A Brief History of Yiddish Literature

Wherever Jews settled for any length of time in the Diaspora, "Jewish languages" emerged, colorful mixtures of the regional language and the traditional Jewish languages, Hebrew and Aramaic. They were always written with the Hebrew alphabet, and read from right to left. The most important of these Jewish languages were Judeo-Spanish (Ladino) and Jewish-German (Yiddish). Yiddish emerged in the Middle High German language area, where Jews had lived since the 9th century (see p. 60 ff.).

Despite the strong similarity of Yiddish to Middle High German, both Jews and non-Jews considered the Hebrew and Aramaic elements the most striking characteristic of the language. Due to persecutions since the crusades, the Ashkenazim had migrated eastward, bringing Yiddish into contact with the east European, particularly the Slavic, languages. And it was here, in eastern Europe, that it developed further and became the everyday language of the shtetls (see p. 86 ff.).

In the 19th century, two movements promoted the emergence of a modern Yiddish literary language: Hassidism and the *Haskalah* (intra-Jewish Enlightenment). Hoping to reach the broadest possible audience, Hasidic writers took up the task of making Yiddish both appealing, by promoting a sense of its lively and unique character, and accessible in a form acceptable to speakers of all Yiddish dialects. The Hasidim brought about a renewed interest in religious folk literature, while their old antagonists, the rationalists, published texts criticizing relationships within the shtetl. They would have much preferred to write in the "pure" Jewish language, Hebrew, but knew that would exclude many potential readers, including almost all women. So, for pragmatic reasons, they fell back on Yiddish.

The fathers of modern Yiddish literature

Convinced by the arguments of the Enlightenment, Mendele Mocher Seforim (Shalom Jacob Abramowitz, 1835–1917) originally wrote in Hebrew. Wanting to reach a broader audience with his fiction, he soon turned to Yiddish. He considered the succeeding generation of authors the creators and founders of the new Yiddish literature; they lovingly called him their *zayde*

121   Page from *Masasot Binjamin Haschlischi* ("The Journeys of Benjamin III") and *Fischke der Krummer* ("Fischke the Crooked") with a portrait of author Mendele Mocher Seforim.

122 The Wedding in the Cemetery. Etching by Anatoli Kaplan from the cycle, *Fischke der Lahme* ("Fischke the Lame"), 1976.

("grandfather"). Mendele had a breakthrough in 1864 with the book *Dos kleine Mentschele*, in which he criticized the heads of the shtetl for unlawfully lining their own pockets. His work is characterized by satirical criticism of conditions in the shtetl alongside humorous descriptions and caricatures of its "reality-strange" inhabitants (**121**, **122**).

Isaac Leib Peretz

Isaac Leib Peretz (1851–1915) began to write in Yiddish in the 1880s, after the cruel pogroms that followed the assassination of Czar Alexander II in 1881. Earlier he had written in Polish, believing that both Yiddish and Hebrew were likely to die out. But the wave of pogroms destroyed the hopes of many Jews, including Peretz, for assimilation. He came to believe that the Yiddish language is an important part of Jewish independence and autonomy in the Diaspora. From 1891 on, he published the Yiddish library which included not just Yiddish literature but also popular science texts for general edification. He was a staff member of many Yiddish newspapers and journals and worked for Yiddish theaters. Among his most important works are volumes of tales written in both Hebrew and Yiddish, as well as Yiddish poetical dramas, such as *At Night in the Old Market* (1907), which was staged at the Moscow Yiddish State Theater in 1925. Peretz was the first author to make Hasidism itself a literary subject. In 1908, he was a key speaker at a conference of Yiddishists, gathered to promote Yiddish literature as both timely and serious. When he died in 1915, an estimated 100,000 mourners gathered for his funeral.

Sholom Aleichem

The Ukrainian-born Sholom Alei-chem ("Peace Be with You," pseudonym of Shalom Rabinovitz, 1859–1916) also cherished the hope of educating and entertaining people with stories in the Yiddish language. He described the stereotype of one who always fails, but never loses hope and strives to keep smiling despite an often dreary life. He

123 Set design model for the opening of *Fiddler on the Roof*, Boris Aronson, 1964.

immortalized this type in his novel *Tevye the Dairyman* (1894) and in the tales collected into *Tevye's Daughters*, which formed the basis for the Broadway musical *Fiddler on the Roof*—those who saw him will never forget Zero Mostel's defining performance as the popular "hero." The show opened on Broadway in 1964 and has been revived many, many times since then on stages around the world (**123**).

Women and Yiddish literature

For less educated men, but especially for women, who were included only at the margins of the traditional education system and were not given the opportunity to master the "cultured" language of Hebrew, an extensive literature emerged in *Weiberdeutsch*, or "Women's German," a common disparaging term for Yiddish. An example of this literature is *Zenne Renne*, a collection of popular, freely embellished bible stories furnished with explanations. Originally compiled and annotated by the Bohemian Rabbi Jacob Ashkenazi (1550–1628), it was first printed

around 1620. In the following centuries *Zenne Renne* became the standard text for the raising and education of Jewish women; its name comes from a quotation from the Song of Solomon (3:11). About the same time, back in the 16th century, the *Tchines* (from *techinna*, "supplication"), personal prayers for women, were written. The style of the prayers was emotional and they were intended for edification. Some were even written by women, which was not common in religious literature.

The *Memoirs of Glückel of Hamelin* (1646–1724) are a Yiddish text of a totally different kind, written by a confident daughter from a rich Hamburg family, wife, mother of

YIVO (the Yiddish Scientific Institute). Founded in 1925 in Berlin with the goal of exploring the Yiddish language, literature and culture, YIVO's main office was in Vilna, Poland, until 1940, and is now in New York. YIVO's archives constitute the world's largest collection of Yiddish culture: books, magazines, posters, records, films, photos, and more. It offers courses in Yiddish, publishes books, and organizes conferences and exhibitions. The political changes of the late 1980s and early 1990s in eastern Europe gave YIVO researchers access to archives in those countries for the first time. Thus, YIVO's efforts in Vilna uncovered large parts of the original YIVO archive, which had been missing since the German Occupation in 1941.

twelve children, and businesswoman. Her memoirs, which she wrote for her children, reflect the everyday life of affluent Jews in northern Germany in the late 17th and early 18th century. Glückel wrote in Yiddish. Only a few decades after her death, in the wake of the Enlightenment demand for linguistic assimilation, western European Jews gradually gave up Yiddish.

125 *In Vald* ("In the Wood"). Title page of a Yiddish children's book by Leib Kwitko (1890–1952) with illustrations by Issachar Ryback, 1922. Kwitko was one of the most important authors of Yiddish children's books in the Soviet Union. He was arrested during the Stalinist purges in 1949 and executed in 1952 along with 30 other Yiddish writers.

Yiddish as a language of world literature

Before the Second World War, Yiddish was the native language of about 12 million people worldwide. The Holocaust in Nazi Germany until 1945 and the Stalinist purges of 1948–52 destroyed the Yiddish language and literature along with its authors and readers in middle and eastern Europe. After the pogroms in czarist Russia and especially the World Wars, the Yiddish-speaking masses emigrated to America.

An active literary scene soon emerged from this community of immigrant authors. Isaac Bashevis Singer (**124**), his older brother Israel Joshua Singer, and Sholem Asch, among others, proved to be important storytellers. Their works have been translated into several European languages and thereby found many readers among gentiles as well as Jews. In 1978, the Nobel Prize for Literature was awarded to Isaac Bashevis Singer, an honor for all of Yiddish literature.

124 Isaac Bashevis Singer (1904–91). After a crisis in his writing career, Singer realized that Hebrew was not the language in which he best expressed himself, but rather Yiddish, his mother-tongue. For the rest of his life he wrote only in Yiddish.

15th – 16th cent.

ca. 1400
The Medici in Florence (their prominence will last up to 1737).

ca. 1477–1576
Titian, most famous painter of the Venetian school.

1527 The sacking of Rome: The army of Charles V conquers and plunders Rome.

1545–63
The Council of Trent launches the Counter-Reformation.

1607 Claudio Monteverdi's *L'Orfeo* marks the beginning of European opera.

1626 Dedication of St. Peter's Basilica in Rome.

1632 Galileo Galilei is cited by the Inquisition and ordered to recant his assertion that the earth revolves around the sun.

127 Base of a glass goblet with gold ornamentation. Rome, 3rd/4th century. The glass goblet, of which only the trimmed base is preserved, was found in the catacombs. This base has two sections: The top shows a Torah ark, open and flanked by two lions; the bottom shows a shofar as well as a *lulav* (palm branch) and *etrog* (citron) between two menorahs.

126 Catacomb of the Villa Torlonia. Rome, ca. 4th century CE The painted rear wall of the Arkoso tomb shows an opened Torah ark between two menorahs. Because of their rich Jewish symbolism, the catacombs of the Villa Torlonia on the Via Nomentana are the most important of six Jewish catacombs discovered in Rome since 1602.

Next to the Greek, Italian Judaism is the oldest strand of Judaism in Europe, with a continuous history from antiquity to the present. Just as the fragmented nature of the city-state system of government was favorable for the Jews in Germany (at times), so, in Italy, the division into city-states and principalities worked in favor of the Italian Jews. When one area expelled them, another, for its own reasons, gave them refuge.

The Jewish community in Rome is, naturally, the oldest such community in Italy. As early as the 2nd century BCE—while the Temple still stood in Jerusalem—Jews were known to reside in Rome. Catacombs and glass goblets marked with Jewish motifs, as well as the synagogue unearthed in Ostia with mikvehs and community rooms, attest to the Jewish presence in ancient Rome and its environs (**126**–**128**). Up to the end of the Roman empire, the Jews in Rome lived relatively undisturbed, though soon thereafter came the first conflicts with the emerging Christian culture. Ultimately, the well-being of the Roman Jews lay squarely in the hands of the popes, who sometimes were tolerant of the Jews, and other times considerably less so.

In the time of the Reformation and Counter-Reformation, the hostility of the popes reached a peak. Under Julius III in 1553, the Talmud was burned on the Campo dei Fiori. In 1555 Paul IV issued a papal bull, *Cum nimis absurdum*, in which he ordered Jews into ghettos, restricted the number of synagogues to one per community (**128**), forced all Jews to wear identifying badges, and prohibited Jews from participating in any commercial activity; the one exception was the junk trade. To make matters worse, that same year, Rome's Jewish ghetto on the banks of the Tiber was frequently overwhelmed by floods.

128 An isometric reconstruction of the synagogue in Ostia, the ancient harbor of Rome. The synagogue was established in the 1st century CE and was redesigned in the 4th century. It is the second oldest preserved synagogue ruins in Europe (the synagogue on Delos is the oldest).

129 Watercolor of the Piazza delle Scuole in Rome, 1837. After the pope limited each ghetto to only one synagogue in 1555, a building complex was erected in Rome housing five synagogues: the Scuola Catalana of the Jews from Catalonia, the Scuola Siciliana for the Jews from Sicily, the Scuola Castigliana for Jews from Castile, and the Scuola Nuova and Il Tempio, the synagogue of the Jewish community in Rome since antiquity. The building of the Cinque Scuole was destroyed in a fire in 1893.

In efforts to force Jews to convert to Christianity, they were compelled to listen to Christian sermons, a practice that continued in Rome until 1847. In 1569, Pius V expelled all the Jews from the pontifical states. They were allowed to remain only in Ancona and Rome. The southern Italian communities, which had exercised leadership in the Middle Ages, had expelled the Jews long before. In the 13th century, Sicily and

15th – 16th cent.

Sardinia were already under Spanish dominion; thus, the Spanish Expulsion Edict of 1492 also applied to the Jews there. Many fled to the Ottoman empire; others took refuge in communities in northern Italy where their rights and freedoms were dependent on the will of the local sovereigns. In general, it went well for the Jews under the Medici in Florence, the Gonzaga in Mantua, and the Este in Ferrara.

At a time when all other Italian Jews were being confined to ghettos, the city of Leghorn (Livorno) followed its own path. The Medici openly recruited the Jews to cooperate in their plans to develop Leghorn into an important seaport. Thus, Grand Duke Ferdinand I, in the *Constituzione livornia* of 1593, granted the Medici unprecedented freedoms: The city never established a ghetto, the Jews were not compelled to listen to conversion sermons, they were not forced to wear identifying symbols, and they enjoyed full property and commercial rights. Leghorn's Jewish community experienced a true economic and cultural blossoming in the 17th and 18th centuries, and Leghorn became the most important Hebrew publishing center in Italy. In 1789, the most magnificent synagogue of Italy was erected there: It was destroyed in the Second World War by a bomb and was replaced in 1962 with a new, smaller building (**130**). It is not astonishing that the early-20th century Jewish-Italian artist, Amedeo Modigliani, was a native of Leghorn.

130 Tempio Maggiore in Leghorn, interior view. The synagogue was designed by the architect Di Castro and dedicated in 1962. The gilded Torah ark (early 18th century) comes from the Tempio Spagnolo in Pesaro.

The world's first ghetto: Venice

Although there were restricted Jewish quarters in Europe even before 1516—the Judengasse in Frankfurt, for example, was built in 1462—the idea of cordoning off a specific area and forcing Jews to live inside it dates back to March 20, 1516. On this day, the Venetian patrician Zaccaria Dolfin demanded publicly that all Jews presently living in Venice be removed to the fortress-like Ghetto Nuovo, and that drawbridges and walls be constructed to contain them. Dolfin's speech apparently touched a public nerve: by March 29, 1516 a corresponding decree was issued.

Thus was born the world's first ghetto—a fateful invention that would become synonymous throughout the world with oppression and genocide. The original meaning of the word "ghetto" is still being debated today. Most scholars trace its derivation to an archaic designation of the Jewish quarter as the site of a cannon foundry: *gettare* means to pour, and *getto* is the Venetian word for foundry.

A contract called the *Condotta* clearly defined the conditions under which the Jews could settle in the ghetto. The Venetian ghetto was divided into three parts (**131**): The Ghetto Nuovo emerged by decision of the Senate in 1516 and was settled by German and Italian Jews; this became known as the "Natione Tedesca." These Ashkenazi Jews were occupied in financial transactions and as pawnbrokers, serving the poorer strata of the Christian community who were in need of credit and could not afford to pay high interest rates. Since the Christian

> The Jews must all live together in the complex of houses found in the ghetto at San Girolamo. And so that they may not roam around at night, on the side of the Ghetto Vecchio, where there is a small bridge, and likewise at the other side of the bridge two gates shall be erected, that is to say one each for both named places. That gate must be opened in the morning at the sound of the Marangona bell and locked in the evening around midnight by four Christian guards, who must be hired and paid for their service by the Jews.
>
> *Decree of the Council of Venice, March 29, 1516*

15th – 16th cent.

131 The ghetto in Venice:
1 The inscription at the entrance to the Ghetto Vecchio, 1704
2 Scuola Spagnola
3 Scuola Levantina
4 The Yeshiva of Simone Luzzatto (1583–1663)
5 Study Center of Leone da Modena (1571–1648)
6 Study Center of Giacobbe Vivante
7 Scuola Italiana
8 Scuola Canton
9 Scuola Grande Tedesca
10 Banco Rosso

132 Under a weather-beaten arcade marked by the street number 2912 is a faded inscription from the site of the Banco Rosso.

leaders were at a loss to solve the population's financial problems themselves, they loosened their religious objections to the Jews and left them to the business of finance. The interest rate for credit and mortgages, however, was determined and strictly controlled by the authority in the *Condotta*. The three banks of the ghetto were named after the colors of their transaction records—red, green, or black—Banco Rosso, Banco Verde, and Banco Negro (**132**).

The Ghetto Vecchio was established in 1541 to receive the "Levantines" (**133**) pouring in from the eastern Mediterranean, and the "Ponentini"— welcomed refugees from Spain and Portugal. The "Natione Tedesca," the "Levantines," and the "Ponentini" all brought with them their own language, history, customs, and economic activities. The residents of the Venice ghetto were moneylenders and lived and worked in the city; those of Vecchio were wholesale merchants who lived near and traveled on the sea.

The last and smallest of the Italian ghettoes, the Ghetto Nuovissimo, with its beautiful palazzi, was started in 1633 as nothing more than a residential area for wealthy Sephardim.

Hebrew book publishing in 15th- and 16th-century Italy

The Jewish family Soncino came originally from Germany (**134**). Samuel and Simeon, the sons of Moses from Fürth, moved to Italy in the middle of the 15th century. The Milanese Duke Sforza in 1454 granted them permission to settle in the small town of Soncino near Cremona. They took the name of this city as their surname, and it soon became the trademark for books of high-quality printing.

The first-born of the family, Israel Nathan Soncino, a physician and Talmudic scholar,

133 Clothes of a Levantine merchant of Venice, 16th century.

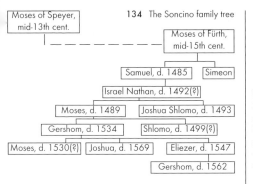

134   The Soncino family tree

Moses of Speyer,
mid-13th cent.

Moses of Fürth,
mid-15th cent.

Samuel, d. 1485 — Simeon

Israel Nathan, d. 1492(?)

Moses, d. 1489 — Joshua Shlomo, d. 1493

Gershom, d. 1534 — Shlomo, d. 1499(?)

Moses, d. 1530(?) — Joshua, d. 1569 — Eliezer, d. 1547

Gershom, d. 1562

135   A page of the Soncino bible. Joshua Shlomo Soncino, Soncino, 1488. The editions of the Soncinos were known for the artfully engraved foliage, animals, and angels worked into initials and page borders.

encouraged his son Joshua Shlomo to take up the printing trade. In 1484, the first book from Joshua's workshop, an edition of the Talmudic treatise *Berakhot*, appeared. This was followed by a Mahzor according to Roman rituals in 1486, a Hebrew bible in 1488 (**135**), and many more titles. The Soncino family publishing house issued a total of 130 Hebrew books, many of which were biblical or Talmudic treatises appearing in print for the first time.

Under the direction of Joshua's nephew, Gershom ben-Moses, the Soncino printing and publishing house grew into a world-famous enterprise. In addition to their Hebrew books, they published works in Greek, Latin, and Italian. The year 1491 saw the first printing of the Hebrew book, *Meshal Hakadmoni*, the "Fable of the Elders," illustrated with figurative woodcuts (**136**). The Soncinos also introduced the handy "pocketbook" format for particularly popular books. Gershom Soncino not only hired excellent typesetters, but also engaged editors and proofreaders, which was

136   *Meshal Hakadmoni.* Meir Parenzo, Venice 1546/50. The "Fable of the Elder" was written in 1281 by Sahula who used biblical and Talmudic dialogues between animals to express his moral lessons. Sahula's fables were widely disseminated and were printed for the first time by Gershom ben-Moses in Brescia in 1491. This was the first illustrated Hebrew edition. The illustrations of this later edition are taken from the first edition of Soncino.

15th – 16th cent.

137 Two hallmarks of Gershom ben-Moses Soncino. The upper one was used in the early Italian printings, the lower in books that were printed in Rimini, Salonika, and Constantinople in 1522–33.

138 Woodcut by Jakob Steinhardt (1887–1968) to selected verses of Yeshu ben Eliezer ben Sirach. Hebrew/German, Soncino company, 1929.

quite unheard of at that time. He personally undertook extensive journeys in search of precious manuscripts to serve as models for his publications. His printing firm operated not only in their hometown of Soncino but also in nearby Casalmaggiore, Ancona, Barco, Brescia, Cesena, Fano, Ortona, Pesaro, and Rimini (**136**).

The proliferation of printing shops, however, was not the result of the Soncinos' desire to expand their business, but came about because, as Jews, they were repeatedly harassed and constrained by the regulations of the local authorities. Finally, Gershom Soncino had to leave Italy completely. In 1527 he founded his new printing house in Salonika (today, Thessaloniki), and in 1530 he built a second in Constantinople (Istanbul). Soncino himself explained that he wanted to ease the lot of the Sephardic refugees by manufacturing important and inexpensive books. His death in 1534 brought the heyday of his publishing house to an end: only a few editions by his sons and his grandson are known.

In the year 1924, the "Soncino Company of the Friends of Jewish Books" was founded in Berlin. Its mission was to produce bibliophile-quality books in the tradition of the Soncinos (**138**). The company was dissolved in 1937 by the National Socialists.

The Christian printer, Daniel Bomberg
Daniel Bomberg (d. 1549/53?), a native of Antwerp, was the most important Christian printer of Hebrew books of his time. In Venice, between 1516 and 1549, with the help of Jewish scholars, he published over 220 Hebrew texts. The Venetian Jews themselves were forbidden–

with some rare exceptions—to work as independent printers or publishers. They therefore became indispensable staff members in the prominent publishing houses owned and/or run by Christians. The house of Bomberg printed the first rabbinical bible in 1517.

This edition contained not only the Hebrew text but also the *Targum* (Aramaic translation) and commentaries of famous medieval exegetes. Bomberg's greatest projects, however, were the first printed complete editions of the Babylonian (1520–23) and the Palestinian Talmud (1523–24). Orders for these volumes came from throughout the Diaspora. The pagination of the Bomberg Talmuds has been retained in all later editions through the present day.

Around 1548 Bomberg discontinued his activities. His famous Hebrew fonts were bought up by other printers, who appreciated their extraordinary quality. After Bomberg, the Venetian families Giustiniani, Bragadin, and de Gara made their names as printers of Hebrew books. The rivalry between Giustiniani and Bragadin was so intense that each denounced the other to the Christian authority, maintaining that the other's publications were blasphemous and riddled with subversive anti-Christian sentiments. These accusations considerably damaged the blooming publishing business; with the defamations of some fanatical converts, the tactics of these arch competitors contributed to the 1553 Talmud burnings on the Piazza San Marco in Venice and on the Campo dei Fiori in Rome.

In 1568, another book burning ended this golden period of Hebrew printing in Venice. No Talmud was ever printed in this city again. The first reprints, complete or in parts, came out of Lublin (1559), Salonica (1563), and Basel (1578).

139 *Yad Ha-Hazakah* ("Strong Hand"), another name for Maimonides's *Mishneh Torah*. Title page of the two-volume Bomberg edition, printed in 1524 in Venice. Bomberg's titles bear the famous epigram, "From Moses to Moses there were none like Moses," in print for the first time.

15th – 16th cent.

7th – 20th cent.

The legal status of the Jews in the Islamic countries was regulated in a pact called the *Dhimma*, attributed in its first formulation to the Caliph Omar (634–644) (see p. 50). The beneficiaries of this pact were called Dhimmis. All non-Muslims who followed a monotheistic, revelation-based religion (i.e., Jews and Christians) were classified as Dhimmis. The Islamic sovereigns guaranteed their Dhimmis—in contrast to the persecuted "heathens"—safety of person and life, freedom of worship, and unlimited access to all professions, as long as they agreed to acknowledge the superiority of the Muslims. The Dhimmis, as a token of this acknowledgment, had to pay a per-capita tax and to submit to a number of restrictions—their clothing was prescribed and they were prohibited from keeping weapons. The construction of religious buildings was also regulated; none could be taller than the mosques.

The purpose all of these rules was to keep the Dhimmi ever mindful of his low status and to emphasize the superiority of the Muslims. A free Muslim in a militarily oriented culture naturally carried weapons and rode on a horse. The discriminatory laws against the unbelievers forbid them to bear these weapons and allowed them to ride only on an ass, and that, only sidesaddle. The clothing regulations also had a discriminatory character. For instance, while the free Muslim women covered their faces as a sign of virtue and decorum when they left the house (*Purdah*), this was forbidden the female Dhimmis and slaves.

The Dhimma model, thus, granted no equality, but it did allow for a peaceful coexistence of sorts. Only in exceptional instances were the Dhimmis forced to choose between exile, conversion to Islam, or a martyr's death (that happened once in Morocco and once in Yemen;

otherwise, it occurred only in Persia), while such no-win choices were the rule for Jews and Muslims in the Christian Spain of the Reconquista. Under Islamic dominion, the Jews were one among many minorities in a widely gradated society governed by a simple guiding principle: Live and let live.

Although all professions remained open to the Jews, they tended to concentrate in certain fields, particularly those that were forbidden the Muslims for doctrinal reasons—because they were seen as impure or lowly: leather work, manufacture and sale of wine and spirits, and menial services. For the orthodox Muslims, any occupation that involved working with precious metals was especially offensive—whether it involved manufacture of jewelry, household implements, coin minting, or working with armor. For this reason, in some Islamic countries, for example, in Yemen, gold- and silversmithing became a highly developed craft of the Jews (140). The Muslims, moreover, shunned all professions in which they would have to work with unbelievers. This afforded many Jews opportunities in diplomacy and international trade and finance.

Jews found opportunity for social improvement not only in finance, but in medicine as well.

140 Torah ornaments for crowning the two wooden dowels of the Torah roll. Gilded silver, Yemen, ca. 1900.

7th – 20th cent.

The merchant Benjamin from Tudela in Spain traveled for many years in the second half of the 12th century into far-flung areas of the then-known world: over the south of France, Italy, Greece, and Asia Minor to Palestine, then through Syria and Mesopotamia to the Persian Gulf, and ultimately to Egypt. His travel journal (*Sefer ha-Massaot*, "The Book of the Journeys"), which contains many detailed statements about the Jewish communities he visited, is an invaluable source for the Jewish history and culture of the time. About Baghdad, for example, he wrote: "In Baghdad live approximately 40,000 Jews, and under the great Caliph, they live in safety, prosperity, and recognition; there are many great scholars among them, who are the leaders of the Torah schools. There are ten Torah schools in the city."

Since Jewish doctors often were masters of several languages and could read the foreign-language technical literature, they occasionally had an advantage over their Muslim colleagues. A successful physician could count high officials and even sovereigns among his patients, and this gave him at times direct access to the seat of power. The Jewish physician, then, could represent not only his own interests, but also those of the Jewish community. The most famous such physician, of course, was Maimonides (see p. 58 f.), who used his influence as personal physician to the vizier of the sultan in Cairo to secure a reduction of the high taxes and duties for his oppressed co-religionists in Yemen.

In the 19th century and at the beginning of the 20th, the Jews in many Islamic countries benefited from the establishment of direct European colonial control: Algeria, Tunisia, and Morocco came under French sovereignty; Aden, Egypt, and Iraq under British control; and Libya under Italian sovereignty. The establishment of colonial powers in these areas gave the Jewish minority in these countries an unprecedented degree of safety, even occasionally European citizenship. Characteristically, during this time, too, when the Jews were no longer willing to be second-class citizens and observe the rules of the Dhimma, violent anti-Semitic riots broke out. The alliance of the Jews with the European rulers ultimately proved fateful, as the colonial powers began to falter and nation after nation reclaimed its independence.

Morocco

The life of the Jews in Maghreb is typical of the history of the Jews in Morocco. Since antiquity, the city was home to Jewish settlements. Their importance increased in the 8th century CE when the country first came under the dominion of a

141 "Great dress." Holiday gown of velvet with gold embroidery. Morocco (Tetouan), late 19th century. The "great dress" of the urbanite was covered—for the first time at the wedding—with jewelry. It consists of a skirt, belts, a richly embroidered Brusttichel, a jacket with long sleeves, a head covering with artificial black hair, and a shawl draped over the headpiece.

7th – 20th cent.

tolerant Islamic authority, and the communities developed close economic and cultural contacts with the Jewish communities in Moorish Spain. The heyday of Moroccan Judaism, however, came about in the 11th century and the first half of the 12th. The capital, Fez, with its many centers of learning, rivaled Cordoba, which was the center of Moorish-Jewish Spain.

Under the rule of the fanatical Almohads after 1147, the situation of the Jews in Morocco and Spain deteriorated drastically. The Almohads brooked absolutely no deviation from Islam and denied the Jews, and the Christians even more so, any religious tolerance. Then came pogroms and forcible conversion to Islam. The Christian communities were completely destroyed. From then on, Morocco's Jews found themselves in a situation that was unique among the Muslim countries: They remained the only religious minority in an otherwise exclusively Muslim society. Here, and in the lands bordering on Morocco, the discriminating restraints of the Dhimma were always more severely enforced than they had been in the original Islamic lands, where different non-Muslim minorities had lived.

After the Almohads in Morocco were supplanted by the Merinids in 1269, Jewish life in the Moroccan cities recovered. The new rulers were more tolerant than their predecessors; occasionally, as late as the early 15th century, Jews were even found at court. The Muslim populace, however, remained hostile, so the sovereigns deemed it necessary to establish *Mellahs*, obligatory Jewish quarters. With the Mellahs, Morocco became the only Islamic country (with the occasional exception of Persia) with a form of ghetto for the Jews.

The first Mellah was established in 1438 in Fez. In contrast with the cramped European ghettos, the Mellah in Fez was initially just a

142 Hair styles and headdress from different cities of Morocco. The Jewish women in Islamic countries, in contrast to the Muslim women, went unveiled. Most carried a trimmed headdress that could be pulled down over the forehead but left the face exposed.

143 *Ketubbah.* Morocco, 1871. A decorated border in the form of a horseshoe arch, a classic motif of Islamic architecture, shows the Islamic influence on the Jewish art.

7th – 20th cent.

144 Eugène Delacroix, "Jewish Wedding in Morocco." Paris, Louvre. Delacroix traveled to Morocco in 1832 and captured his impressions in sketches. He used these sketches as bases of paintings later, in Paris.

7th – 20th cent.

normal municipal district. From the 18th century, however, the Mellahs invariably decayed into over-crowded places stained by poverty and backwardness. Finally, in 1912, under French colonial legislation, they were abolished.

In the 14th and 15th centuries, a large wave of Spanish and Portuguese Jews immigrated to Morocco, as well as to all the countries of the Maghreb—the area of northern Africa that today includes Morocco, Algeria, Tunisia, and sometimes Libya. These immigrants soon assumed a prominent part in the cultural, economic, and community affairs of their new home. In the 16th century, the Ottoman empire expanded into North Africa; only Morocco remained independent. While the Jews under Ottoman dominion in the 15th and 16th centuries experienced a new period of relative ease, the life of their fellow Jews in the Mellahs was one of growing poverty and abasement, and even marked by a deterioration of learning. It was here, in 1860, that the "Alliance Israélite Universelle" was formed. The activity of the Alliance involved not just pedagogic and cultural renewal but medical care and professional restructuring as well. Two years after its establishment, the Alliance opened its first school in the city of Tetouan, with instruction conducted in French. In 1867, the first two graduates of this school went to France for teacher training, in order to open schools for the Alliance. In 1882, the first girls' school was opened in Tetouan.

These innovations led to conflicts within the Jewish communities; the local rabbis often bitterly resisted the initiatives of the Alliance. Until now, they had been the sole authorities in all individual or collective questions. They now saw their hegemony threatened, not only by the Muslims but more bitterly by the west European Jews and their pupils. In 1912, when Morocco became a French colony, the Moroccan Jews became French citizens. During the Second World War, when Casablanca became the most important Jewish community in North Africa through the arrival of European refugees, the sultan Muhammad V protected his Jewish subjects from the Vichy authorities' efforts to deport them. In Tunisia, in contrast, the German invasion in 1943 led to the deportation of Jews to the death camps back in Europe.

After the proclamation of the State of Israel in 1948, and on the occasion of the wars of 1956, 1967, and 1973, there were anti-Semitic riots in all three states of the Maghreb. Most of the remaining Jews emigrated to Israel or to France. Today, approximately 35,000 Jews still live in Morocco, and the Alliance still runs thirty-one schools and training facilities.

Yemen

The beginnings of Jewish life in Yemen are cloaked in darkness. According to legend, Jews had already come to Yemen at the time of Solomon (10th century BCE), but the authenticated evidence—dated epitaphs—comes from the 3rd century CE. In 629 CE, Yemen was conquered by Muslims. The imams who ruled from the end of the 9th century up to 1962 strictly observed the instructions of the Dhimma.

Some Yemen Jews were dealers and petty merchants in coffee and spices, but

145 *Labbe*. Woman's gold necklace, Yemen, 19th/20th century.

146 "Tapestry page" from a Pentateuch. Yemen, 1469. The illuminated manuscript shows the skill of Yemenite scribes. The outlines of the six-pointed star, composed of ten fish in a circle with the triangles of scales, are drawn in micro-script of verses from Psalms 119 and 121.

7th – 20th cent.

147 Teva. A carved and painted wooden lectern, Yemen, 18th century. In Yemenite synagogues there was no platform (bimah) for Torah reading; instead, a portable wood pulpit was used. The pullout bench for small boys is illuminating. In Yemen a boy could read from the holy writings even before the bar mitzvah in the presence of the community. The only criterion for this honor was intellectual maturity.

148 At study in the synagogue of Sanaa. Photo by Hermann Burchhardt, Yemen, between 1907 and 1909.

most worked as laborers (tanners, weavers, blacksmiths) or traveled as peddlers. They lived for the most part in modest, often poor conditions. Still, the reputation of the Yemenite gold- and silversmiths had spread to Europe in the Middle Ages (**145, 149**). They were among the wealthiest and most respected members of their communities.

Despite the poverty of the communities and despite their isolation in the far south of Arabia, the Yemenite Jews protected their traditions and maintained contact with the centers of Jewish learning in North Africa, Egypt, and Palestine. The thought of a return to the Holy Land always remained peculiarly real to them. In 1165, the ruling imam tried to forcibly convert his Jewish subjects to Islam. In this time of persecution and despair, a messianic movement emerged. A self-appointed messiah promised to lead the sufferers out of the Diaspora to the Holy Land. The leader of the Yemenite Jews turned to the authority of the time, Maimonides, in Fostat. Maimonides responded in the "Letter to the Jews in Yemen," copies of which were distributed to all the Jewish communities in the country. He comforted his fellow Jews and exhorted them to hold fast to their time-honored beliefs and to reject the false messiah. Maimonides also provided practical help and used what influence he could bring to bear upon the imam to reduce the Jews' heavy taxes.

Under Ottoman dominion (1546–1911), the Jewish minority in Yemen once more found themselves between a rock and a hard place: Suspected by the conquerors of conspiring with the indigenous rebels, they were in turn accused by their gentile countrypeople of collaborating with the new rulers.

hey endured mistrust and harassment from
both sides. In the 1880s, news of the first
Jewish settlements in Palestine reached the
Yemenite Jews; the news was followed by the
first significant wave of emigration to the Holy
Land.

With Yemen's independence in 1918, the
Jewish situation worsened further: Considered
the "property" of the imam, the Jews were
forbidden to leave the country. Thousands of
Yemenite Jews, having learned of the establishment of the State of Israel, fled to the British
protectorate of Aden; from there they were
airlifted, in "Operation Flying Carpet," to Israel.
Through the end of 1950, approximately
50,000 Jews from Yemen were resettled in this
way. In their new home, they nonetheless kept
their Yemenite traditions: Their rituals, songs, and
dances, their arts and their crafts have greatly
enriched Israeli culture.

Similar rescue operations were undertaken in
other Islamic countries: In 1950–51 approximately 110,000 Iraqi Jews (Operation Ezra and
Nehemia), in 1983–84 and 1991 approximately 25,000 Ethiopian Jews (Operation
Moses and Operation Solomon) were brought
to Israel.

The Ottoman empire

In the 16th century, the Turkish sultans had
already conquered large territories in the
Balkans, in the Slavic countries, in the Near
East (including Palestine in 1516), and in
North Africa. The population of this vast empire,
thus, was composed of many different ethnic,
national, and religious minorities, of which the
Jews were but one. The conditions granted by
the Ottoman sovereigns—religious freedom,
freedom to settle, free choice of job, and
community autonomy—appeared very promising

149 Jewish woman from
Yemen in traditional wedding
garb. The bride is fitted with
splendid robes and rich
jewelry, which, according to
national customs, includes
chains, earrings, bracelets,
brooches, and forehead
ornaments.

7th – 20th cent.

The great Turkish empire, boundless as the unwinding sea, opened before us. Open before you, son of my people, stand the gates of freedom: You may enter without shame for your belief, you can begin a new life, shake off the yoke of the inverted doctrines forced on you by the people ... and find the way back to the original truth of your ancestors.

Samuel Usque, 1552

to the Spanish and Portuguese Jews and Marranos fleeing from the Inquisition, torture, and pyres. They flooded into the empire and, within a short time, numerically and culturally surpassed the domestic Greek-speaking "Romanis" and the earlier Ashkenazi immigrants. In Istanbul (Constantinople), Izmir (Smyrna), Edirne (Adrianople), and Salonika (Thessaloniki)—where the Jews constituted half of the population in the 16th century—considerable communities developed.

In their new home, the newcomers guarded a strong feeling of solidarity and cultivated their religious, cultural, and economic traditions as well as their own language, an archaic dialect of Castilian that the Judeo-Spanish called Ladino. The peak era of the Sephardim was the 16th century, which was also the peak of the Ottoman empire. The Turkish rulers' confidence in their own authority made it easy for them to be tolerant and to relax their enforcement of the Dhimma. The Jews were, to them, useful subjects whose wealth, international trade connections, and capabilities were completely at their service. The sultans considered the Jews more loyal than the Christian Dhimmis, whose many conflicts with the empire quickly fostered rumors that they were collaborating with foreign Christian powers. Jews, though, were appointed to high posts in economy and politics, as ministers, diplomats, tenant overseers, and physicians to the sovereigns.

Don Joseph Nassi and Dona Gracia

The careers of Don Joseph Nassi (ca. 1515–79) and Dona Gracia (ca. 1510–69) (**151**), his aunt and later mother-in-law, exemplify the possibilities for the Sephardim to rise under the Ottomans. Don Joseph and Dona Gracia came from a rich Portuguese banking family of New Christians. After an odyssey that brought them through Antwerp, Venice, and Ferrara, they settled in 1553 in Istanbul, where they openly returned to Judaism. Here they worked as successful merchants.

With his fine education and his diplomatic talent, Don Joseph Nassi soon came to the attention of the sultan Sulayman II and was entrusted with important state affairs. Perhaps the best-known project associated with his name was the administration of Tiberias and some adjacent villages which the sultan entrusted to him in 1564. Don Joseph wanted to establish a sanctuary there for Jews from all over the world. He had the city reconstructed and arranged mulberry plantations to develop a silk industry. Despite the large financial outlays and the unstinting efforts of Don Joseph Nassi and Dona Gracia, the ambitious project failed.

When Selim II became sultan in 1566, Don Joseph's star rose still higher. He was responsible for all of the sultan's foreign policy and was named the Duke of Naxos. He and Dona Gracia founded new synagogues, promoted Jewish learning, and erected a printing office specifically for the dissemination of Jewish writings. With the death of Selim II, however, the star of his protégé also fell. In his latter years, Don Joseph devoted himself only to patronage.

After Don Joseph, no Jew in the empire ever climbed to such a height and other minorities began to compete with the Jews for positions in Ottoman services.

150 Jewish cloth trader in Istanbul. Watercolor by A. Preziosi, 19th century. Cloth trade and textile manufacture were among the most important businesses of the Sephardim in the Ottoman empire. The main center of trade was Salonika.

7th – 20th cent.

151 Dona Gracia, Bronze medaillon, ca. 1552.

7th – 20th cent.

The art of printing

The Jewish merchants, who did a lively business with the important cities of Amsterdam, Leghorn, and Venice, are only one example of the striking financial accomplishments of the Ottoman Jews. In cultural areas such as medicine and typography, their success was impressive. The first Hebrew printing house was founded in 1493 in Istanbul—a pioneering effort, if one considers that the first printed book in Turkish did not appear until 1728.

In the 16th and 17th centuries, Istanbul ranked as one of the most important centers of Hebrew printing. Experts on the art of printing met here, as did the owners of valuable manuscripts, which could be printed here and distributed with little interference. It was to Istanbul and to Salonika that the Italian Gershom Soncino and his son Eliezer (1527–47) brought their prestigious and well-established family printing business (see p. 104 ff.).

A false messiah: Shabbetai Zevi

The Jewish mysticism of the 16th and 17th centuries, with its centers in cities in the Ottoman empire, stirred excitement in the entire Jewish world. Messianic expectations were aroused and the eschatologically expectant began consciously to prepare for the messianic age through studied exercises in asceticism, meditation, and meticulous fulfillment of all liturgical precepts.

This period of mysticism found a base in the small Galilean city of Zafed. The studies of the scholars living there focused exclusively on determining exactly when—what year, month, day, hour, minute—the messiah would appear. The eschatological expectations fanned by the mystics were exploited by Shabbetai Zevi (1626–76) (152), born in Izmir, the son of a

Der Große betrieger und falsche MESSIAS
SABATAI - SEVI.
König der Juden.
Anno 1666.

152 Portrait of the false messiah Shabbetai Zevi. Contemporary German engraving. On the top left is the ship in which he came from Izmir to Istanbul; the top right shows Shabbetai as a prisoner of the sultan.

prosperous merchant. Shabbetai's great claims at first did not meet a great response. He was banished from Izmir because of unlawful acts (his adversaries reproached him for "speaking aloud the divine name, as it stands written"—a deed reserved for the messiah at the moment of deliverance), and came to Jerusalem by way of Salonika, Istanbul, and Cairo. In Jerusalem, he led the life of a religious-mystical ascetic, constantly alternating between bouts of depression and periods of spiritual exaltation (perhaps a case of manic-depression). He studied with the kabbalist Nathan of Gaza, who he hoped would cure him of his depressions. Instead, Nathan came to believe that Shabbetai Zevi was indeed the messiah, and became his prophet.

In 1665, Shabbetai Zevi publicly declared himself the messiah. Nathan of Gaza sent out missives from Amsterdam to Yemen, proclaiming the beginning of the messianic time and calling for remorse and penitence. This led to Shabbetai's exile from Jerusalem. He returned to Izmir, where he allowed himself to be celebrated as royal messiah and determined that the day of deliverance would be June 18, 1666 (**153**).

From Izmir, messianic enthusiasm spread to the whole Jewish world: to the Polish and Ukrainian Jews escaping the Chmielnicki massacres and the oppressed Yemenite Jews, as well as to the comparatively free and wealthy Sephardim in Amsterdam and in the Ottoman empire. Many of his followers

153 Prayer book of the followers of Shabbetai. Amsterdam, 1666. The upper section of the title page shows Shabbetai Zevi as crowned king, surrounded by angels; the lower half shows the twelve princes of the reunited twelve tribes of Israel at the table. According to the printer's entry, the work appeared "in the year of the Messiah 5426" (1666), year 1.

7th – 20th cent.

154 Man's festive tunic. Turkey, 19th century. Embroidery with gold and silver threads was greatly treasured by the Sephardim in the Ottoman empire.

155 *Tik*. The Tik is common in countries of the Orient to protect the Torah scrolls, instead of the fabric mantles common in Europe. It is made mostly of wood and is covered with velvet or with silver. The scroll is securely installed in the round Tik. It is opened for reading but the scroll is not removed. The Torah essays are inserted at the side, but not attached to the scroll staffs.

7th – 20th cent.

sold their property in order to journey to the Holy Land and, before long, a long, embittered fight erupted between the followers of Shabbetai Zevi and his adversaries.

In the "messianic" year 1666, Shabbetai was arrested by the Turkish authorities and offered a choice between execution and conversion to Islam. He chose conversion and lived, with a Turkish pension, first in Edirne and later, until his death, in a fort in Albania.

Most Jews were shocked and despondent when they learned of their so-called messiah's betrayal. Their hopes collapsed. Nevertheless, neither Shabbetai's renunciation of Judaism nor his death put an end to the false-messianic movement. Nathan of Gaza managed to integrate Shabbetai's conversion into his theology and explained it as a necessary part of the process of salvation: The messiah must overcome evil in the world and can only free himself and Israel when he has gone through impurity and deep abasement.

This doctrine lived on in radicalized form in the movement of the Dönmeh (a Jewish sect that converted to Islam with Shabbetai Zevi) and the Frankists (an 18th-century Jewish sect that converted to Catholicism with their founder Jakob Frank). The appearance of this false messiah agitated the Jewish world, promulgating an enduring instability with consequences (e.g., denial of mysticism) still perceptible in our time.

With the continual decay of and the increasing European influence in the Ottoman empire from the 17th and 18th centuries, conditions for the Jews worsened. The legal emancipation of 1856 and the activity of the Alliance Israélite Universelle were essentially insignificant. Economic and religious concerns renewed the tensions between Jews and Christians.

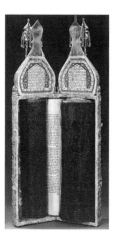

The increasing European influence strengthened the position of the Christians, who applied pressure on the positions of the Jews. The Christians had a few significant advantages: They were more numerous and they enjoyed the protection of the Occident, which preferred them to the Jews. The tensions persisted through the 19th century, giving rise to renewed accusations of ritual murder (the Damascus Affair in 1840) and yet more persecutions.

Before the 19th century, the slanderous claim that Jews used human blood for ritual purposes was almost unknown in the Islamic countries. There is little doubt that such ideas sprang from a Christian-European source. They remained unheard of for a long time even in the traditionally more anti-semitic countries (Morocco, Yemen, Persia), presumably because there were few or no Christians and the European influence was slower in coming. Although Christian in origin, the claims of ritual murder became a standard theme of anti-Jewish Islamic literature.

After the territorial reorganization of the Balkans and Near East at the beginning of the 20th century, the Ottoman Jews came under the dominion of at least four different national states. The Jews living in the Turkish Republic escaped the Holocaust, while almost all the Jews of Greece, Yugoslavia, and Rumania were murdered by the Germans. From Salonika alone, for example, a city that had been for centuries a center of Jewish culture, approximately 44,000 persons were deported to Auschwitz in 1943, and murdered.

156 Amulet. Silhouette of under- and overlaid paper of many different colors. David Algranati, Turkey, 19th/20th century. The amulet illustrates the text of Zechariah's vision (Zech. 4:1–7): "The angel who talked with me came again, and wakened me ... He said to me, 'What do you see?' And I said, 'I see a lampshade all of gold ... there are seven lamps on it ... And by it there are two olive trees, one on the right of the bowl and the other on its left.'" This text appears in the medallions of the frame, while the menorah bears the text of Psalm 67.

7th – 20th cent.

In traditional Judaism, no distinction is made between religious and secular areas of life, for religion permeates every aspect of daily life. How one dresses or what one eats is as much a part of religious practice as prayer and service of God. In a traditionally led household, the observance of the dietary laws which derive from divine commandments found in the Bible and the Talmud, clearly demonstrate this integration.

What may be eaten?

All foods must be kosher, which literally means "right" or "fit." Animals are classified into three groups—land animals, sea animals, and "air," or winged, animals (fowl)—and must meet certain criteria to be considered pure, or kosher.

☛ For land animals, the bible names the following features: "Any animal that has cloved hoofs and is cleft-footed and chews the cud—such may you eat" (Lev. 11:3). If either of the two features is missing, it is forbidden to eat the animal's flesh. As examples of proscribed animals, the Torah cites camels, rabbits, and hares, which are ruminants but do not have cloven feet. The pig, on the other hand, has split hooves but is not a ruminant and therefore is explicitly forbidden. As far back as the times of the Maccabees, eating pork was considered a repudiation of Judaism.

☛ Regarding sea animals, the bible prescribes: "These you may eat, of all that are in the waters. Everything in the waters that has fins and scales, whether in the seas or in the streams—such you may eat. But anything in the seas or the streams that does not have fins and scales, of the swarming creatures in the waters ... they are detestable to you .... Of their flesh you shall not eat, and their carcasses you shall regard as detestable" (Lev. 11:9–12). Accordingly, shrimp, eels, oysters, lobsters, crabs, mussels, and snails, as well as a few other species, are forbidden.

☛ Most fowl are considered pure and may be eaten. The bible specifically enumerates the impure birds in Lev. 11:13–19 and Deut. 14:12–18. Insects, with the exception of four species of grasshoppers, are impure (Lev. 11:20–22).

Animals must be specifically slaughtered as food: "You shall not eat anything that dies of itself" (Deut. 14:21). Dead and sick animals—roadkill or animals wounded by predators (the literal biblical proscription is against animals "torn" by another animal)—may not be eaten.

Butchering and dressing kosher animals

Because the bible prohibits the enjoyment of blood (Lev. 7 and 17) and the consumption of animals that either died naturally or were "torn,"

57 Ritual butchering of oxen and fowl. Illustration for the Law Codex Arba Turim of Jakob ben Asher (around 1270–1340), Mantua 1435. The animal is hung with its head down so that the blood, which the Torah repeatedly forbids one to imbibe, can drain well.

Jews follow the method of kosher butchering called *shehitah*. A specially trained butcher, the *shohet*, uses a sharp knife to cut through the carotid artery, trachea, and esophagus in a single motion so that the blood can drain out completely (**157**). The shohet is assisted by the *menakker*, who cuts away the forbidden fat and removes the hip socket and sciatic nerve, which is forbidden in Genesis 32:33, owing to Jacob's fight with the angel. Shohets and menakkers are supervised by rabbis, who may examine slaughtered animals to make sure that they are kosher. For example, an animal with adhesions may be considered "torn" and hence unfit for consumption. When questions arise, the shohet consults a rabbi, who makes the final decision (**158**).

In traditional homes, the housewife is responsible for removing the final residues of blood. To "kosher" the meat, it is soaked for half an hour in lukewarm water, patted dry, salted on all sides, and then set on a slanted or a perforated draining board so that any blood can run down unhindered. After an hour, the

158 A kosher stamp of the rabbinate for foods that have fulfilled the demands of the *Kashrut* supervision, Germany, 2nd half 19th century. The stamp's surface reads "kasher" (Hebrew for "fit" or "proper").

159
A plate
for dairy
foods with the Yiddish
inscription "*milschtig.*" Niederwiller, France,
19th century.

מילשטיג

salted pieces of meat are washed three times in water. They are then considered ready for meal preparation. Since fish is not considered a meat, it does not have to be made kosher through shehitah and salting.

The prohibition against mixing meat and milk

"You shall not boil a kid in its mother's milk" is repeated three times in the bible (Ex. 23:19 and 34:26 and Deut. 14:21). This threefold repetition has been interpreted by rabbis as three prohibitions: one may not cook meat and milk together; one may not eat meat and milk together; and one may not profit from the mixture of meat and milk, for example, by selling it to non-Jews. Out of later tradition evolved a complete separation of meat and dairy products. After a meat meal, for example, one must wait for the meat to be digested (as a rule, six hours) before consuming any dairy products. (For dessert or in coffee, milk substitutes such as soy milk or nondairy creamers may be used.) After milk-based meals, which are more quickly digested, it is only necessary to wait half an hour. The separation of meat and dairy includes rinsing the mouth between meals. A kosher kitchen is equipped with two separate sets of pots, dishes, utensils, cutlery, tablecloths, and kitchen linens for meat and dairy (except for glass, which is considered neutral) (159).

Since fish is considered *pareve* ("neutral"), it may be eaten with both meat and dairy but must have been prepared in appropriate cookware—that is, in the dairy pots for a dairy meal, and in the meat pots for a meat meal. Fruits and vegetables, eggs, vegetable oils, and margarine are all considered pareve and may be eaten with both meat and milk.

Alcohol

Wine and all spirits that are produced from fermented grapes (cider, champagnes, Cognac) must be kosher—that is, harvested and processed under rabbinical supervision. Spirits that do not come from the vine—beer, whiskey, vodka, and liqueurs—are subject to no particular instructions.

160 A plate for kosher food from Cologne's Gürzenich Concert Hall. Late 19th/early 20th century. The blue decorative band is interrupted by the words "*kasher*" (in Hebrew letters) and "Gürzenich."

Regional differences

Under observance of these dietary laws, Jewish cuisine developed certain idiosyncrasies, largely due to the influence of various regional culinary traditions. Typical of Sephardic cooking is plentiful use of olive oil, lemon, and garlic, as well as intense and often hot spices. Ashkenazi cooks often use wild goose and chicken fat to prepare nutritious stews, more mildly seasoned with considerably less garlic.

To accomodate the prohibition of all work, including lighting a fire, on the Sabbath, typical dishes evolved in various regions of the Diaspora: the Ashkenazi prepare *tsholent*, the Sephardim *dafina*, and the Jews of the Ottoman empire make *hamin*. All three are slow-cooked stews that are prepared before the Sabbath begins—before sunset on Friday—and are left overnight in a warm oven at low heat to cook until Saturday noon. The Spanish Inquisitors considered slow-cooked stews a treacherous sign of "judaized" New Christians.

On holidays, symbolic foods that underscore the meaning of the celebration are often served. The best example is the Pesach (Passover) celebration, the seder (see p. 20 ff.).

Dispersion of the Sephardic Jews

16th – 18th cent.

Amsterdam, "Jerusalem of the West"

After the expulsion of the Catholic clergy in 1578, only one religion could be officially practiced in the Netherlands—Reformed Calvinism. Other believers (Catholics, Lutherans, Mennonites, and Jews) were not persecuted, however, and were free to exercise their beliefs in private. For instance, houses of worship of the religious minorities could not be recognizable as such from the outside. This regulation applied to Jews until 1670. The first Jews came to Amsterdam in the late 16th century, and the first Jewish community was founded in 1602 by Portuguese immigrants. Twelve years later, they acquired a piece of land outside Amsterdam, in Ouderkerk on the Amstel, where they laid out a cemetery (161).

The legal position of the Jews in the United Netherlands was never precisely defined. In 1619, the two wealthiest provinces—Holland and Westfriesland—determined that each city should decide whether and under what conditions to accept Jews. However, the cities that chose to accept Jews were allowed to demand that a mark of differentiation, or "Judenfleck," be worn. This regulation held sway in the remaining provinces as well until the civil equality of the Jews took effect in 1796. Prompted primarily by economic considerations, Amsterdam authorities accepted Jews into the city despite their many religious reservations. The Sephardic refugees were often wealthy merchants and bankers who brought their international contacts with them, or they were respected literati and scientists. Along with the Huguenots, who came slightly later, the Jewish immigrants helped strengthen Amsterdam's economic power.

161 Jewish cemetery of Ouderkerk. The marble tent sarcophaguses are typical of Sephardic graves.

Sephardim and Ashkenazim

After the Sephardim were established in Amsterdam, the Ashkenazim came in 1635, forming a second "Jewish nation." Coming from the countries of central and eastern Europe, they brought their own language, Yiddish, and their own customs, many of which were different from those of the Sephardim. Unlike the Sephardim, the Ashkenazim had not participated in the cultural development of western Europe but had completely concentrated on life within their own communities. For them, Amsterdam represented a peaceful sanctuary after years of persecution.

The Ashkenazi community grew quickly and soon outnumbered the Sephardim. However, while the small group of rich Sephardic merchants and intellectuals were scarcely distinguishable from their Dutch peers in mode of dress or lifestyle, the poorer Ashkenazim were first integrated (and perhaps assimilated) into Dutch society sometime in the 18th century (162).

162 Francisco Lopes Suasso (1641–1710). Painting, Netherlands, ca. 1685. From his father, Francisco Lopes inherited influence, wealth, and a title. The members of this originally Portuguese merchant family were at home among the cream of Amsterdam society. In his right hand, the nobleman holds an orange, an allusion to his relationship with the ruling dynasty of Orange.

Jews in the economic life of Amsterdam

Many Sephardic Jews were wholesale merchants or bankers whose dense networks of contacts extended to the Iberian peninsula, the Ottoman empire, and even to Brazil. They traded in sugar, raw woods, tobacco, and diamonds. The Ashkenazi Jews were primarily tradesmen and street vendors.

In 1632, however, fear of competition led the Dutch citizens of Amsterdam to pass an ordinance banning Jews from membership in trade guilds and limiting retail trade. The only exceptions were in professions where gentiles were not

16th – 18th cent.

Sephardic Dispersion: After the expulsion of the Jews from Spain (1492) and Portugal (1496–97), the Inquisition with its pyres remained a constant danger for New Christians, or Marranos, especially when they secretly practiced Jewish customs. Many left in the 16th and 17th centuries for countries where they might live without danger and even return to Judaism, such as areas in the Ottoman empire (see p. 115f.), the Netherlands, England, and South and North America.

163 A diamond factory in Amsterdam. Photo, ca. 1925.

concerned about competition: pharmacists, physicians, Hebrew printers, and kosher butchers. The Ashkenazi Jews were hard hit by the restrictive ordinance. It had much less impact on the Sephardic community, since they earned their money in wholesale trade—outside the guilds. In 1674, the average per capita income of the Ashkenazi Jews was 3.48 guilders; for the Sephardim, it was 1,448.72 guilders. When diamond cutting emerged in the 17th century as a new form of handwork, there was no guild for it; nor was there a guild for textiles. Many Jews therefore found work in these trades (163).

Baruch De Spinoza

From its founding, the Jewish community of Amsterdam brought together Jews of many different backgrounds. Many Marranos from Spain and Portugal who had been raised as Christians returned to Judaism, but had to be "re-Judaized." Anxious not to fail at this important task, rabbis and community officials were very strict about the religious practice of re-Judaized Marranos and punished severely even the slightest suggestion of free thought, the smallest deviation from orthodoxy, and any action that could disturb their good relationship with local authorities. The worst punishment was *herem*, or banning from participation in the religious community: a banned person could not enter the synagogue, and community members were forbidden personal or commercial contact with him (or her).

The imposition of the *herem* on Baruch De Spinoza (1632–77) (164) is perhaps the most famous example of banishment. In 1656, the Amsterdam-born rationalist philosopher—a rabbi by the age of twenty—was banned by the community because of his heretical views (165). The *herem* could only be lifted through public penitence

164 Portrait of Baruch De Spinoza by Rembrandt van Rijn. Oil on linen. Netherlands, ca. 1670.

and payment of a fine. Spinoza, however, made no attempt to make amends, and when the ban brought his career as a merchant to an end, he lived in seclusion in different places in Holland. Shunning material possessions and believing that he should earn his own keep, Spinoza worked as a lens grinder and lived on a modest annuity that enabled him to pursue his philosophical writing. His *Tractatus Theologico-Politicus* (Treatise on Religious and Political Philosophy), which appeared anonymously in 1670, deals with freedom of philosophy and belief. In *Ethics*, which was published posthumously, he presents his view of God as a unitary, indivisible, and endless substance and postulates a pantheistic unity of God and nature. He continued to be reviled after his death until the German men of letters Gotthold Lessing (1729–81) and Johann von Goethe (1749–1832) took an interest in his works and helped establish Spinoza's reputation as one of the great thinkers of western civilization.

The Ashkenazi synagogues of Amsterdam

In 1670, Amsterdam's Jews were first allowed to build recognizable synagogues (**166**). The first representative place of worship of the Ashkenazi community, the "Great Synagogue," was erected according to plans by the municipal architect

165 The *herem* ("ban") on Spinoza, written in Portuguese in the Jewish year 5416 (1656). "The chiefs of the council make known to you that having long known of evil opinions and acts of Baruch Spinoza, they have endeavoured by various means and promises to turn him away from evil ways. Not being able to find any remedy, but on the contrary receiving every day more information about the abominable heresies practiced and taught by him, and about the monstrous acts committed by him, having this from many trustworthy witnesses who have deposed and borne witness on all this in the presence of said Spinoza, who has been convicted; all this having been examined in the presence of the rabbis, the council decided, with the advice of the rabbi, that the said Spinoza should be excommunicated and cut off from the Nation of Israel."

16th – 18th cent.

166 The synagogues of Amsterdam. Copper engraving of Adolf van de Laan, Amsterdam, ca. 1710. Left is the "Portuguese," right, with five arched windows, is the "Great Synagogue" of the Ashkenazi community. On the far right, in the house with a pointed roof, was a mikveh.

167 Interior of the Great Synagogue. Today this room houses a permanent exhibit of Judaica.

16th – 18th cent.

168 The Museum for Jewish History in the Ashkenazi Synagogue complex. On the right is the Great Synagogue (1671); on the left the New Synagogue (1752).

Daniel Stalpaert and was dedicated on Passover in 1671 (**166, 167**). The constant need for more space soon made it necessary to build two smaller synagogues behind it: the "Upper Synagogue" (1685) and the "Third Synagogue" (1700). As the membership of the community grew, they decided to build yet a fourth synagogue. This "New Synagogue" was larger than the three already in use and was dedicated in 1752. All four buildings served as centers of prayer and study until 1943.

In 1935, the Ashkenazi community celebrated the tricentennial anniversary of the "Great Synagogue." A mere ten years later, however, all four buildings showed the ravages of war and anti-Semitism: copper ornaments and lamps had disappeared, as well as everything of wood that could be detached: The floors, galleries, and entire balconies were torn out for firewood during the "hunger winter" of 1944/45. The few Holocaust survivors from Amsterdam obviously lacked the means to restore the buildings after the war, and they sold the entire complex to the city of Amsterdam in 1954. While the "Great Synagogue" served temporarily for storage, the "New Synagogue" housed the laboratory for urban development of the city's public works department.

In 1974, the city of Amsterdam decided to turn the Ashkenazi synagogues into museums of Jewish history. After careful restoration, the Jewish Historical Museum was opened in 1987 (**168**).

The Portuguese Synagogue of the Sephardim

The great Portuguese Synagogue (**169**) was built in 1675 from plans by Elias Bouman. This synagogue is

one of the most important baroque synagogues in the world and is authentically preserved to this day. The high building with its symmetrical baroque facade stands in a court, surrounded by low wings. This configuration goes back to the Jerusalem Temples. Architects had been trying since the Renaissance to reproduce its appearance.

169   Southwest view of the Portuguese Synagogue (1675). Anonymous, early 18th century.

The design of the Portuguese Synagogue might have been influenced by a book that appeared in 1642 in Middelburg, *Afbeeldinge van den Temple Salomonis*, and the accompanying Temple model by Jakob Jehuda Leone. Leone traveled through the Netherlands and made regular appearances with his wooden model, which earned him the surname "Templo." The similarities between the synagogue and Templo's model suggest that Bouman drew his inspiration from it.

As is usual in Sephardic synagogues, the Torah shrine stands in the east, the *bimah* in the west, and the benches are placed along the northern and southern walls (**170**). The magnificent Torah shrine, like the rest of the furniture, is carved from dark Jacaranda wood imported from Brazil (**171**). Moses Curiel, who donated the shrine,

170   Interior view of the Portuguese Synagogue showing the Torah shrine in the east and the *bimah* in the foreground. Anonymous, 17th century.

16th – 18th cent.

was one of the founders of the Dutch trading company "Brasiliaans Compagnie." The building served as a model for numerous Sephardic synagogues around the world, including one in London (1701) and another in Newport, Rhode Island (1763).

Amsterdam's decline

In the second half of the 18th century, Amsterdam lost its position as a leading world seaport. The general decline also affected the city's Jewish residents. Even the once wealthy bankers and wholesale merchants tried to stave off the encroaching poverty. By the end of the 18th century, 87% of the Ashkenazi and 54% of the Sephardic Jews were reduced to accepting charity from the community.

171 The Portuguese Synagogue in Amsterdam: The magnificent Torah shrine of Jacaranda wood with opened doors.

The 19th century, by contrast, brought the flourishing of the diamond industry and, with it, the rise of the Jewish proletariat. The first Dutch union of Jewish workers, the "Algemeene Nederlandse Diamantenwerkers Bond," was founded in 1894.

The Holocaust

Dutch Jews had been fortunate enough to live in freedom, without crippling discrimination or fear of persecution, for centuries. The German occupation in the spring of 1940 came as a shock. The anti-Semitic measures of the German occupying forces came fast and furious: kosher butchering was outlawed, Jewish officials were dismissed from their positions, and in May 1942, in preparation for the deportations (to the camps) that were sure to follow, Jews were forced to wear a six-pointed Star of David on their clothing at all times. From July 1942, the trains rolled from Westerbork station to the extermination camps. Of the 140,000 ews who lived in the Netherlands before the war, over 100,000 were murdered.

England

In 1290, the English monarch Edward I had expelled all Jews from England. Their resettlement in the 17th century began through the initiative of the Amsterdam Rabbi Manasseh ben-Israel (1604–57) (**172**). Manasseh and his family fled from an Auto da fé (heretic burning) in Lisbon and settled in Holland. While still quite young, he gained a reputation as a scholar, printer, and publisher. Manasseh cultivated good relationships with gentile scholars and artists. He was a neighbor of the great Dutch painter, Rembrandt van Rijn, who painted his portrait and contributed illustrations to his book, *Piedra Gloriosa*.

172 Portrait of Manasseh ben-Israel. Govaert Flinck, Amsterdam, 1637.

Manasseh believed that the messiah would come as soon as the Jews had settled everywhere, even the ends of the Earth, and he spent much of his life trying to find new places where Jews might settle. Manasseh and his followers came to the conclusion this must be England, which they considered the "End of the Earth" (based on the Norman designation, "Angleterre"). Thus, he strove for the resettlement of Jews there. He dedicated his pamphlet *The Hopes of Israel* to the English Parliament and decided to travel personally to England to convince Oliver Cromwell (then head of the Puritan Commonwealth) to revoke the prohibition on Jewish resettlement.

The prospect of economic prosperity through the influence of the supposedly money-wise Jews swayed Cromwell in Manasseh's favor, and he did decide to rescind the ban on Jews in England in 1656. Because of popular resistance, however, the decision was never disclosed publicly or put into law. Jews were simply tacitly allowed to enter Great Britain, where they were given economic equality, freedom of movement in the country, and

16th – 18th cent.

freedom of worship. By the middle of the 19th century, the only sphere of British life still closed to them was public office.

The first Jews to come to England were Sephardim from Amsterdam. It is no surprise that they modeled their London Synagogue (1701) on the Portuguese Synagogue of Amsterdam. The original plans were modified only slightly in the Bevis Marks Synagogue to include a row of columns along the western wall in addition to those on the north and south.

An Ashkenazi community developed in London as well in 1693. Typically far less affluent than the Sephardic immigrants, many of the poorer Ashkenazim settled in the provincial centers, such as Liverpool, Portsmouth, Bristol, and Plymouth. Around 1700, there were scarcely 2,000 Jews in England, but by the mid-18th century the number had grown to 10,000 (8,000 of them in London); near the end of the century, the number had climbed to 20,000 to 25,000.

Brazil

Sephardic Jews from western Europe founded the first Jewish communities in the Americas. Marranos had come to the continent with Spanish and Portuguese conquerors. In 1630, the Netherlands conquered Pernambuco in northeastern Brazil, while the capital Recife was conquered by the Portuguese. Dutch Jews settled in both areas and established a blooming trade center. Some owned sugar cane plantations (**173**) or traded in sugar, tobacco, and woods. By 1645, Brazil's Jewish community had 1,450 members, a synagogue, and an important rabbi, Isaac Aboab de Francesca—the first on the American continents.

The Portuguese takeover of Brazil in 1654 meant expulsion for the

173 Sugar production on a Brazilian sugar plantation. Frans Post, ca. 1650.

Jewish community. Some returned with their rabbi to Holland; others moved to Central or North America. Jewish communities emerged in Surinam, on Curaçao, Barbados, and Jamaica, and in the colony of New Amsterdam, today New York City.

North America

In September 1654, twenty-three Jews reached the colony of New Amsterdam. The governor, Peter Stuyvesant, a strict Calvinist, wanted them to move right on again. In his letters to the Dutch West Indies Company, he described the new-comers as enemies of Christ, repulsive and deceitful. The company turned down his request for permission to expel them, in part (and no small part, perhaps) under the influence of its Jewish share-holders. Likewise, his attempts to forbid the Jews from holding services and establishing a cemetery failed. In 1656, the Jewish community of New Amsterdam was granted permission to acquire its own land. The right to settle, however, was not sufficient for the Jews of the New World, and they fought for their civil rights. They did not accept that they had to pay a special tax in place of serving in the city militia, from which they were prohibited. In 1655, they sued for this right and won it. When Asser Levy was denied his full civil rights, he complained to Amsterdam, and, since he was a Dutch citizen, he obtained his rights. Thus, the first Jewish settlers laid the foundations on which later immigrants would build.

Shortly after 1680, a group of Jews founded a community in Newport, Rhode Island. They suffered a temporary decline around 1750, but grew steadily thereafter. Their leader was Aaron Lopez, a Marrano from Portugal. In 1763, a Sephardic synagogue was dedicated there; like the one in London, it was modeled after the Portuguese Synagogue in Amsterdam, and is the oldest preserved synagogue in North America (**174**).

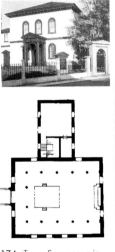

174 Touro Synagogue in Newport, Rhode Island, 1763.

16th – 18th cent.

Enlightenment and Emancipation

17th – 19th cent.

In the late Middle Ages, the Jews had been expelled from almost all the large cities of Europe (see p. 72f.). In the 16th and 17th century, most German Jews lived in small suburbs or in the country. They worked as cattle dealers, peddlers, money lenders, and pawnbrokers. While most of the Jews lived in relative poverty, a rich Jewish minority, the Court Jews, Hofjuden, developed after the Thirty Years' War.

After 1648, Germany consisted of a number of small principalities, and the influence of the emperor was slight. Regardless of the religion of the princes—some were Catholic, some were Protestant—they all tried to establish their own absolute authority and to maintain a splendid court. The wealthier class of Jews were indispensible to the ambitious courts—as bankers, financial advisers, court troups, purveyors to the court, and as diplomats. In return for their services, they were exempted from the restraints that regulated the lives of ordinary Jews. The Court Jews had freedom of travel and settlement, often owned wonderful palaces, lived in luxury, and dressed in the latest fashion. Since they were allowed to keep their family and servants with them, their presence often became the seed of a new Jewish community.

The Court Jew was often able to use his relationship with the sovereign to advocate for his community. On the other hand, a Court Jew who fell into disfavor could bring an entire community with him into ruin: In 1573, the Court Jew Lippold was executed in Berlin, and all Jews were forbidden thenceforward and "for eternal time" to live in Brandenburg.

Despite their wealth and influence, the Court Jews remained "mighty slaves" whose safety depended on the favor of the prince. Without his protection, they were vulnerable to the enmity of the wider population—all the more so, since among their responsibilities in the princes' service, they often had to enforce unpopular measures such as currency devaluations or tax increases.

Josef Süss Oppenheimer—the "Sweet Jew"

The most famous German Court Jew was Josef Süss Oppenheimer (1698–1738), called "Jud Süss," whose character and spectacular demise have fascinated writers and composers. In 1732, Oppenheimer entered the service of Duke Karl Alexander of Württemberg and soon became the prince's most important financier and consultant. He grew wealthy, was known as a gallant courtier, and owned magnificent houses. As the duke's secret financial adviser, he enforced a new fiscal policy that rescinded the old privileges of the landowners and merchants and was supposed to promote a modern, centralized mercantilist state.

175 Josef Süss Oppenheimer. This contemporary engraving shows him surrounded by instruments of torture; under him is the cage in which he was hung.

When Karl Alexander died suddenly in 1737, supposedly during a night of debauchery, his favored Jew became the target for everybody's resentment. All of the duke's excesses (and Karl Alexander's life had been full of them) and his unpopular politics were blamed on Oppenheimer, the convenient (and surviving) scapegoat for the duke's autocratic rule. Oppenheimer was accused of high treason, embezzlement, and a

We, Frederick William, by God's grace Margrave of Brandenburg ... herewith publicly admit ..., that We, under special circumstances and on a most humble basis, authorize Hirschel Lazarus, Benedict Veit, and Abraham Ries, Jews, for the advancement of trade and commerce, to bring some fifty Jewish families relocated from other places into Our country ... and under Our special merciful protection We take on and accept ... 6. They shall not be permitted to have a synagogue; however, they may assemble in their houses for prayer and ceremonies, ... and shall abstain from all vices and blasphemies under threat of severe punishment. *

Edict of the Great Elector, May 21, 1671

137

number of other crimes. He was condemned to death and hung in 1738 on the gallows (**175**).

Berlin

In the 17th century, Jews were still banned from the larger German cities; in about 1670, they were expelled from Vienna. In 1671, Frederick William, the elector of Brandenburg known as the Great Elector, took fifty of the richest families of expelled Viennese Jews into Prussia. Noble as this sounds, his decision should not be misunderstood as particularly tolerant or Jewish-friendly (the fact that they were the *wealthiest* Viennese Jews is cause enough to suspect the Great Elector's motives); he and his successors expressed their anti-Semitism often enough.

The Prussian sovereigns were always ready, however, to throw out convention if it meant strengthening the position of the state. Jews were admitted because they might prove "useful," but the authorities took great pains to keep the number of Jews small: the Prussians sought to have as few Jews as possible perform as many economically important services (money and credit trade, establishment of manufacturers) as possible. The Jews themselves were subject to petty regulations (1671, 1714, 1730, and 1750) regarding exactly which taxes, protection monies, and other duties they had to pay, how many children they could bring with them under the letter of protection, which professions they

176 Porcelain ape similar to the "Mendelssohn Apes." Under Frederick II, on specified occasions—buying a house, assessment, death, or marriage—Jews had to purchase the overpriced remainders of the Royal China Factory in Berlin and, of course, were not allowed to choose for themselves but suffered at the pleasure of the manufacturer. Thus, Moses Mendelssohn involuntarily came to acquire 20 porcelain apes.

17th – 19th cent.

His Royal Majesty in Prussia ... has for the promotion of porcelain manufactured by His Porcelain Manufacturer ... resolved, that each time Jews apply for, or receive permission, to acquire a house, they shall be required to purchase a certain moderate quantity of Porcelain. A Jew who applies for ... a general privilege, shall make a purchase worth 500 reichstaler; one who applies for ... an ordinary protection shall make one worth 300 reichstaler, and one who applies for ... a concession for house purchase or any other benefit, likewise, shall make one worth 300 reichstaler.   Frederick II, Kabinettsorder of March 21, 1769

could choose, and the conditions under which they could marry. Under Frederick II especially, the Jews were asked to add to the state's coffers. New orders were constantly being added to the many special taxes already in place. Perhaps the most famous such discriminatory order in this period was the "Kabinettsorder an das Generaldirektorium" of March 21, 1769. This order, designed to help the foundering Royal Porcelain Manufacturer (KPM) achieve a better balance sheet at the expense of the Jews, compelled Jews to purchase KPM products: The philosopher Moses Mendelssohn, for one, was obliged to "accept" twenty porcelain apes in exchange for a concession (**176**).

Berlin's Jews were allowed to enter the city through only one gate where they were required to pay a special, and particularly humiliating, body toll, levied only on Jews and cattle—all symbols for the "privileged powerlessness" of the Berlin Jews, some of whom were in fact the wealthiest persons of central Europe. The state's extreme financial demands led to an abnormal structure within the Berlin community. Only the richest Jewish families were issued an unrestricted residence permit and residential and labor rights equal to those of gentile merchants. They began at first to assimilate, to some extent—to mimic the habits of the Christian upper class; at the same time, the meanings of the traditional custom began to fade. This process of assimilation has characterized Jewish populations to greater and lesser extents throughout the world, often having a considerable impact on their acceptance and fate in the face of conditions to come.

177 The first Berlin Community Synagogue in the Heidereutergasse. Engraving by F.A. Calau, 1795. After furious quarrels among competing private synagogues, a synagogue was built for the whole community. The simple, rectangular assembly hall with high, round, arched windows and hip roof was erected in 1712–14 by Michael Kemeter.

17th – 19th cent.

178 Portrait of Moses Mendelssohn by Johann Christoph Frisch, ca. 1780.

179 Gotthold Ephraim Lessing (1729–81) was a close friend of Moses Mendelssohn and worked with him as an author and publisher. Colored copper engraving of 1773 by Johann Friedrich Bause from a painting by Anton Graf.

180 Photo from a 1981 Hamburg production of Lessing's Nathan the Wise.

There were poor Jews. They were the public servants (rabbis, shohets, choir masters, religion teachers) and the house servants, whose residence permits were valid only for as long as they remained in a particular position.

It was not only the Prussian king who ensured that just a few rich Jews received renewed letters of protection. Some leaders of the Jewish communities themselves supported this restrictive policy since all community members were required to help pay the high taxes, and the wealthy would have to subsidize those who were less able to shoulder the tax burden. Thus, the influx of poor foreign Jews complicated life in the Jewish Prussian communities.

Moses Mendelssohn

In the autumn of 1743, the fourteen-year-old Moses Mendelssohn, son of a poor Torah scribe from Dessau, came to Berlin. As a pupil of David Fränkel, Mendelssohn followed his teacher to Berlin where Fränkel became rabbi at the Synagogue Heidereutergasse (**177**). The legal status of the students was only vaguely understood and depended on the approval of the city officials. For the first seven years, Mendelssohn led a hand-to-mouth existence. Beside the traditional Talmud study, he applied himself to secular learning: German, French, Latin, Greek, mathematics, philosophy, and natural science. He earned his livelihood from 1750 from the silk manufacturer Isaak Bernhard, first as a private tutor, later as an accountant, and then as partner. Until 1763, he did not have his own letter of protection and could only remain in Berlin, since he was employed by the "legal Jew" Bernhard. Mendelssohn remained faithful to scientific work for the rest of his life.

The German dramatist Gotthold Ephraim Lessing (1729–81) was an outspoken champion of religious freedom and tolerance. He was largely responsible for establishing the reputation of Spinoza among the world's philosophers, and, likewise, his personal relationship with Moses Mendelssohn was a critical factor in the latter's development and acceptance. Lessing had written a protest against the anachronistic prejudices against the Jews in 1749 in his comic play *The Jews*. He and Mendelssohn were lifelong friends, and this friendship influenced the literary work of both men. Along with author/publisher Frederick Nicolai, they developed German literary criticism as a scholarly discipline. Lessing left his friend a monument in his poetic drama *Nathan the Wise* (1779): The character of Nathan is clearly based on Moses Mendelssohn.

With his philosophical work, *Phaedon* (1767), Mendelssohn became famous as a German philosopher. He had already received the first prize of the Royal Prussian Academy of Sciences in 1763 for his "Treatise on the Evidence in Metaphysical Sciences." In 1771, the Academy voted in favor of his membership, but the "enlightened" philosopher-king Frederick II did not confirm him. As a proponent of Enlightenment ideals, Mendelssohn sought an end to the social and cultural isolation of his fellow Jews. If the Jews could play a part in German culture, this could lead to their social integration and prepare the ground for engagement with gentiles. The majority of the Prussian Jews, however, spoke Yiddish, wrote in Hebrew letters, and hardly spoke German. To open the gate to the German-speaking country to his co-religionists, Mendelssohn translated the Hebrew bible into German. The text first used Hebrew letters, to facilitate access to the Jewish readers. The reactions to Mendelssohn's translation in the Jewish community were quite strong: Most people greeted it enthusiastically; three editions ap-

181 Frederick II (1712–86). Drawing by Johann Heinrich Ramberg, 1786.

If my translations were to be accepted by all Israelites without objection, they would be superfluous. The more the so-called wise men of the time oppose, the more necessary they are. I have done these translations primarily for the common man and find, however, that they are even more necessary for rabbis.
Moses Mendelssohn, 1779

17th – 19th cent.

> If the civil union cannot be held alive under any other conditions than by deviating from the laws which we all still accept as binding then we regret from the bottom of our hearts what we are forced to state: then we should rather renounce this civil union.
>
> Moses Mendelssohn

peared in Mendelssohn's lifetime. The orthodox rabbis, on the other hand, were angered and threatened Mendelssohn with *herem*, or banishment. For them, translation of the holy scripture into a secular language was blasphemous.

In "Jerusalem, or On Religious Power and Judaism," Mendelssohn objected to every kind of religious pressure and defined Judaism as revealed law (in contrast to the Christian religion, which rests on revealed doctrine). Judaism offers binding instructions and laws for living, but not instructions for thinking. With this definition, Mendelssohn provided support for the view of Judaism as a primarily ceremonial-legal religion, but he believed that it was a more enlightened, rational religion in comparison to the dogmatically bound Christianity. Although it was very important to Mendelssohn to integrate the Jews into western culture, he was adamant that this could not happen at the price of giving up Judaism. His own life was consistent with the model he espoused for all Jews: Hold fast to the rites and laws of the Jewish tradition and simultaneously participate fully in the surrounding culture. The younger Jewish rationalists saw it differently. For them, integration into western culture meant also breaking with time-honored beliefs and rites. As father of the *Haskalah*, Mendelssohn remained the great idol of the younger generation of rationalists and became—despite the example of his own life—the figure head of German-Jewish assimilation.

182 A Jewish cattle dealer sells a dairy cow to a gentile. Anti-Semitic bronze figure, Germany, ca. 1840.

The rocky road to legal equality

Under the influence of the Age of Enlightenment, the American Revolution, and the French Revolution—with their strongly egalitarian rhetoric—the impulse to change the Jews' legal position had been in the air since the end of the 18th century. Jewish communities, with enlightened politicians and leading civil servants, advocated full civil rights for Jews. In Germany these efforts were organized under the ideas of "civic improvement" or "naturalization." In the 1830s, the idea of "emancipation" emerged. Demands for equality for the Jews (like demands for freedom for the peasants) had become an element of civil rights for all. But such enfranchisement, in Germany no less than in many other countries, would require dissolution of the status quo, of longstanding and entrenched law and custom.

Toward the end of the struggle for emancipation, two essential concepts developed: One was a liberal-revolutionary kind of emancipation that sought to establish the equality of the Jews by means of a single legislative act. Implicit in this view was a conviction that a legislative act could elicit an integrating response from society and lead to a gradual dissipation of all differences between Jews and gentiles without additional regulations or laws. This idea corresponded to legislation passed during the French Revolution: The "Law of National Unity of September 28, 1791" made the French Jews free, equal citizens of the new republic overnight. With this law, all disadvantages, but also all privileges such as community autonomy or freedom from military service, were eliminated.

The second possibility for emancipation of the Jews in early 19th-century Germany revolved around an enlightened establishment conception that equality could only be attained in a lengthy legislative process. A progressive civil program would be responsible for the "improvement" of the Jews through educational measures. This social integration would culminate in full equality. It was this notion of a slow emancipation process that predominated in Germany, and so emancipation was drawn out over a period of nearly a hundred years, until the constitution of

> What is ... the great task of our time? It is emancipation. Not only for the Irish, Greeks, Frankfurt Jews, West Indian blacks, and such oppressed people, but for the whole world, particularly for Europe, which in its maturity must liberate itself now from the iron reins of the privileged, the aristocracy.
>
> Heinrich Heine, 1828

183 Heinrich Heine (1797–1856). The son of a Jewish textile trader in Düsseldorf, Heine became a merchant before he began his Jewish studies in 1819. Shortly before his graduation in 1825, he converted to Protestantism. Subsequently he worked as a freelance author and editor. In 1831, he went to Paris. Jewish themes recur throughout his poetical work, especially in the story fragment *The Rabbi of Bacherach* (1840) and in the *Hebrew Melodies* from the *Romanzero* (1851).

17th – 19th cent.

143

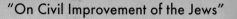

the German empire in 1871. Progress was not steady, but like the liberation movement of the middle class, with which it is inherently connected, came in waves. Times of revolutionary upheaval produced significant advances, while reactionary times brought backsliding.

"On the Civil Improvement of the Jews"

With his written argument, "On the Civil Improvement of the Jews" (Berlin, 1781) (**184**), the Prussian official Christian Wilhelm von Dohm raised the "Jewish question" before the general public, paving the way for emancipation in the German states. Dohm expressed the view "that the Jews just as well as all other people can be useful members of civic society," and that everything for which one reproaches the Jews "is caused only by the political situation in which they live." "Improvement," however, would have to be mutual. The state should lift the limitations on residency, the prohibition of certain professions, and degrading special taxes, and give the Jews full civil rights. The Jews, for their part, should be more flexible in relation to the surrounding culture, keep their accounts in the national language, and put aside their "still too mercantile spirit."

Followers of Dohm's "physiocratic" doctrine tried to steer the Jews toward agricultural occupations, because "for the state as for himself, in most cases it is better if the Jew labors more in the workshops and behind the plow, than in the chancellery." Unlike later "improvers," however, Dohm wanted to leave the Jews authority in their own community and over their own religious questions.

Dohm's argument sparked furious debates for and against civil equality for the Jews. Only a few months after its publication came the first state measures toward Jewish emancipation.

Ueber

die bürgerliche Verbesserung

der

J u d e n

von

Christian Wilhelm Dohm.

Mit Königl. Preußischem Privilegio.

Berlin und Stettin,
bei Friedrich Nicolai,
1 7 8 1.

184 Title page of the treatise of Christian Wilhelm von Dohm (1751–1820). With Mendelssohn and the publisher Nicolai, Dohm was among the most important Berlin rationalists. His programmatic writing sparked lively debate in France and Vienna as well as in his home town.

17th – 19th cent.

oseph II in Vienna proclaimed the Tolerance Charter, lifting the most severe limits on the Austrian Jews, though by no means granting emancipation in any modern sense.

The Prussian emancipation edict

The Prussian Reform Act, which included the Edict of 1812, was the result of Prussia's shattering defeat by Napoleon. Enlightenment statesmen such as Karl August von Hardenberg and Wilhelm von Humboldt recognized that Prussia could be restored to economic and military power only through modernization. For this, serfdom and guild limitations, as well as special privileges for the Jews, had to go. On March 11, 1812, the controversial Emancipation Edict was issued, granting the Prussian Jews civil rights and the right to settle anywhere, to acquire property, and to serve in the military (**185**). Permission to hold public offices, it was believed, required a special law. That law never came, and Jews remained excluded from public office. The edict, moreover, applied only to Jews who already had a privilege or a letter of protection; all foreign Jews remained disenfranchised (**186**). The emancipation process was hampered, however, by the fact that the reforms came from above, through enlightened officials, and were not based on a broad political movement.

Similar emancipation laws were passed in other German states. With the Edict of 1812, Jewish emancipation in Germany reached its first peak. The Jewish communities reacted to their new legitimacy with, among other things, demands for internal reform (see p. 151).

Reaction: The Congress of Vienna

Many Jews believed that civil equality brought them closer to the goal of integration into society. This hope soon proved illusory. The Congress

185 A Jewish militia member says goodbye to his parents and steps into the row with his Christian comrades. Woodcut of L. Pietsch based on an oil painting of Oskar Graf. As Frederick William III called his people to arms in March 1813 to expel the French occupying forces, 170 Prussian Jews were for the first time—since the Edict of 1812—also conscripted as citizens. Another 561 Jews volunteered.

17th – 19th cent.

186 Document declaring the banker Simon Wolf Oppenheim according to the Edict of 1812 a Prussian citizen and establishing his surname. The status of citizenship was tied to a series of conditions: One must, for example, as "In-länder and Staatsbürger" (resident of country and state), have established a family name. Until the era of emancipation, Jews usually limited themselves to a first name, to which they may have added a patronymic ("son of …") form.

17th – 19th cent.

of Vienna rescinded the rights established during the Napoleonic era and the concessions of the Edict of 1812: Article 16 of the Viennese Closing Acts allowed each state to restore the earlier legal status of the Jews. Many states where the Napoleonic wars had brought equal rights for Jews took advantage of the Acts' provisions.

The Hepp-Hepp riots

With the Hepp-Hepp riots, many Jews in the German states lost their wealth and often enough their life. The war cry, "Hepp-Hepp", was supposedly formed from the initials of the crusaders' cry, "Hierosolyma est perdita" (Jerusalem is lost). Young unemployed laborers, and farmers and merchants deep in debt, imagined that Jewish equality threatened their own livelihoods, their own survival. They stormed Jewish houses and businesses and set fire to the synagogues. Some city and town administrations actually instigated these attacks, or at least tolerated them, and the German Jews faced a popular revival of violent anti-Semitism just at a time when they believed legal emancipation was within their grasp.

A way out: Emigration

For many young Jews, the Congress of Vienna and the Hepp-Hepp riots were representative of a bleak future. They chose to heed the warnings and to leave what they considered the backwardness of Europe and its burdensome, indeed life-threatening, fetters. Drawn to America by visions of unlimited freedom, central European Jews immigrated in waves, and the Jewish population in the United States grew between 1820 and 1860 from 6,000 to 150,000.

187 The Hepp-Hepp riots in 1819 in Frankfurt and other German cities were marked by pogroms, with vandalism, looting, beating, and murder.

Exemplary of the ascent of many German-Jewish immigrants in the second half of the 19th century is the career of Levi Strauss (1829–1902) who came from Buttenheim (Bamberg District). Levi emigrated with his mother and siblings in 1848; some years later, he recognized the need for a new kind of clothing to suit the rugged demands of life in the new country and designed pants for gold prospectors and farmers made of blue cotton canvas (denim) with copper rivets: the famous "Levi's" (**188**), which became synonymous for years with the new—and eternal—American fashion, blue jeans.

Not all immigrants, of course, attained this level of affluence, but the United States, nonetheless, became home to the largest Jewish community of the Diaspora. American Jews have had to face anti-Semitism here as elsewhere, but they have also been able to flourish in many walks of life since the first wave of immigration in the 19th century.

"Entréebillet to European culture"
These setbacks to enfranchisement were particularly painful for the members of the upper class. Because they were Jews, they were allowed into neither civil service nor the universi-

188 Advertisement for work clothing of Levi Strauss, San Francisco, after 1875. Levi Strauss, the inventor of blue jeans, was born on February 26, 1829 in the house at Marktstrasse 33 in Buttenheim, district of Bamberg. He was one of countless German-Jewish emigrants who left Germany in the mid-19th century. His American career began in 1853 in San Francisco, where he produced the first Levis.

17th – 19th cent.

189 Ludwig Börne (1786–1837). Börne grew up as Juda Löw Baruch in the Frankfurt ghetto, studied first medicine, then law and political science. After graduation, he worked as a police registrar in the Frankfurt city administration. In 1815, after the end of the Wars of Independence, the old pre-Napoleonic restrictions were reactivated, and, as a Jew, Börne was dismissed. Three years later, he had himself baptized Ludwig Börne in the hope of being able to write more freely. In 1830, he settled in Paris. Through his letters from Paris (1832–34), Börne became popular as a excellent stylist and radical champion of intellectual and social freedom.

190 Rachel Varnhagen, née Levin (1771–1833).

ties. For some, the only "entréebillet [ticket] to European culture" appeared to be conversion to Christianity.

Ludwig Börne, born Juda Löw Baruch in Frankfurt, felt first hand the ramifications of the Congress of Vienna's turning back of the clock. In 1815, Baruch was suddenly dismissed from his post in urban administration because he was a Jew. He turned to journalism. In 1818, he took the name Ludwig Börne and had himself baptized. This was, he believed, the only way he would be free to pursue a career as a journalist (189).

Others, such as the well-to-do salon ladies Rachel Levin and Brendel Mendelssohn, did not change faith out of what they considered practical or economic necessity, but, to some degree, out of religious conviction and because they wanted to marry Christian men. Rachel Levin became Antonie Friederike Varnhagen von Ense (190). Brendel, the daughter of Moses Mendelssohn, had already dropped her Yiddish names in 1794 and renamed herself Dorothea. In 1804, she married the German Romantic philosopher Friedrich von Schlegel (it was her second marriage), and converted to Protestantism. Her search for the true religion did not end with her conversion. Like many other Romantics, she and her husband were drawn to the Catholic church, which they ultimately joined.

Regardless of their motives, conversion apparently did not ease the life of the convert. On her deathbed, Varnhagen was tormented by doubts over the meaningfulness of her conversion. German Romantic poet Heinrich Heine and Ludwig Börne both regretted their baptism and felt tied to Judaism for their entire life.

The conversions to Christianity in the 19th century were hardly a mass movement but, rather, a trend among young, educated, and assimilated

Jews. The atypical structure of the Jewish community in Berlin, where these Jews were especially dominant, meant that there were proportionally more converts in Berlin than elsewhere in Germany.

The Revolution of 1848

After the July Revolution of 1830 in Paris, liberal currents also began to stir in Germany. Gabriel Riesser (1806–63) (**191**), among others, saw in the political fight for Jewish emancipation an alternative to conversion or emigration. After the March Revolution of 1848, Riesser was chosen for the Frankfurt National Assembly and strove to convince the liberal representatives that their own freedom and equality of necessity demanded equality for Jews. Thanks to his efforts, an emancipation clause was included in the "Basic Rights of the German People", the German constitution: "The enjoyment of civil and state rights is neither limited nor conditioned by religious creed."

The defeat of the revolution, however, ended another period of optimism. The ensuing reactionary period revoked whatever rights had been acquired in the revolution. Another two decades would pass before the process of legal emancipation was completed. In 1869, the area of the North German League passed a law stating that: "All still-existing limits on civil and state rights because of the diversity of religious beliefs are hereby lifted. In particular, the qualification for participation as community and state representatives and as holders of public office is independent of religious beliefs." After the founding of the German empire in 1871, this also became the law of the empire. Unlike France and England, Germany had required waves of legislation and debate before arriving at full legal equality for the Jews.

> But after everything that I wanted, I received in return only one of the three Louis d'or, which I paid the minister for my Christianity. For eighteen years I've been baptized, and it has never helped me a bit. Three Louis d'or for a cookie in the German madhouse! It was a foolish waste.
> Ludwig Börne, 1836

191 Gabriel Riesser (1806–63) advocated the equality of the German Jews and denounced the reproach that the Jews were loyal to another "nation" beside Germany: "But where is this other state, for which we have to fulfill duties? Where is the other authority which dared to put their commands in the way of the commands of legal authority? Where is the other country which calls us for its defense? To hold it against us that our fathers, centuries or millennia before, were immigrants is as inhuman as it is absurd. ... We are either Germans, or we are homeless."

17th – 19th cent.

149

19th – 20th cent.

By the second half of the 18th century, Judaism had not undergone much religious reform. The rationalists of this time strove to rejuvenate the Jewish educational system. Their goal was to educate young men not only in traditional Talmudic study and scholarship, but in secular languages and literature as well and to give them a general "worldly" education. The rationalists attributed the tenacious prejudices against Jews to their Yiddish colloquial speech. They hoped that if the German Jews, for example, became accustomed to using German colloquial speech, this might go a long way toward dispelling the prejudices against them, as well as toward eradicating the legal restrictions. Inspired by Moses Mendelssohn and informed by this belief that linguistic change could bring about social reform, David Friedländer (192) and Daniel Itzig in 1778 founded the Jewish Free School in Berlin; here German and French were taught alongside Hebrew and lessons were conducted in German.

Secular subjects were central to the curriculum. For the first time, Hebrew and religious instruction became peripheral. In the traditional Jewish educational system, a child (boy) was inculcated with the principles of Judaism through gradual introduction to biblical and Talmudic sources, while his home life was shaped by religious law, which reinforced the education system at home from an early age (and the latter constituted essentially the sole form of education afforded young girls). At the Jewish Free School, Judaism was "taught" as just one subject of study, and newly prepared textbooks were substituted for the study of traditional primary sources.

With the founding of more reformed schools, a new era of Jewish educational theory began.

Religious reforms

There never was anything like *the* Judaism. The absence of a central educational authority even in ancient times enabled the evolution of different streams of Jewish life. As an example it is easy to cite the obvious distinctions dating back to the Middle Ages between Sephardic and Ashkenazi Judaism (see pp. 50 f. and 60 f.). Even today, groups descended from these two strands differ in practice and in ritual; there are even two independent rabbinates in Israel. More fundamentally, the differences fall under the umbrellas of Reformed, Conservative, and Orthodox Judaism. This three-pronged division stems from reform efforts that germinated in central Europe toward the end of the 18th century.

192 David Friedländer (1750–1834). Pupil and acknowledged successor to Moses Mendelssohn. As a dedicated agent of the Enlightenment and champion of Jewish emancipation in Prussia, he strove to define Judaism as a creed formed by ethics. In 1778, he founded the Jewish Free School in Berlin; in 1779, he wrote a text for Jewish children.

Reformed Judaism

It was doubtless impossible for Jews to gain entry into the broader civil communities without sending reverberations throughout the Jewish communities. Many "civic" Jews, finding the traditional Jewish forms of expression inappropriate, demanded reform. Among their demands, they sought from the beginning to reorganize the synagogue service. The traditional service seemed like a cacophony of praying voices that

193 Synagogue on the Roonstrasse, Cologne. Interior, ca. 1920. The innovations of the Jewish reformers changed the conception of space in synagogue architecture. For example, the bimah was moved from its traditional place in the center of the room to the east in front of the Torah ark. With this change, prayer was oriented to a certain direction in the synagogue. Seats were now no longer grouped around the bimah; instead, rows of benches were set up facing the east. The sermon, moreover, was given in the vernacular, and required a pulpit, which often was similar to a church's chancel. The sexes, however, despite demands to end their segregation, remained separated, and the women continued to be seated in galleries above, and out of view from, the men.

19th – 20th cent.

151

194 New Synagogue in the Oranienburger Strasse. Emile de Cauver, oil on linen, Berlin, 1865. On September 5, 1866, the largest synagogue of Germany was dedicated. Its Reformed ritual—organ, mixed choir, some prayers in the national language—was the expression of an established Jewish German middle class. During the 1938 November pogroms, the courageous chief of police Wilhelm Krützfeld protected the place of worship against greater damage. In November 1943, the synagogue, which held up to 3,000 persons, was bombed; in 1958 Krützfeld's ashes were sprinkled there by order of the government of the German Democratic Republic. Restoration of the lobby through the "New Synagogue Foundation" began in 1988; on May 7, 1995, it was dedicated as a center for research and meetings. The issue of reopening the synagogue as a place of worship remains open, although Jerzy Kanal, currently chairman of the Berlin residents' Jewish community sees no need to reconstruct the original prayer room: "We do not want to build any monuments that are not used, and there simply is no need for such a large synagogue at the moment." The original synagogue, thus, remains only an open space laid out in stone; within, lies a small room for 80 people. Says Kanal, "We have not rebuilt the synagogue room. If required, the next generations can decide on a new building."

often drowned out the prayer leader. To the reformers, this individual and informal service was no longer appropriate in a culture that valued "decency" and reserve. Instead, they wanted a service that would be "worthy and uplifting." Their model for what constituted a "worthy and uplifting" service was the Protestant church service, for it was in the Protestant culture of northern Germany that the reform efforts took root.

The reformers introduced a synagogue order that prescribed the conduct of the prayers precisely. The sing-song of the cantor, who leads the congregation in prayer, was replaced by hymns from a trained choir with organ accompaniment, the *drasha*, the biblical lesson, through an edifying sermon in German. And, since the reformers thought of themselves as Germans rather than as exiles from Jerusalem, they edited out of their services references to the hope of a return to Israel, of rebuilding the Temple, and of reintroducing burnt offerings (**194**).

The first Reformed services took place privately. The first Reformed temple was founded in 1818 in Hamburg. The designation "temple" was intended to underscore differences from the traditional synagogue. The orthodox in the communities opposed all innovations and accused the Reformists of sectarianism before the state authorities in Prussia. In response to such protests, the Reformed service was forbidden in Berlin in 1823 by royal order.

Abraham Geiger

Abraham Geiger (1819–74) (**195**) was the leading Reformed rabbi. He was a reformer, historian of Judaism, and famous preacher who did not consider living by religious law the driving force of Judaism but, rather, the prophetic tradition of social justice. Throughout his life, he emphasized the high moral rank of the Jewish religion and strove to show modern Jews how they could strike a balance between their old beliefs and a new world.

Geiger sought to articulate general principles to distinguish the fundamental from the more marginal dogmas in Judaism. He therefore insisted on approaching the question of Jewish tradition in a scientific, systematic manner, and on giving up the restrictions and customs that formed no essential part of Mosaic law but were products of later periods and therefore unfitted to modern society. Geiger was a co-founder of the liberally oriented University for the Science of Judaism in Berlin in 1872.

195 Abraham Geiger (1810–74), leading theoretician of the Reformed movement, rabbi in Wiesbaden, Breslau, Frankfurt on Main, and Berlin. At the 1845 and 1846 synods of the Reformed rabbis, Geiger was a dominant personality.

The gathering of the rabbis

During the 1840s, reform-minded rabbis gathered in three conventions—in Braunschweig in 1844, Frankfurt in 1845, and Breslau in

The situation of the Religion: "We have brought back the current situation of Judaism upon this basis, that it will be practiced merely through observation of the Laws. The reader him or herself will observe, certainly from the preceding meeting description, that the law still serves us as a peripheral authority, and that it is destined to lose this stature as well with increasing enlightenment and at the current movement of things.

"I have given some hints about what evil consequences this may have not only for the education of our nation but also for our beliefs. I ask thus: Can one see me as a heretic or enemy of our faith, if I maintain for moral reasons that our nation can have no practicable improvement, unless we undertake a positive reformation of the Law?"

Saul Ascher (1767–1822), one of the earliest advocates of Jewish religious reform, 1792

196 *Zacharias Frankel (1801–75). Founder of so-called Conservative or positive-historic Judaism. Since 1854, Frankel was director of the Jewish Theological Seminary in Breslau as well as founder and publisher for 17 years of the* Monthly for the History and Science of Judaism.

1846. They convened to address the most important questions before them and to try to generate consensus. The majority of the rabbis wanted to continue to celebrate the Sabbath on Saturday, even though it was a work and a school day for Jews in the Christian society. Only extremist Reformed rabbis such as Samuel Holdheim spoke in favor of moving the Sabbath to Sunday. At the first conference in Braunschweig, some sought permission to perform mixed marriages between Jews and Christians. At the Breslau convention, some suggested leading steps toward religious emancipation of Jewish women, who had always been considered unequal in the synagogue.

The most significant change to issue from the rabbinical conferences was thanks to the Bohemian rabbi from Dresden, Zacharias Frankel (1801–75) (**196**), who proclaimed a "positive-historic Judaism." This eventually developed into its own religious current somewhere between the extreme positions of Reformed Judaism and Orthodoxy. Frankel left the Frankfurt gathering in 1845 to protest the adoption of a resolution proclaiming the Hebrew language unnecessary for worship in the synagogue.

Conservative Judaism

Under Zacharias Frankel, Conservative Judaism emerged—advocating a positive-historic Judaism, a Judaism that, though subject to historic development, retained an inviolable kernel of the revealed religion on which it relied for protection against all historic criticism. Frankel, thus, accepted that current demands might prompt certain modifications in Judaic practice or custom, but he nonetheless held fast to his conviction that the traditional rituals also were profoundly meaningful for contemporary Jews. Essential to preserving the fundamentally meaningful traditions was a thoroughgoing understanding of their sources and development; for this reason, to abolish Hebrew as the primary language of prayer in the synagogue was unthinkable.

Frankel also made a permanent mark on the history of the Jews in Germany and central Europe by establishing two institutions: In 1851 he founded the *Monatsschrift für die Geschichte and Wissenschaft des Judentums* (Monthly for the History and Knowledge of Judaism), and in 1854 he became director of the Jewish Theological Seminary in Breslau. In its eighty-three years of publication, the monthly became the largest international organ of the study of Judaism, until the Gestapo confiscated the last volume, edited by Leo Baeck, in 1939 (this issue finally appeared in 1963 as a reprint). The Jewish Theological Seminary, under Frankel's direction, was the first academic training facility for rabbis in Germany. There, famous scholars educated generations of students. Among these lecturers was the historian Heinrich Graetz (1817–91), who during his tenure wrote a monumental eleven-volume *History of the Jews from Ancient Times to the Present*. The Breslau school required its students to acquire an academic degree from the Breslau University in addition to their seven-year course in traditional rabbinical studies.

The Breslau seminary became the model for similar institutions worldwide. One of the most famous offspring is the Jewish Theological Seminary in New York, founded in 1887. The New York seminary became the intellectual center of Conservative Judaism in the United States as well as a world-famous center for Judaic research (**197**).

197 The Jewish Theological Seminary in New York. Photo, 1993.

19h – 20h cent.

The Neo-Orthodoxy
The most important innovator of Orthodox tradition and founder of the so-called Neo-Ortho-

doxy was Samson Raphael Hirsch (1808–88). His motto, and that of the whole Neo-Orthodoxy, was a sentence of Rabbi Gamaliel from the *Sayings of the Patriarchs* (2:2): "Jafé Talmud Torah im Derekh Erez" (Beautiful is the study of the Torah united with worldly education).

For Hirsch, the Torah was the essence of Judaism; he demanded strict observance of all, even the most seemingly slight, religious precepts. Despite his loyalty to tradition, however, Hirsch conceded that worldly education was also important and, despite his adherence to messianic hopes, he welcomed legal emancipation. The abolition of legal and political pressure created greater possibilities and freedom for the fulfillment of religious law. But, felt Hirsch, it must not elicit the opposite effect among Jews—it must not become a license to ignore or misuse divine commandments. Hirsch's ideal was the rational person who continues to keep the commandments of Judaism.

In 1851, Hirsch became rabbi of the Orthodox Israelite Religious Order in Frankfurt, which he expanded into a model community. At first, he saw no reason to split the Jewish community, but when the Reformed leaders decided after the rabbinical conference in Braunschweig to nullify the Jewish dietary and marriage laws, he changed his mind. In 1876, he succeeded in pushing the so-called Withdrawal Law through the Prussian state legislature. With this law, Jews could leave their own Jewish community for religious reasons and merge with separate communities of their own social and legal persuasion to build their own synagogues, cemeteries (**198**), and schools. Few of these "withdrawal" communities based on Hirsch's ideas actually developed. The established communities, rather, started to show more respect for their more traditionally minded members, who comprised

198 The cemetery of the Orthodox Cologne congregation of dissidents Adass-Jeschurun. Photo by Maren Heyne. In 1910, the Cologne congregation of dissidents acquired a property in Cologne-Deckstein to set up its own cemetery. The funerals there strictly followed Jewish law and Jewish burial rites. The 1911 Burial Ground Ordinance forbids burial in coffins and funerals with ashes. Gravestones were allowed (besides name and dates of birth and death) only Hebrew inscriptions.

mostly a minority in the metropolitan centers. The traditional minorities were offered particular services (in synagogues without organ music), and communities often hired more traditional rabbis. This solution, first hammered out in Breslau after long debate, was adopted by many large communities. The beauty of the solution was that it preserved the traditional principle of the united congregation, which continued to be a fundamental value among the Jewish communities.

In 1873, the Orthodox community founded its own Rabbi Seminary in Berlin, but even here, students now demanded a secular education in addition to traditional religious instruction. The knowledge base of the future Orthodox rabbis in Germany, it was generally felt, should extend beyond the narrow sphere of the Yeshiva.

The rabbi-doctor

Through the 19th century, the rabbi had always been an excellent scholar with a thorough grounding in the Talmud and in the literature of religious law. He was first of all the *halakhish* authority whose advice was sought in case of doubt, the judge in all things that fell under the authority of religious law (such as family law), and the last word in all questions of the Kashrut (dietary laws, see p. 122 ff.). As a Torah scholar, naturally, he was also a teacher; usually he directed a school where he taught the Talmudic literature. He was not, however, expected to direct the service or to give regular lectures in the synagogue.

To the new generations toward the end of the last century, this traditional rabbinical type seemed outmoded and ill-suited to lead a modern community. To many rationalist Jews, Talmudic scholarship appeared secondary or nearly worthless for it no longer had a direct

199 Leo Baeck (1873–1956). Oil painting by the Jewish artist Ludwig Meidner (1884–1966), 1931. Baeck was a typical "rabbi-doctor." He was one of the most important agents of Reformed Judaism, and, since 1912, instructor at the University for the Study of Judaism in Berlin. In 1933, he was named president of the "Reich's Agency of German Jews" (see p. 180). He refused to emigrate and officiated as the last rabbi in Berlin, until he was deported to Theresienstadt in 1943. After the camp was liberated, Baeck settled in London, though he also occasionally taught at the Hebrew Union College in Cincinnatti. In 1955, an institute for research into German Jewish history since the Enlightenment was named after Leo Baeck as the last great representative of German Judaism. The Leo Baeck Institute, with offices in New York, Jerusalem, and London, owns the world's most important collection of material about the history of German Judaism.

19th – 20th cent.

200 Regina Jonas, Germany's first woman rabbi. She was ordained on December 27, 1935.

influence on their lives. Instead, the direction of the worship service and preaching were emphasized among the duties of the modern rabbi.

This meant a new leader personality was needed. A modern rabbi—whether liberal or orthodox—should have a broad education, verified by his holding a university degree, and should be a good speaker; he should represent the Jewish community worthily to the outside world. Thus emerged a new type of rabbi—in Germany, in western Europe, in America—who was educated at one of the new rabbinical seminaries: the "rabbi-doctor."

Women rabbis?

The rabbinical conventions of the 1840s heard arguments in favor of granting full religious equality to women: such arguments were, of course, expected among the most radical Reformed and liberal communities, but they were also heard, and with almost equal force, in Conservative camps. Still, the first woman was not ordained as a rabbi until the 20th century: on December 27, 1935, Regina Jonas (**200**) received the *Hattarat Hora'a* (scholarly authorization and authorization for the decisive questions on religious law) from Rabbi Max Dienemann. Dienemann had been asked by the liberal rabbi organization to administer the rabbinical examination for her.

Regina Jonas had studied since 1924 at the liberal University for the Study of Judaism in Berlin. In 1930, she presented two final projects, one a biblical study of *The Lexical of Rashi in the First Book of Moses*, the other a Halakhish paper entitled *Can a Woman Assume the Office of Rabbi?* It took five more years before a rabbi dared to give her rabbinical authorization.

It goes without saying that the ordination of Regina Jonas was controversial. Newspaper articles from the time reflect the different positions. She received support largely in Jewish liberal papers, while objections in Orthodox organs were vociferous. The Orthodox press mocked the ordination as the deed of a rabbi who "now also deems it proper through his kind chivalry toward the ladies, to freely give up the pulpit and the office of the rabbinical authority."

In 1942, Regina Jonas was deported to the concentration camp at Theresienstadt. Survivors report that up to the time when she was transported to Auschwitz in October 1944, she dedicated her energy to Jewish knowledge and spiritual welfare among her fellow prisoners. She remained faithful, for she had become a rabbi, she averred, because of "my belief in God and the divine calling and my love for humanity."

The first woman rabbi in the United States was Sally Priesand, who was ordained in 1972 at the liberal Hebrew Union College in Cincinnati. In 1984, the Conservative Jewish Theological Seminary in New York ordained its first woman. At present, there are over 200 women Rabbis active in Israel, the United States, and Europe.

Today, the three currents that began in Germany are strongest in the United States: Reformed, Conservative, and Orthodox Judaism are organized here into their own synagogues, schools, and seminaries—Hebrew Union College, the Reformed wing, was established in Cincinnati in 1875, while the Conservative Jewish Theological Seminary was established in 1887 and the Orthodox Yeshiva University in 1897, both in New York City.

201   A cover page of *Reform Judaism*, a quarterly publication of the organization of the Reformed community in the United States, Summer 1991.

Unlike in the United States, where membership in some congregations is larger than the national organization in Germany, the survival of the Jewish community for us can only be guaranteed by a united community.

Ignatz Bubis, chairman of the Central Council of the Jews in Germany, 1995

19th – 20th cent.

Circumcision (*berit milah*)

According to the *Halakhah* (religious law), a Jew is someone born of a Jewish mother. Thus, children of a Jewish-gentile marriage are Jewish if the woman is Jewish, but not when the man is the Jewish partner. Even babies born Jewish, however, must be actively accepted into the community.

For boys, this is achieved through circumcision, the removal of the foreskin, which is an indelible "sign of the flesh" marking membership in the covenant between God and Abraham.

The bible commands that it be performed on the eighth day of life, even if it falls on the Sabbath or a high holy day. The circumcision may only be delayed if the baby is too weak or sick, for respect for life takes precedence over all other commandments. A *minyan* of ten Jewish men, representing the community of Israel into which the child is received, should be present at the ceremony. The festively clothed baby is placed on the "Elijah's chair." According to tradition, the prophet Elijah, because of his zeal for the "Covenant of the Lord" (1 Kings 19:10), is an invisible guest of honor at every *Bris*

202 Circumcision plate, 20th century.

203 A Mohel's instruments: cutting knife and bowl, clamps, vial with styptic powders, and a manual with instructions and the special prayers.

(and at every Passover seder). The Bris is led by the *Mohel*, who has both religious and medical training (**203**). The godfather has the great honor of holding the baby on his lap during the actual circumcision. After the circumcision, the baby's Hebrew name is said aloud for the first time (in many Diaspora communities, he is also given a name in the national language). The boy is called by his Hebrew name on all religious occasions: at the call to the Torah reading (the bar mitzvah), at his wedding, and on his gravestone.

The circumcision is followed by a banquet at which the newborn is given presents and repeatedly blessed. Those gathered respond: "As this child has entered into the covenant, so may he enter into the Torah, the *huppah* [nuptial canopy], and good deeds." This prayer may be embroidered or painted on the Torah cloths, which in some groups are made of the circumcision diaper and given to the community by the boy at his first visit to the synagogue. The cloths are used to bind the Torah scroll, wrapped on two rods (204).

A newborn girl's Hebrew name is proclaimed on the first Sabbath after her birth before the gathered community, when her father is called to read the Torah. In France, Holland, and Germany, it was custom to proclaim the girl's name at the "Hollekreisch" cere-mony, at which the children of the community lifted the cradle of the newborn and called out "Holle-kreisch" or "haut la crèche" (raise

205 Hollekreisch. Oil painting by Alice Guggenheim, 20th century.

204 Torah cloths. Illustrating the words, "to the Torah" and "to the *huppah*," an open Torah scroll and a bridal pair under a grape arbor is embroidered on a strip of linen.

the cradle), "What should the child be called?" The father then called out the baby's name. This was repeated three times, after which the children were given presents (205).

Coming of age: bar mitzvah or bat mitzvah

"A five-year-old is ripe for the bible, a ten-year-old for the Mish-nah, a thirteen-year-old for the fulfillment of the Commandments" (*Sayings of the Patriarchs* 5:24). According to Jewish tradition, a Jewish boy becomes mature, a *bar mitzvah* ("son of the com-mandment"), with the completion of his thirteenth year. He becomes a full member of the community with all rights and duties deter-mined by religious law. For the first time he may be counted in a minyan and say the morning prayers with *tefillin* (206).

Coming of age is celebrated in the synagogue on the following Sabbath. The high point of the celebration occurs when the bar mitzvah is called for the first time to read the Torah. He says the opening prayer, reads part or all of the week's reading, and often the excerpt from the prophets.

206 Bar mitz-vah, etching, after 1900.

After the Torah reading, the boy's father says: "Blessed be He who hath freed me from the responsibility of this child." This prayer suggests that the father is dismissed from the responsibilities of child rearing, and the boy is now responsible for his own deeds and for their consequences.

At the meal that follows, it is common for the boy to give a short lesson about the paragraph he has read (*Drasha*) (**207**), showing those gathered what he has learned up to that day and thanking his parents and teachers for their work in his upbringing.

Girls are considered of age when they complete their twelfth year, by which time it was expected that they would be familiar with homemaking and the *Kashrut*. To free them for domestic duties, girls and women are not obligated to fulfil religious commandments within a firm time

208 Girls read from the Torah. Photo by Bill Aron.

frame. Since the 19th century, in Reformed Judaism circles, girls have participated in a course of study and celebration similar to the bar mitzvah. Orthodox communities reject the so-called bat mitzvah ("daughter of the commandment") as well as the public reading of the Torah by women (**208**).

Wedding and Marriage

To marry and have children is considered part of the natural and God-given order of life in Judaism. Newborns are blessed with the wish that they "enter into marriage," and the rabbis state in the Talmud (*Yevamot* 62b–63a) that a person is not complete without a marriage partner.

Just before her wedding, a bride goes to the *mikveh* for the first time. On the wedding day itself, the couple fast until after the ceremony to make themselves worthy for the event. The wedding is usually performed by a rabbi, though it may be performed by any learned person who is versed in the instructions for marriage. The ceremony may take place anywhere; many marry out-

207 Bar mitzvah lecture. Phototype from a painting of Moritz Oppenheim.

doors or in the synagogue. A minyan is desirable but not imperative; two male witnesses not related to the bridal couple are required.

At the wedding, the man and woman stand under the *huppah*, a traditional canopy that symbolizes the couple's home (**210**). In the first part of the ceremony, the *erusin* (promise), the rabbi says the blessing over a goblet of wine, from which both bride and groom drink. The legal ceremony follows in the presence of the two witnesses: the man places a ring on the index finger of the woman's right hand and says: "With this ring you are promised to me according to the law of Moses and Israel" (**210**). The rabbi then reads the *ketubah*, the marriage contract.

After the reading, the groom hands the marriage contract to the bride. This is followed by the real marriage ceremony (*nisuin*). The Rabbi speaks the seven wedding benedictions, and the bridal pair again take a sip of wine while the groom crushes a glass with his right foot to recall the destruction of the Temple even on this joyous occasion, the guests shout *Mazel tov!* (much luck). At the end of the official ceremony, the

210 The wedding. Phototype from a painting of Moritz Oppenheim. The pair under the canopy wear traditional wedding belts. The rabbi reads out the wedding contract, the groom places the wedding ring on the bride's right forefinger.

pair withdraw briefly together to a private room to symbolize the marital unity.

Traditionally, having children is an essential goal of marriage. "Be fruitful and multiply" (Gen. 1:28) is an important commandment; for Orthodox Jews, it is a sin to choose not to have children.

The marriage contract

Without a ketubah, a written marriage contract, no marriage is valid. The oldest preserved ketubbot date from the 5th century BCE from Elephantine, an island in the Nile in southern Egypt. The Aramaic text of the contract was standardized over time. Only the personal details such as names, date,

209 Gold wedding ring, early 20th century.

and place vary. In it, the man obligates himself to honor his wife, to clothe her, to nourish her, and to satisfy her sexual needs. He also promises to give the bride a specific sum of money. If the bride is widowed or divorced, he pays only half—not because a widow or divorcee is worth less, but because she was already paid the ketubah by her previous husband, and it is assumed that she already has some financial security. These minimum amounts can be increased by the man at will. The woman's dowry, which the husband administers and may use, is also specified. The ketubah amount is signed by the groom and the two witnesses.

The rabbis achieved two things with this marriage contract: the woman's financial welfare was secure, and it was harder for a man to get a divorce. If the man dies or initiates divorce, the woman receives the entire amount named in the ketubah before the marriage contract is revoked. If the wife initiates divorce, she gives up her claim to the ketubah sum, but not to her dowry. These terms were very progressive in contrast with the usual treatment of women in antiquity and the Middle Ages.

Death and burial

Since the Middle Ages, almost every community has had a *Chevra Kaddisha*, a "holy brotherhood" (or sisterhood) whose task is to visit the sick, to stand by the dying in the hour of death, and assure a proper burial. They are also responsible for the washing of the dead, which must follow exact instructions. Most Jewish cemeteries have a special building for this, the *tahara* ("cleaning") house. After washing, the dead are laid out in simple linen burial clothes. The fringes are torn off a man's prayer shawl, which is draped around his shoulders. Since, in the traditional rabbinical view, Jews buried in Jerusalem will be the first to arise with the messiah, many hope to be buried there even today. This is obviously not possible for most Jews in the Diaspora, but a sack of earth from the Holy Land is often placed under the head. Except in Israel, the deceased are no longer put directly into the grave, but are laid in a narrow coffin made of plain boards. Traditionally, the funeral should be held on the day of death. Thus, in Israel, deaths are announced immediately on slips of paper pasted on trees and walls, to allow burial to take place within hours. Outside Israel, the funeral and burial are generally held within forty-eight hours of death. Most funeral services are held in a mortuary. Modern convention allows the rabbi to give a eulogy, although historically eulogies were given only at funerals of great scholars or community leaders. The son of the deceased or other near relative says the *Kaddish*, the prayer for the dead, praising God the King. At the cemetery, the family rends their clothing in a symbolic act of separation and mourning—today, a necktie or a ribbon is often worn for this symbolic purpose. The deceased is then accompanied to the grave. Escorting the dead is considered a *mitzvah*, a religious duty and good deed. When leaving the cemetery, everyone washes their hands, without drying them, to extend the memory of the deceased. After the burial, the mourners return to the house of the deceased where they observe a rite called sitting *shivah* (literally, "seven," for the custom lasts seven days). During this time, the mourners remain at home, perform no work, sit on low stools, wear no leather shoes, and do not bathe, shave, wear makeup, cut their hair, or engage in sexual intercourse. Torah study—considered a source of delight—is forbidden. Only mourning texts like Hiob, the songs of mourning, and parts of Jeremiah may be read. With the end of *shivah*, the less intense period of *shloshim* begins (it lasts thirty days from the burial). Children of the deceased observe a year of mourning. On the anniversary of the death or the funeral, the family observes the *yahrzeit*. They visit the synagogue and say the Kaddish. A special anniversary light, the yahrzeit candle, is lit and left to burn the whole day. The gravestone is often unveiled on the first anniversary of the person's death.

The cemetery has a particular status in the Jewish community as the place where the dead are commemorated. As the "house of eternity," it cannot be dissolved; according to Talmudic instruction, the dead should rest in peace for eternity. This explains the resistance, especially among Orthodox Jews, to any kind of building on cemetery land, even ancient cemeteries no longer in Jewish hands.

211 Death and burial. Three paintings, originally in the conference room of the Prague Burial Brotherhood, ca. 1780.

1870 – 1933

In 1879, a few years after the German empire formally granted legal equality to Jews (see p. 149), an anti-Jewish journalist named Wilhelm Marr published *The Victory of Judaism over Germanism*. Marr postulated that the problems of the state amounted to a life-and-death struggle between Jews and Teutons, and the Jews were winning. Out of this period and this climate came the now common term for anti-Jewish prejudice: anti-Semitism (**212**). Marr's thesis articulated a new slant on the demonization of Jews—a new take on an old theme, as it were. The new demonization merely grew outward from the centuries-old hatred based on religious and economic preconceptions, for this was now the age of Darwin and Marx, and the old arguments faded into the background, replaced by pseudo-scientific views that grounded the cultural norm of Jew-hating in new "biological" bases. Germany's anti-Semites of the 1870s drew heavily, and expediently, upon eugenic theories formulated in the early 19th century: German idealist philosopher Johann Gottlieb Fichte and Friedrich Ludwig ("Turnvater") Jahn had invoked "biological" factors to explain the superiority and/or inferiority of certain peoples or ethnic groups. To this climate were added the racial theories of Arthur von Gobineau and his successors. Through works typified by Gobineau's *Essay sur l'inégalité des races humaines* (1854), racism became an ideological element of anti-Semitism. Jews became defined more rigidly as a race, rather than a religious group. Negative "racial attributes" were associated with the so-called Semitic race, and these, to the anti-Semites, were innate and unchangeable. The medieval stereotype of the diabolical Jew, far from disappearing in the "enlightened" 19th century, reemerged.

Eugen Dühring and Houston Stewart Chamberlain, the son-in-law of the German composer Richard Wagner, were among the best-known propagandists of racial anti-Semitism in Germany. Dühring, in his popular work *The Jewish Question as a Racial, Moral and Cultural Question* (1881), described an insurmountable gap between the Nordic-Aryan and the Semitic "races." To answer this "question," he called upon the "Aryans" to bring back ghettos.

In Chamberlain's book, *The Foundations of the 19th Century* (1899), the "noble Aryan race" is presented in opposition to the "depraved Semitic." Once upon a time a creative and constructive voice, Chamberlain later became injurious and destructive. His book, which utterly lacked any scientific basis, was repeatedly reissued. William II, Emperor of Germany, supposedly read it to his children and suggested that it be adopted into the curriculum of the Cadet Academy.

There was also an anti-capitalist component to anti-Semitism (this is often forgotten in the impression common today that German anti-Semitism, mostly of the 20th century, claimed the Jews were co-conspirators in international communism). Let us remember that the 19th century was the peak of the industrial revolution. In the face of ever-growing industrialization and urbanization, members of the nobility, the clergy, the rural farming classes, and the lower middle class—those segments of the population who had little or no share in industrialization and moderniza-

212 Journalist Wilhelm Marr (1818–1904) wrote several anti-Semitic books and in 1879 founded the "Anti-Semites' League."

1870 – 1933

Aliyah, pl. **aliyot**: Literally, "ascent," designates immigration to Israel.
Zion/Zionism: Zion was originally a hill in Jerusalem with a castle on its peak, which David conquered and renamed City of David, ca. 1000 BCE. When this city expanded northward, the adjacent Temple district became known as the central holy place, Zion. Later, Zion became a poetic designation for Jerusalem and then, more broadly understood, for the entire Holy Land. The goal of the Zionists in the 19th and 20th century was the acquisition of Zion as a homeland for the Jewish people.

tion—watched with envy the Jews' putative success in business (obviously, they never saw the far more common spectacle of the entrenched poverty of the shtetls a stone's throw away from their own lands). Jews were caricatured and stereotyped as nothing but agents of capitalistic trade and were blamed for any and all economic crises, as well as any and all negative phenomena in the rapidly changing world.

Anti-Semitism grew first in the political arena. From 1880, political platforms staunchly included anti-Semitism within a world view that opposed both progress and democracy. The early political influence of these anti-Semitic factions peaked in 1893 when they boasted sixteen representatives in the German Parliament. While their importance within the parliament continually declined, anti-Semitism became a rallying ideology within many national associations and an integral element of the popular culture, where it became increasingly acceptable to express such prejudices vocally and openly.

213 "Le Traître" (The traitor). Dreyfus as a dragon. Anti-Semitic caricature from the poster series, "Musée des Horreurs," Paris, 1899.

France: The Dreyfus affair

In France, anti-Semitism came to a head on December 22, 1894 when Captain Alfred Dreyfus, an Alsatian and a Jew—therefore a doubly "dubious character"—was convicted of treason based on falsified papers, and was condemned to life imprisonment on Devil's Island. Although his innocence was soon proven and the true traitor was found, reactionary military circles opposed reopening the case.

This judicial scandal led to an unprecedented polarization of the French public. Families were divided into "Dreyfusards" and "Anti-Dreyfusards." To Dreyfus's adversaries—the military, royalists, and the Catholic church—the infamous "affair" served as a welcome pretext for anti-

emitic arguments and riots (213). They
damantly opposed a retrial. Republicans
hat is, French people in favor of a
emocratic government), civil rights ad-
ocates, socialists, and intellectuals, on the
ther hand, proclaimed Dreyfus's inno-
ence or, at the very least, his right to a
ew trial. Perhaps the most famous of the
Dreyfusards was Emile Zola, the French novelist
and social critic, whose 1898 letter to the pre-
ident of France became legendary: "J'accuse,"
Zola wrote, as he accused the military staff of
covering up the truth and protecting the real spy.
A year later, Dreyfus's case was reopened
(214), but it took seven years before he was
acquitted and freed.

214 Dreyfus before the court martial in Rennes. Anonymous steel engraving, 1899. Dreyfus's retrial was held in Rennes, after the dubiousness of the evidence against him had become undeniably clear.

   The Dreyfus affair was a critical moment in the
history of Zionism: Theodor Herzl, a reporter for
the Vienna *New Free Press*, covered the case
from Paris. Influenced by the drawn-out history of
the Dreyfus proceedings and the popular reaction to the ensuing events, Herzl wrote *The
Jewish Nation*.

Institutionally sanctioned anti-Semitism

In Russia, the brutal anti-Jewish policies of Czar
Nicholas I (1825–55) were eased somewhat
under Alexander II (1855–81): military service
for the Russian Jews was reduced from twenty-

215 After the pogrom of 1881, this Jewish street is a scene of desolation.

1870 – 1933

five years to only five; rich Jewish merchants were permitted to live outside the Pale of Settlement (see p. 85); and their children were allowed into secondary schools and universitie·

The assassination of the czar on March 1, 1881, however, changed this relatively stable period overnight—bringing trouble to the Russia Jews. To dispel the growing discontent among the people, and to divert their attention away from the government's incompetence and the decadence of the Russian monarchy, reactiona· circles spread assertions that Russia's difficulties were the result of exploitation by the Jews. The Jews, moreover, were rumored to be involved i·

216 Pogroms within the "settlement radius," 1881–1906.

the czar's assassination. More than a hundred Ukrainian Jewish communities were besieged by a wave of pogroms (**215**)—indeed, the very word "pogrom" originated at this time to describe the lootings and murders of Jews in czarist Russia. The authorities were either unwilling or·unable to protect the Jewish population. Who started the pogroms was never quite clear, but the fact that they spread with lightning speed suggests that they were instigated, or at best tacitly condoned, by the chief authorities in the Russian empire (**216**).

Extremist anti-Semitism became a staple of Russian politics. On May 3, 1882, Alexander III wanting to "protect the leading citizens from Jewish exploitation," announced the "provisiona· ordinances," which limited the Jews' freedom of movement and imposed restrictions on trade and occupations, forcing them into even worse poverty. These ordinances were expanded in the last two decades of the century through additional prohibitions and remained in force up to the Revolution of 1917.

1870 – 1933

For the Russian rulers, anti-Semitic legislation became a political instrument. They feigned improvements in their relationships with those segments of the populace who were "needy of protection." The repeated pogroms—in Kishinev and Gomel in 1903, in Bialystok and Siedlce in 1906, among many, many others—were considered an appropriate pressure valve for social discontent (people were "just letting off steam"); in 1905, anti-Semitism was blatantly used as propaganda to combat the revolution. It was no accident that the *Protocols of the Elders of Zion* was published in 1905 for the first time in Russia. The czar's secret police used these spurious writings about supposed plans to establish "Jewish world domination" as anti-Semitic bait, which again fomented bloody pogroms.

Reactions to the catastrophic living conditions in the Russian empire varied: a common response was migration westward, for example, to America. Thousands of Russian Jews flooded through the turnstiles at Ellis Island in New York Harbor. Many of the younger generation responded to oppression by joining the radical political forces who concentrated on overthrowing czarist rule. Yet another response was a growing Jewish national movement. The thought of returning to Zion had far greater appeal for the east European Jews who faced deteriorating circumstances, than it had for the Jews of western Europe. For those facing pogroms, discriminatory laws, and expulsion, there was little expectation that emancipation could come from outside the Jewish community or that their problems could be solved by somehow melting into mainstream Russian society.

In 1897, the BUND, the first Jewish Socialist party, was founded in the Lithuanian city of Vilna. The BUND rejected the Zionist idea that the Jews could only end their oppression by estab-

217 Wall poster for the BUND ("United Yiddish Workers' League in Lithuania, Poland, and Russia"), Kiev, 1918. The Yiddish motto reads: "Where we live, there is our country!"

1870 – 1933

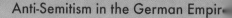

218 Adolf Stoecker (1835–1909), photo 1902. In 1878, the well-respected preacher and politician Adolf Stoecker founded the anti-Semitic "Christian Social Workers' Party." His sermons and speeches provoked anti-Jewish riots. One press notice read: "In Stettin on the 15th and 16th of August, tumultuous demonstrations erupted against the Jews. Fortunately, in the Pomeranian capital there are sufficient police and military powers, and so they succeeded in dispersing the crowd in a short time. The founders of the movement, Dr. Henrici and preacher Stoecker, now deny responsibility for these disgraceful riots."

219 Maccabea, a Zionist student organization, ca. 1906. In reaction to the increasing anti-Semitism at the universities, Jewish students established their own student organizations at the end of the 19th century, patterned in many ways after the apprentices' unions. The spectrum of these unions ranged from German nationalists to leftist-Zionists.

lishing their own homeland and believed that full equality for the Jewish work force should and could be fought for only in the countries where the Jewish masses were already found. The goal of the BUND was to establish a single national-cultural entity in eastern Europe with Yiddish as its official language (**217**).

Anti-Semitism in the German empire

In Germany, Wilhelm Marr, along with the evangelistic preacher Adolf Stoecker and the history professor Heinrich von Treitschke, devoted themselves to the spread of anti-Semitism. Stoecker used anti-Semitic slogans, influenced by the theology of Martin Luther, to reunify the discontented middle classes and the social democratic work force under the leadership of the church and the monarchy during the economic crisis that followed the establishment of the German empire. Stoecker preached repression of Jewish civil rights, exclusion of Jews from public office, and elimination of Jewish influence in the banks and the press. With the establishment of his anti-Semitic "Christian Social Workers' Party" in 1878, he made a decisive contribution to the political instrumentalization of anti-Semitism (**218**).

In 1879, Treitschke, a respected historian, published the first of a series of articles about the "Jewish question" (the very fact that so many assumed without challenge that a Jewish question existed is an expression of fairly deep-seated anti-Semitism). Treitschke did not see himself as an anti-Semite, but his partisanship for the anti-Semitic movement lent respectability to their propaganda.

ewish unions and organizations

Although the new empire initially allowed Jews greater freedom than they had ever enjoyed within Germany, and many Jews were employed in general political organizations, the rising tide of anti-Semitism in the 1890s dragged the emancipatory process to a crawl, if not a halt. In their own defense, the Jews responded by establishing their own organizations to fight anti-Semitic propaganda and to strengthen Jewish self-esteem (**219**).

The most important of these Jewish unions was the "Central Union of German Citizens of Jewish Belief," founded in 1893 in Berlin. The Central Union represented the majority of assimilated, middle-class liberal Jews and was grounded in the belief that a synthesis of Germany and Judaism was both possible and desirable. These Jews emphasized their German ethnic origins and rejected the emerging national Jewish movement and the hopes for a Jewish state. For the Central Union, such hopes only undermined the German Jews' chances of establishing their position in Germany. The Union considered its main task the defense against attacks on the civic and social equality of the German Jews: They organized campaigns to oppose anti-Semitic political parties and their candidates, sought legal reparations for Jews who were publicly slandered, and tried through education to expand understanding of Judaism and to strengthen Jewish self-confidence (**219**).

Zionism

Although the religious longing for a return to the Holy Land had always been a current in Judaism, it was not until the 19th century that this current crystallized into a political movement. Interestingly, Zionism grew almost simultaneously and independently in eastern and western

220 *Im Deutschen Reich* (In the German Empire), until 1922, the mouthpiece of the Central Union. This was succeeded by the *Central Union Newspaper* which continued publication until 1938. Each month, a special edition focused on the enlightenment of Christian fellow-citizens and was sent to people of all religious and political orientations.

1870 – 1933

221 Moses Hess (1812–75). The "Communist Rabbi" Moses Hess influenced Marx and Engels, though the latters' views about class were somewhat more radical. During his collaboration with Marx, Hess's attitude toward Judaism was ambivalent. The failure of the revolution of 1848 and the continuation of Jewish persecution, however, reminded him of his Jewish background, which steered him toward the idea of a modern national state.

Europe. The positive example of nationalist movements that reache their goals was not lost on Jewish thinkers. Moses Hess was one of the first who, in *Rome and Jerusalem* (1862), promulgated the idea of the "rebirth of the Jewish people" with a "concentra tion in their homeland." After the unification of Italy in 1861 and the imminent unification of Germany, Hess considered the Jewish question "question of nationality" (**221, 222**). He assumed that the Jews constituted a community with a shared destiny from which no one Jew can separate him or herself simply at will. Each Jew is a constituent member of the whole nation of Jews. This implied that every Jew in the Diaspora would have to renounce the notions of emancipation and assimilation. Although Hess laid out much of what would decades later become the essential tenets of Zionism, in his own day he remained relatively obscure.

The pogroms in Russia also convinced the assimilated intelligentsia that integration with the Russian majority was problematic. From the winter of 1881/82, unions sprang up in many communities promoting "self-liberation" and colonization of Palestine. They adopted names such as the "Lovers" or "Friends of Zion" and strove to create a new homeland for their "oppressed fellow tribesmen." In 1882, the first *aliyah* (immigration wave) of Russian and Romanian Jews arrived in Palestine. The number of immigrants was not large (for most, the preferred destination was still the United States; only 3,000 emigrants traveled to Palestine), but they came with the clear goal of establishing agricultural colonies as a foundation for Jewish resettlement in their historic

Rom und Jerusalem

die

letzte Nationalitätsfrage.

Briefe und Noten.

Von

M. Hess,

Correspondirendes Mitglied der Soziatey philosophischen Gesellschaft.
Redakteur der ehemaligen Rheinischen Zeitung etc.

Zweite unveränderte Auflage.

Mit einem Bilde des Verfassers

und einer Vorrede von Dr. Bodenheimer.

Leipzig.
M. W. Kaufmann.
1899.

1

222 *Rome and Jerusalem: The Last Nationality Question.* Title page of the second edition of 1899. In Europe's nationalist age, Moses Hess proposed a Jewish nation-state organized according to socialist principles in Palestine.

1870 – 1933

omeland. A group of Russian students who alled themselves the "Biluim" (drawn from aiah 2:5 "O house of Jacob,/come let us walk in the light of the Lord!"), with the help of the riends of Zion, founded the first agricultural olony *Rishon Le-Zion* ("First in Zion") (**223**).

Following the 1903 pogroms in Kishinev, in entral Moldavia (**224**), and during the revolu-on of 1905, a second aliyah (1904–14) rought 40,000 young Russian Jews to Palestine. By 1914, the Jewish population of Palestine was approximately 85,000.

Jewish self-esteem in western Europe grew tronger and the numbers of the Zionists grew correspondingly. In Vienna in 1882 the Jewish student organization *Kadima* ("Eastward"—i.e., o Israel—and "Forward") was founded. The driving force of the Viennese circle was Nathan Birnbaum, a native of Vienna. In *The National Rebirth of the Jewish People in their Land* (1893), Birnbaum called for international legal equality for Jews and coined the word "Zionism."

While people everywhere responded enthusi-astically to the idea of an autonomous Jewish people's society, it was Theodor Herzl's book *The Jewish State: Search for a Modern Solution to the Jewish Question* (1896), written largely as a reaction to the Dreyfus affair, that gave the first decisive push toward the unification of the exist-ing national Jewish unions. The result was what we understand today as political Zionism. Herzl had seen France as a country of progress and culture and was shocked by the rampant anti-Semitism that exploded during the Dreyfus affair. His response was to grapple thoroughly with the so-called Jewish question and to search out pos-sible solutions. Herzl at last concluded that anti-Semitism would never go away and that hopes of assimilation into Christian culture were futile. The Jewish question could only be answered when

223 Development and colonization in Palestine, 1881–1914.

224 *The Martyrs of Kishi-nev.* E.M. Lilien, 1903. In the Easter pogrom of Kishinev, 45 people were killed and approximately 700 houses and 600 businesses were destroyed. Shocked by these events, the Jewish graphic artist Lilien (1874–1925) designed a page to com-memorate the victims of the pogrom.

1870 – 1933

> For me, the Jewish question is neither social nor religious ... It is a national question ... We are a people, a *people*.
>
> Theodor Herzl

225 Theodor Herzl (1860–1904). Photo by E.M. Lilien, taken during the Fifth Zionist Congress in Basel, 1901. Herzl, founder and first chairman of the World Zionist Organization, grew up believing that assimilation was desirable and possible for the Jews. His experiences of anti-Semitism, especially during the Dreyfus affair, prompted him to work for the establishment of a Jewish national state.

1870 – 1933

the Jews were organized and settled in their own country. Herzl's remarks make it clear that 19th-century nationalist thinking was a far more pressing concern than was traditional religious thinking. Herzl himself was, in principle, indifferent about where the Jewish state should actually be. He was just as ready to build the Jewish state in East Africa or South America as in Palestine.

With his book, Herzl generated great support for the Zionists from around the world, which allowed him to assemble an international organization in a short time. The First Zionist Congress met on August 29, 1897 in Basel and was attended by approximately 200 delegates. Those present were allied with the "Basel" or "Zionist program," which declared: "Zionism aspires to the creation of one publicly and legally secured homeland for the Jewish people in Palestine."

Herzl thought this goal could be achieved by political and diplomatic means. He led many talks with, among others, the Turkish sultan and Wilhelm II, but was unsuccessful and brought criticism upon himself from his own group. His critics firmly believed that the deliverance of the Jewish people would only occur by their own hand and could not count on external authorities.

After Herzl's death in 1904, the "political" and the "practical" Zionists were constantly engaged in furious disputes. The latter rejected the ability of the former to achieve independence (as evidenced by Herzl's lack of success) and sought instead through de facto creation—that is, the energetic colonization of Palestine—to promote the emerging Jewish state.

That the Zionist movement was characterized by diverse ideologies is hardly surprising, since the Zionists were no more monolithic than the worldwide Jewish community itself: The Jews who professed Zionist ideals came from different social classes, cultural spheres, and milieus.

Most prominent among the various splinters within organized Zionism were four ideological directions: the socialists, the neutral bourgeois, the religious, and the people's national parties.

Outside the international Zionist movement, resistance to the idea of a Jewish state came from both Orthodox and assimilated Jews. The former reviled Herzl as a heretic who opposed the "divine fate of the exile," while many among the latter still saw anti-Semitism as a curable disease and believed that the restoration of a Jewish state was neither possible nor necessary—they felt they were treated as equal citizens in their own countries and were afraid that Zionism would threaten their situation. The Zionist movement, thus, tended to have fewer followers in countries where assimilation appeared to have succeeded better than in eastern Europe; in Germany, before the First World War, there were never more than about 9,000 active Zionists.

At first, the First World War put a deep dent in the settlement work in Palestine. The money from Europe only dribbled in, and the dispute between Turkey and Great Britain had devastating consequences for the settlers, who could remain in the country only if they assumed Turkish citizenship. Leading Zionists such as Chaim Weizmann, however, recognized a political opportunity in the war. Through his influence, the British foreign minister Arthur J. Balfour declared in 1917 that the British government, as explained by Baron Lionel W. Rothschild, would consider "the creation of a national homeland in Palestine with good will" and "make the greatest efforts to facilitate the accomplishment of this goal." The Balfour Declaration constituted the first official recognition from any national power of the national hopes of the Jews in Palestine. In 1922, the declaration was incorporated into the preamble to the People's Mandate for Palestine.

> In Basel I have founded the Jewish state. If I said that out loud today, I would be answered by universal laughter. Perhaps in 5 years, in any case in 50, all will see it.
>
> Entry in Theodor Herzl's diary after the First Zionist Congress in Basel

226 *Die Welt* (The World). Central organ of the Zionist organization from 1897 to 1914.

1870 – 1933

1919	Establishment of the German Workers' Party, which became the National Socialist German Workers' Party in 1920.
1920	Right-wing extremists attempt a coup.
1933	Adolf Hitler elected German chancellor.
1935	The Nuremberg Race Laws. Carl Ossietzky, imprisoned in a concentration camp, receives the Nobel Peace Prize.
1938	Annexation of Austria.
1939	Battering of Czechoslovakia and invasion of Poland.
1939–45	World War II.
1941	Japanese attack on Pearl Harbor. The United States enters the war.
from 1942	Thomas Mann gives a radio address to the Germans from exile in the United States.
January 27, 1945	The (Soviet) Red Army liberates Auschwitz.

In the years of the Weimar Republic established at the end of the First World War, German Jews, like other citizens, enjoyed improved conditions and scrambled through the postwar chaos. The war was followed at first by an economic and cultural upswing during which there were earnest attempts to fight anti-Semitism, but this bucolic picture is misleading. Few Germans loved the republic; many blamed the government for the humiliating Treaty of Versailles, which they blamed for the country's economic woes. After the stock market crash in October 1929 and the worldwide depression that followed it, the German people were particularly ripe for extreme ideologies. Many were quite ready to exchange the young democracy for an authoritarian regime—anything that promised a restoration of order and ascendancy. Such hopes appeared to be fulfilled, with Hitler's nomination as chancellor on January 30, 1933.

The marking of the Jews

Under the National Socialist (Nazi) regime, latent and more or less passive anti-Semitism turned into state-dictated terror. The methods of the new regime quickly became apparent. In March 1933, the first concentration camp was set up to accommodate political dissidents in Dachau near Munich, but the coercive tactics the regime used against its political opponents were also used, from the beginning, against the Jews. On April 1, 1933, a general boycott was staged against Jewish doctors, attorneys, and businesses. Members

227 The boycott of April 1, 1933. Jewish merchant Richard Stern, decorated with military medals, stands in front of his Cologne business beside a German stormtrooper (SS). Stern distributed a leaflet in which he reminded passersby of the service of Jewish front-line soldiers in World War I and appealed to the solidarity of the Cologne population: "We are not worried, because we know there is still in Cologne today the courage once demanded by Bismarck, and German loyalty, which now applies to us Jews."

1933 – 1945

of the SS (Hitler's elite corps) posted themselves in front of Jewish offices and businesses and harassed anyone who wanted to enter (**227**). The laws of discrimination came in a flood. On April 7, the "Law for the Restoration of the Civil Service" excluded Jewish officials from civil service. The Nuremberg Laws, passed on September 15, 1935, defined the Jews as second-class (or worse) citizens. Moreover, they established a racial definition of a Jew—a Jew was any person who had three or four Jewish grandparents, regardless of his or her religious practice. Henceforth, citizens of "non-German or kindred blood" were excluded from the "Reich's citizenry" and stripped of all political rights, including the right to vote. Marriages and sexual relationships between Jews and persons of Germanic blood were forbidden under threat of prison; and no German domestic employee under the age of forty-five could be engaged in a Jewish household.

'Racially'-motivated legal proceedings and convictions became routine. Occupational prohibitions and the "Aryanization" of Jewish organizations destroyed the Jews' economic base. Many could no longer support themselves. In the last prewar winter, one-quarter of the German Jews received support from the Jewish Winter Aid (**228**).

228 Advertisement for "Stew Sunday" to benefit Jewish Winter Aid, December 1937. Even before 1933, a Jewish Winter Aid organization was set up within the general Winter Aid. Jewish Winter Aid became an independent agency in October 1935 when the Jewish needy were excluded from the regular German Winter Aid activities. On selected sundays, Jewish families were asked to have stew as a midday meal instead of the usual expensive roasts. The money they saved was then collected by Jewish Winter Aid volunteers.

1938

Germany's "annexation" of Austria in March 1938 delivered the Austrian Jews over to the German racial laws. As of August, each Jewish man had to insert the word "Israel" on official documents between his first and surname, and each

1933 – 1945

Holocaust/Shoah: *Holocaust* (from the Greek and Latin meaning "fire victims, total sacrifice"), used predominantly in Anglo-Saxon cultures, and the Hebrew idea of *Shoah* ("destruction") describe the ideologically grounded and systematically accomplished murder of six million Jews during the Nazi regime in Germany between 1933 and 1945.

229 The passport of Kurt "Israel" Rubin, January 19, 1939. On the top left is the "J" stamp.

230 The destroyed Cologne synagogue in the Glockengasse. Photo, no date.

1933 – 1945

Jewish woman had to add "Sara." In October, the passports of German Jews were called in and given back marked with a "J" (**229**).

At the end of October 1938, the Germans rounded up approximately 15,000 Polish Jews living in Germany. They were loaded into trucks and driven to the Polish border. The Polish authorities refused to take them back into Poland, and Germany would not allow them to return to their homes, so the Germans dumped them on the spot. Freezing and hungry, they wandered on foot until enough political pressure was applied to Poland to open its border (as time would prove, the reprieve was a short-lived blessing). Among the people who were pushed out in the "Polish Action" were the parents of seventeen-year-old Herschel Grynszpan, who, upon hearing of it, murdered the German ambassador von Rath in Paris.

The news of the ambassador's death served as a pretext for Goebbels, Hitler's propaganda minister, to organize a series of pogroms on November 9, before a gathering of the Nazi Party in Munich. The pogroms were carefully orchestrated but were carried out to look like a spontaneous reaction to the murder in Paris. The night of November 9, 1938 became known as *Kristallnacht*, or the "Night of Broken Glass." Hundreds of synagogues in Germany and Austria were set on fire (**230**), about 7,500 Jewish businesses destroyed and plundered, dozens of Jews murdered, and the next morning around 25,000 Jews were arrested and forced into concentration camps. Adding insult to injury, Goebbels managed to hold the Jews themselves responsible for the ravages of *Kristallnacht* and the Nazi authorities demanded "reparations" from them of one billion marks.

Jewish self-assertion

Ironically, the Germans' persecution of the Jews during the Third Reich—designed in all details to undermine, impoverish, weaken, and ultimately exterminate the Jewish community—actually helped strengthen the bonds between the individual Jew and his or her Jewish community. In September 1933, a group of Berlin Jews founded the "Reich's Advocacy for the German Jews," to represent the Jewish community. The main tasks of the Advocacy were to arrange emigration, to provide training for new professions, to maintain Jewish schools, and to support Jews whose ability to practice many professions had been curtailed.

Their expulsion from cultural life prompted the Jews to create Jewish Cultural Leagues that organized concerts, theater productions, lectures, and exhibitions. The establishment of the Cultural Leagues was also a reaction against the establishment of the National Socialist Reich's Cultural Council, from which the Jews were, of course, excluded. Artwork, nonetheless, could only be displayed in public if the artist was a member of the Reich's Cultural Council—in short, no Jewish artists were allowed to show their work.

Although the Zionist movement had never been very popular with the majority of German Jews, Hitler's ascension to power changed this. Membership in Zionist parties and organizations climbed from 7,500 in 1932 to 43,000 two years later.

The Second World War

With the invasion of Poland in September 1939, the Second World War began. In the following years, Germany invaded and occupied countries that were home to several million Jews. In Poland alone, approximately three million Jews came under the Germans' authority. The Germans met little official opposition. Far from meeting resistance, in some countries—Poland, Hungary, Ukraine, Rumania, Lithuania, and other Baltic states—they found considerable support. Even the Christian churches within Germany, Italy, and the Nazi-occupied na-

> We want to give Jewish artists bread so that they can again work as artists, and thus materially and spiritually help ...
> We will ourselves prepare the way, as we must in times such as these when our spirits are brought so low.
>
> Dr. Paul Moses, chairman of the Jewish Cultural Alliance of the Rhein-Ruhr in the fall of 1933, on the idea and purpose of the cultural alliances.

231 Pope Pius XII. During the Nazi regime, the Vatican never once spoke out against the murder of the Jews. In December 1942, Pius refused to join a resolution of the Allies condemning the Nazi crimes. When the Germans invaded and occupied Rome (September 1943 to June 1944), approximately 2,000 Jews were deported to Dachau, Bergen-Belsen, and Auschwitz, under the pope's eyes.

1933 – 1945

232 "Reich's Bishop" Ludwig Müller greets Hitler at the Nuremberg Reich's Party Day in 1934. After Hitler assumed power, many Protestant ministers joined the German Christians, which sought a "Reich's Church" that would overcome the fragmentation of German Protestantism through the "Führer Principle." Non-Aryans were excluded from the communities, indicating how closely the German Christians were aligned with Nazi racist ideology. When the Allied powers after the war decided which German organizations would be banned, the German Christians were on the list.

233 Anne Frank (1929 –45) hid with her family from July 1942 to August 1944 in the attic of an Amsterdam spice dealer, with the help of Dutch Christians. On August 4, 1944, they were discovered by the Gestapo and deported to various camps. All except Anne's father, Otto, died either from illness, gassing, or on the Death Marches. Anne's diary afforded the world a disturbing picture of the life of a Jewish family during the Holocaust.

tions offered no loud protest against the Jewish policies, whose violent nature was now in plain view. This tolerance was surprising to some, but for others it was predictable (**231, 232**). Only in the Netherlands, Finland, Bulgaria, and Denmark did any numbers of citizens try to save their Jewish fellow-citizens (**233**). These efforts were, it should be noted, often quite remarkable: In Denmark, the underground, with the help of the Danish people, succeeded in smuggling approximately 7,000 Jews into neutral Sweden.

From December 1, 1939, the Jews in occupied Poland were required to wear a blue Star of David on a white armband and were forced to move into ghettos. The Lodz Ghetto was fenced off in May 1940, the Warsaw Ghetto in November. The ghettos not only isolated the Jews from the rest of the population but, by the forced ghettoization of Jews from all over Poland, became so overcrowded that many people died because of the hygiene conditions and the dire shortages of food. In the Warsaw Ghetto in 1941, an average of thirteen persons lived in in a single room; the allotment for each ghetto inhabitant was 183 calories per day (**234**)—nothing short of starvation rations.

The German invasion of the Soviet Union in 1941 led to a catastrophic acceleration of the exterminationist actions against Europe's Jews: After the invasion, Vilna, Kovno, Riga, Bialystok, Minsk, and other cities suffered mass executions by special squads following on the heels of the regular army. The shtetls and vil-

233 Street scene in the Warsaw ghetto. Photo by German soldier Heinz Joest, September 1941.

lages of eastern Europe were systematically attacked and their residents either murdered on the spot or sent to the camps. According to the meticulous German statistics, by the end of the summer, 250,000 White Russian and Baltic Jews had been murdered.

The approximately 220,000 German Jews who were still alive under direct German jurisdiction fell subject to the Nazis' eliminationist policies. From September 1, 1941, all Jews were required to wear an identifying yellow star (**235**) on their clothing. On October 14, the authorities began the systematic deportations from the ghettos in the east. On October 23, 1941, Himmler, head of the Gestapo, issued a ban on Jewish emigration (**236**, **237**). It was clear by now that accomplishing the Nazi goal of making Germany *judenrein* (free of Jews) by expulsion or by their voluntary emigration would not suffice as a solution to the perennial "Jewish question." From mid-1941, the Germans set up extermination camps in the eastern territories of the Reich. The first death camp was Chelmno, but it was soon followed by Auschwitz-Birkenau, Belzec, Majdanek, Sobibor and Treblinka. The concept of the "Final Solution" as the Nazis' euphemism

> Every day we see destitution, hunger-swollen figures; we see children emaciated like skeletons, covered with sores, lying helpless on the street. Only death remains to the people on the street.
> *Polish Underground Press, April 1942*

235
Star of David. On September 1, 1941, the German Reich decreed that Jews must wear this mark.

236 Felix Nussbaum, self-portrait with Jewish passport, 1943. The painter's attempt to escape the Nazis by constantly changing his place of residence failed. He was arrested with his wife in the summer of 1944, sent to Auschwitz, and murdered.

237 Among the 280,000 German Jews who fled Nazi Germany were many famous scientists and artists, including Martin Buber, Erich Fromm, Walter Benjamin, Ernst Bloch, Albert Einstein, Else Lasker-Schüler, Lion Feuchtwanger, Arnold Zweig, and Nelly Sachs (from top to lower right).

1933 – 1945

183

238 Photomontage of a group of young people at the ovens of the crematory of Auschwitz.

for the murder of millions of European Jews was now manifest. At the Wannsee Conference of January 20, 1942, the "Final Solution" was organized bureaucratically and "the different kinds of 'solution possibilities' were discussed." What the Nazis euphemistically called "solution possibilities" were the gas chambers and crematoria of the extermination camps (**238**). The Germans experimented to find the most efficient means of murder and disposal, with the least psychic cost for the squads assigned the actual task of execution. For example, the use of vans that killed by piping engine exhaust fumes while the van itself was driven to a dumping ground in the woods, was superseded by the chambers erected at Auschwitz from which bodies could be easily loaded into adjoining crematoria; much of this work could even be performed by the prisoners themselves, who would soon become victims as well. In 1942, on Himmler's order, the liquidation of the ghettos began. As of July, the Jewish Council of the Warsaw Ghetto had to assemble about 6,000 Jews daily for transportation to Treblinka; this was called "resettlement in the east." The euphemism fooled few.

The Warsaw uprising

Contrary to the common and mistaken belief that the Jews "went like lambs to the slaughter," that they accepted their fate passively, there were in fact many Jewish individuals and groups organized into an active resistance to the genocidal policies. The most important such action was the Warsaw Ghetto uprising. In the early months of 1943, after approximately 300,000 ghetto residents had been "resettled," and word of their actual fate in the death camps trickled back to Warsaw, a group of young people calling themselves the ZOB ("Jewish Fighting Organization") exhorted the Jewish ghetto inmates not to go to the railroad cars. This was the seed of organized resistance in

They understand that death is not the most important thing, that how one dies and for what is much more important. Therefore the Jewish fighters have determined ... to die with a weapon in their hands. They did not deceive themselves over the end of the desperate fight there [in the Warsaw Ghetto]. The Jews had to die, but they did not have to die a miserable death, useless to anyone; they could die a death in defense of human dignity and their own honor. They decided to follow the example of Bar Kochba.

    Maria Kann, Before the Eyes of the World

1933 – 1945

the ghetto. On April 19, 1943, when German troops entered the ghetto to deport its remaining inhabitants, they met armed resistance from approximately 750 young people. The resisters were cut off from the outside world, half-starved, and armed in only a makeshift manner, yet they managed to stave off the liquidation of the ghetto for a month. They never expected to overpower the Germans through this action, but organized the uprising as a symbolic gesture, to shame the world. On May 16, 1943, the Germans announced: "The previous residential quarter in Warsaw no longer exists. The total number of certifiably destroyed Jews is altogether 56,065."

The Holocaust changed the Jewish world radically (240). An estimated six million Jewish people fell victim to the "Final Solution." It represented the largest systematic, state-led program of genocide in the history of humankind, making the two thousand years of Jewish oppression and persecution that preceded it nothing but a protracted prelude. The destruction of east European Judaism meant not only the murder of millions but also the end of a centuries-old culture with its own language, religious traditions, and customs. Any attempt to mitigate the singularity of the Holocaust, to grant it a veneer of normality by comparing it with other regimes—how horrifying they may be—is to mock both the dead and the survivors.

239　Captured insurgents in the Warsaw Ghetto.

240　Jewish population before the war, and numbers of Jews murdered from 1939 to 1945.

▌ Jewish population before the war

▐ Jewish population after the war

Chart Y-axis: 3.5 M, 3 M, 2.5 M, 2 M, 1.5 M, 1 M, 0.5 M, 0

Chart X-axis: Poland, USSR, Germany, France, Belgium, Austria, Czechosl., Hungary, Yugoslavia, Rumania, Bulgaria, Greece, Latvia, Lithuania

241　Bea Wyler, the first woman Rabbi in postwar Germany.

1933 – 1945

1948	Founding of the State of Israel and War of Independence.
1951	Murder of Jordan's King Abdulla in East Jerusalem.
1952	Reparation agreement with West Germany.
1954	Gamal Abdal Nasser deposes King Farouk and becomes president of the republic of Egypt.
1956	Suez Crisis.
1965	Diplomatic relations between Israel and West Germany.
1967	Six Day War.
1973	Yom Kippur War.
1978	Nobel Peace Prize awarded to Anwar al-Sadat and Menachem Begin.
1981	Assassination of Egyptian President Anwar al-Sadat.
1987	Beginning of the Intifada.
1995	Assassination of Israeli Prime Minister Yitzhak Rabin.
1996	Election of Prime Minister Benjamin Netanyahu.

For many Jews in the Diaspora, messianic visions and the dream of reestablishing a Jewish state were always alive. Over the centuries, individual Jews had returned for religious reasons to Palestine. But these more or less isolated instances of immigration bore no political meaning. The latter years of the 19th century brought the first line of a modern, secular-based nationalist movement for Jews—Zionism, at the heart of which was the goal of establishing a Jewish homeland in Palestine (see p. 173 ff.). Between 1881 and 1948, more waves of immigration changed the demographic structure of Palestine. The Jewish population grew from 24,000 to around 630,000 and, shortly before the State of Israel was proclaimed, constituted more than one-third of the total population.

The "aliyot" up to 1948

The first wave of immigration, or *aliyah* (**242**), brought approximately 250,000 east European Jews to Palestine between 1882 and 1904. The first immigrants were interested in establishing an independent agricultural life. The approximately 40,000 immigrants who came in the second aliyah, many of them from Russia, left their homeland because of the pogroms and because of the revolution of 1905. These immigrants brought with them ideas about social reform and social revolution. In 1909, they founded the first kibbutz in Deganya and the first Jewish city, Tel Aviv, in modern Palestine. The third wave, from 1919 to 1931, brought 35,000 immigrants from Poland and Russia; the fourth, from 1924 to 1931, about 80,000 people, mostly from eastern Europe. The aliyot also brought to Palestine the beginnings of private enterprise in the

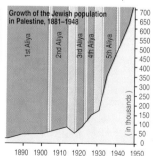

Growth of the Jewish population in Palestine, 1881–1948

1st Aliya · 2nd Aliya · 3rd Aliya · 4th Aliya · 5th Aliya

(in thousands) 0 50 100 150 200 250 300 350 400 450 500 550 600 650 700

1890 1900 1910 1920 1930 1940 1950

1881 – today

242 Growth of the Jewish population in Palestine, 1881–1948.

residential area of the Jewish community, called the *Yishuv*. The fifth wave, between 1932 and 1939, brought over 200,000 people fleeing from Nazi Germany and central Europe. The latter group contributed to the growth of the Israeli cities; many of these immigrants were academics and pursued independent academic careers.

Palestine under British Mandate

During the First World War, with the Balfour Declaration the British government promised the Zionists a "national homeland in Palestine" (see p. 177). The Arabs, however, also hoped to incorporate Palestine into an independent greater Arab empire. Conflict was inevitable. After the war, Palestine became a British Mandate. The Arabs saw their national hopes dashed and began to oppose the increasing Jewish immigration. The gathering force of opposition climaxed in the 1920s and 1930s, with a massacre in 1929 in the Jewish community in Hebron and a great Arab uprising that lasted from 1936 to 1939. In July 1937, the Peel Commission proposed partitioning Palestine into a Jewish and an Arab state. Shortly before the outbreak of the Second World War, however, Britain's policy toward Palestine shifted from a pro-Jewish stand to a pro-Arab orientation. The British government issued a White Paper limiting Jewish immigration.

The Nazi era sent ever more Jewish refugees to Palestine. In order to curry favor with the Arab world, the British attempted to hinder Jewish immigration. Jewish underground groups therefore began to organize illegal immigration, bringing about 100,000 people to Palestine between 1940 and 1948. After the war, the British government intensified its restrictive policies. Moreover, the survivors of the Holo-

243 German Jewish immigrants in Nahariyah, 1938. The container in the background, in which the property of the family was shipped to Palestine, served at the time the photo was taken as lodging; a second was set up as a temporary opthalmologist's office.

> As of April of this year, over the next five years 75,000 immigrants shall be allowed ....
> After five more years no more Jewish immigration will be permitted; ... His Majesty's government is determined to put a stop to illegal immigration.
>
> British White Paper of May 17, 1939

caust at first were not allowed to immigrate. An American statement issued in the fall of 1945 aptly described the plight of the camp survivors in Germany: "They are liberated, but not free." In fact, most of the survivors in the early postwar years found themselves again in camps, the displaced persons camps, which they could not leave without permission.

The "Exodus" affair

The incident involving the refugee ship *Exodus 1947* (**244**) opened the eyes of the world to the critical plight of the displaced persons held in Germany. The *Exodus* carried about 4,500 displaced Jews who wanted to build a new life in Palestine. Before it arrived at the Palestine coast, the *Exodus* was boarded by the Royal Navy and, after a brief struggle, which claimed more casualties among people who had survived years of terror and persecution, was brought into port in naval custody. Britain's foreign minister intended to adhere to the letter of the immigration restrictions and wanted to teach the refugees a lesson: Thus, instead of stranding them in Egypt, as was standard practice with other illegal immigrants under British rule, they were sent back to Germany.

The founding of the state

The *Exodus* affair, along with other tactics by radical Jewish groups, stirred protest from around the world, convincing Britain to find a solution to the Middle East problem expeditiously. Members of the United Nations Special Committee for Palestine later explained that the international scandal of the *Exodus* affair substantially influenced their decision to propose a plan for dividing Palestine. During Jewish efforts to secure agreement for the plan, the Arabs objected. On November 29, 1947,

244 The gravely damaged refugee ship *Exodus 1947* in the harbor at Haifa. The British did not allow the refugees to disembark, but sent them back to Germany.

The United Nations General Assembly agreed to the division of Palestine, and, on May 15, 1948, the British Mandate was terminated by a U.N. accord. Because of the approaching Sabbath, on Friday afternoon, May 14, 1948, the State of Israel was proclaimed by David Ben-Gurion (246). On May 15, the armed forces of Egypt, Transjordan, Syria, Lebanon, and Iraq attacked the new State of Israel. The first Israeli-Arab war, the War of Independence, began.

The wars with the neighboring Arab States and the Palestinians

The State of Israel has, to date, fought five wars with its neighboring Arab states: the 1948 War of Independence, the 1956 Suez Crisis, the 1967 Six-Day War, the 1973 Yom Kippur War, and the 1982 Lebanon War. Since December 1987, it has been engaged in a struggle with the *Intifada* (the "Pushed Aside"—i.e., persons displaced by Israeli occupation) in the occupied territories. The permanent state of war, the anxiety in the face of terror and force, has, like the Holocaust, permanently scarred the consciousness of Israeli society.

At the end of the War of Independence in 1949, Israel possessed an area that was larger than the U.N. plan had outlined, but its boundaries were not advantageous. West Jordan was annexed by Transjordan, and the total area was now called Jordan. Tel Aviv lay only 12.5 miles away from the first Jordanian military posts. The Gaza Strip came under Egyptian administration. Most Arabs had fled from the Israeli-conquered territories (estimates range between 600,000 and 1,000,000). This flight was in part due to Arab propaganda, which promised a return after a

245 The plan to divide Palestine drawn up by the United Nations Special Committee for Palestine, which was ratified by the U.N. General Assembly with a two-thirds majority.

246 On May 14, 1948, Israel's first prime minister, David Ben-Gurion (1886–1973), declared Israel an independent state.

1881 – today

189

247 Soldiers' dance at the Wailing Wall. New Year's Card on the victory of 1967. Since 1948, the Jordanian authorities had barred Jews' access to the Wailing Wall. With the taking of East Jerusalem in the Six Day War, the Old City came under Israeli control. Beyond its religious significance, the Wailing Wall has become a national symbol.

248 Golda Meïr (1898–1978) was Israeli prime minister from 1969 to 1974. International political conflicts over her administration before and during the Yom Kippur War prompted her retirement. She was succeeded as prime minister by Yitzhak Rabin, who held the office from 1974 to 1977, and again from 1992 until his assassination in 1995.

quick victory, in part due to panic in the face of Jewish extremist organizations, and in part due to Israeli pressure. The refugees were not accepted into the neighboring Arab countries, but accommodated in camps. The refugee problem in the Middle East has persisted ever since and seems to defy all efforts at resolution.

In May 1967, Israel found itself encircled by battle-ready Arab forces. On June 5, 1967, the country launched a preventive strike against Egypt, planned by then-General Chief of Staff Yitzhak Rabin. In the Six Day War, Israeli troops took the Sinai, the Gaza Strip, West Jordan, the Syrian Golan Heights, and East Jerusalem (**247**, **250**). The war, however, exacerbated the Palestinian problem within Israel as it placed hundreds of thousands of Palestinians under Israeli occupation and military power.

On October 6, 1973, on Yom Kippur, the Jewish high holy day, the Egyptians and Syrians launched a surprise attack on Israel. After the Arab forces' initial success, the Israeli military seized the upper hand and pushed the Arabs almost all the way back to Cairo. In 1974–75, U.S. Secretary of State Henry Kissinger mediated a ceasefire between Israel and Egypt. The Yom Kippur War—particularly Israel's vulnerability at the beginning of the conflict—showed the nation the limits of its military might. This fourth war in the Middle East brought a new approach to Middle East politics. This meant, especially for Israel's protector, the United States, that Israel would have to adopt a more flexible position toward the Arabs, but it also persuaded the moderate Arab states of Egypt and Jordan to recognize Israel as a sovereign state.

Egypt was the first Arab country to brave recognition for Israel. This breakthrough set in motion a complicated negotiation process.

Through the mediation of U.S. President Jimmy Carter, Israel and Egypt reached an accord in September 1978 at Camp David, the President's retreat (**249**); on March 26, 1979, the peace agreement was signed by Israeli Prime Minister Menachem Begin and Egyptian President Anwar al-Sadat on the White House lawn.

249 (Left to right:) Anwar al-Sadat, Jimmy Carter, and Menachem Begin in Camp David, 1978.

Since the end of the 1970s, the north of Israel was the frequent target of terrorism by the Palestinian Liberation Organization (the PLO), whose base of operations was in southern Lebanon. On June 6, 1982, Israel used this as a pretext for a military incursion into Lebanon. Israeli troops struck Beirut and attacked the military infrastructure of the PLO. For the first time in the history of Middle East warfare, this military action did not have the undivided support of the Israeli people. On September 25, 1982, 350,000 people streamed into the streets of Tel Aviv to protest the Israeli military's toleration of the massacres perpetrated by the Lebanese Christian militia against the Palestinian refugee camps of Sabra and Shatila near Beirut, and to demand that Israel withdraw from Lebanon. The 1984 Coalition of National Unity, comprised of members of the national conservative Likud block and the Labor party in the Knesset (the Israeli parliament), advocated withdrawal as a foreign-policy priority. Israel withdrew from Lebanon in June 1985.

Israel did not allow itself to be drawn into the Persian Gulf War between the United States and Iraq (1990–91). Despite their trifling military consequences, however, the Scud missiles launched on Israel from Iraq stirred traumatic memories for

250 Israel since 1967.

251 Israel's irrigation network. Today, Israel uses 85–90% of its available water, a peak value that does not meet the country's increasing need. For this reason, people are experimenting with purification and reuse of waste water, desalination of sea water, deep boring, and rain making.

Israel: the land, the people, the language, the government, and foreign policy

Israel covers an area of 7,992 square miles. This includes the 1967 incorporated East Jerusalem, but not the occupied Arab territories of the West Bank, the Gaza Strip, and the Golan Heights. Roughly the size of New Jersey, Israel is one of the most water-poor nations in the world. Its present water resources are unevenly dispersed geographically and seasonally: Approximately three-quarters of the country's rain falls in the north of the country during the four winter months. In order to bring water to the areas in the south, Israel needed to install an irrigation network and to develop economical water systems (**251, 253**). These make it possible for the Israelis to use land for agriculture that otherwise would lie fallow. Israel's experience in the struggle against the desertification, which also threatens other countries in the region, could be an arena for future cooperation.

The population of Israel—5.46 million people who come from 80 different countries (as well as native-born)—is ethnically, religiously, and culturally more diverse than is usually supposed. 81.1% of the population are Jewish, 18.9% non-Jewish (of these, 14.2% are Muslim, 3% Christian, and 1.7% Druze). A very small percentage is made up of other minorities along with members of Jewish sects of Karaites and Samaritans. 90.4% of the Jewish and Arab population live in cities, 5.8% in communal settlements (such as the 280 kibbutzim and 400 *moshav ovdim*), and 3.8% in villages. Israel has defined itself as the historical homeland of the entire Jewish people. For this reason, the law that extends the oppportunity of settling in Israel to every Jew in the world and grants those who do immigrate Israeli citizenship is not called an "immigration" law, but a "return" law, meaning a return after two thousand years of exile. The law was passed on July 5, 1949, by the first Knesset. In the first four years after the founding of the state, Israel experienced a mass immigration, approximately doubling its population. Thereafter the influx slowed down, but an ever smaller wave of immigration continued. After the 1980s, during which scarcely any immigrants came to Israel, the liberalization of the emigration laws in the former Soviet Union led to a sharp increase in immigration. Of the 634,000 Jews who "returned" to Israel in 1990–93, about 90% came from the former Soviet Union. Another 300,000 people from the former Soviet Union will be welcomed into Israel from 1995 to 1999.

Since 1948, the official language is New Hebrew, with Arabic the second official language. In an immigrant country whose population has come from 80 different countries, the modern Hebrew language is an essential element in the stability of a unified Israeli nation.

Israel is the only functioning parliamentary democracy in the Near and Middle East. To date, no single constitution has been instituted due to the lack of agreement among religious and nonreligious parties; instead, a series of basic laws govern the civic life of a single district. They must be accepted by the Knesset, the Israeli parliament, with an absolute majority. The Knesset is made up of 120 delegates, all of whom are elected for a term of four years. There is no explicit separation of religion and state. For example, for Jewish Israelis, all questions of marriage and divorce are settled not by secular courts but by the rabbinical court. Similar autonomy over matters of religious custom is extended to Muslims, Christians, and Druzes, who also have religious courts like the Jewish Bet Din.

As far as foreign policy is concerned, Israel's most important relationship is and has always been with the United States. For more than two decades, the United States has given Israel extensive military assistance and has collaborated with Israel in many areas (news service, counter-terrorism, to name a few). While the U.S.-Israeli relationship rests on any number of political and ideological concerns, its strength is due in large part to the American Jewish community, which, with about 6 million people, is the largest Jewish community in the world. In 1952, the Federal Republic of Germany (formerly West Germany) signed a reparations accord with Israel, while the German Democratic Republic (formerly East Germany) denied any responsibility for the Nazi atrocities. The West German acknowledgment that Holocaust survivors were entitled to reparations opened the door to a relationship between West Germany and Israel. This process, however, only crawled forward. In 1960, West German Chancellor Konrad Adenauer met with Israeli Prime Minister David Ben-Gurion on neutral territory in New York, setting the stage for positive relations with "another" Germany (252); in 1965, West Germany and Israel established full diplomatic relations.

many people, all the more so since Saddam Hussein had repeatedly threatened to destroy Israel with poison gas. (The trauma was only deepened by the knowledge among Israelis that Iraq was using German technology to produce its poison gas.)

252 Chancellor Konrad Adenauer and Prime Minister David Ben-Gurion at their historic meeting on March 14, 1960 in New York City.

The hard road to peace

Immediately before he was shot to death on November 4, 1995, Israeli Prime Minister Yitzhak Rabin attended a peace demonstration with some 100,000 participants, where he spoke eloquently for the last time in favor of the peace process in the Middle East (254). Rabin's murder was the consequence of a dramatic radicalization that had begun in 1992 with the electoral

253 Precipitation in Israel.

Precipitation:
mm/year
850
700
550
400
250
100

> For 27 years I was a military man. I have fought war, so long as there was no chance of peace. I believe that now there is this chance, and we must use it for those who are here today and for those who could not come—and of these there are many.
> Excerpt from Prime Minister Rabin's final speech, November 4, 1995

1881 – today

254 Beaming faces at the end of the peace demonstration in Tel Aviv on November 4, 1995. The one-time political rivals Shimon Peres and Yitzhak Rabin embraced in friendship and waved to the jubilant crowd, just a few minutes before the gunshot that killed Rabin.

victory of the Labor party. During his campaign, the new prime minister had declared that the peace process was the only solution for the Middle East conflict. His opponent, the Israeli right and especially the hard core of messianic settlers, suddenly had to recognize, since the majority of Israelis believed that it was better to proceed according to the formula "Land for Peace," than to hold on to the occupied territories at any price. Shortly after Rabin took office, the government ordered a freeze on construction of new settlements in the occupied territories. Rabin tackled the most sensitive question of Israeli internal politics—a question that directly addresses Israel's security and the fate of the 120,000 Jewish settlers in the 144 settlements in the Gaza Strip and West Jordan. For them, West Jordan (which they call Judea and Sumeria) is unquestionably part of "Greater Israel," as it was called in the bible, and "no Jew may ever deny, that the Lord gave the land to the Jewish people." That many Israelis are willing to defend this position by any means is shown by the assassination of Rabin, just as it is shown by the blood-bath unleashed by the extremist Jewish settler Baruch Goldstein in February 1994 among praying Muslims in the Ibrahim Mosque in Hebron.

The solution to the settlement problem will only be decided by the peace process in the Middle East. An integral issue in the quest for peace will be reaching an accord with Syria, for Damascus holds the key to resolving the conflict between Israel and all its Arab neighbors, with the possible exception of Lebanon.

A chronicle of peace, 1991–96

In Madrid, on October 30, 1991, under the auspices of the United States and the Soviet

Union, a Middle East Peace Conference was held. Syrians, Jordanians, Lebanese, and Palestinians (as a Jordanian-Palestinian delegation) sat down at a single table with Israelis. The year 1993 brought a remarkable turn of events. On September 13, PLO Chief Yassir Arafat and Israeli Prime Minister Yitzhak Rabin signed the so-called Oslo Accord in Washington, DC, in the presence of U.S. President Bill Clinton. After decades of bitter enmity, they officially recognized each other and signed a Principle Statement on Ongoing Self-Rule for Palestinians in the Gaza Strip and in Jericho. In May 1994, the autonomy agreement for Gaza and Jericho was ratified in Cairo, fulfilling a central goal of the ground-breaking Washington agreement.

On October 26, 1994, Israel and Jordan made peace. Thus, Jordan, after Egypt, became the second Arab nation that has undertaken an agreement to maintain secure, orderly relations with Israel. On September 28, 1995, Rabin and Arafat signed another Autonomy Agreement (Oslo II) for West Jordan, which was ratified by the Knesset on October 6, 1995 by an extremely narrow margin. After Rabin's murder, his successor Shimon Peres (who, however, was defeated in the 1996 elections) reinforced his strong stand on peace policy: on November 13, 1995, after twenty-eight years of occupation, Israeli troops left the city of Dshenin in West Jordan and handed over autonomy to the Palestinians.

In June 1996, however, Peres was defeated in a general election by the right-wing Benjamin Netanyahu. The world waits, mixed in its opinions, to see what this political shift will mean for the progress of peace in the Middle East.

Population of Israel in 1992:
mainly Jewish
mainly Arab

255 Israel and occupied territories in 1992. Jewish and Arab population.

1881 – today

Glossary

Aliyah, pl. aliyot: Emigration to Israel.

Ashkenazi, Ashkenazim: Ashkenazi was originally the name of a tribe mentioned in Genesis 10:3. In the Middle Ages, Ashkenazi became the Hebrew designation for Germany and northeast France. From the time of the crusades, the term also applied to Jews who had fled to Russia and Poland and their descendants.

Bar mitzvah: Literally, "son of the commandments." Designation for a boy who reaches religious maturity at the end of his 13th year. At that time, he is considered a full-fledged member of the community with all rights and duties, according to religious law. The religious coming of age is celebrated with a bar mitzvah party.

Bat mitzvah: Literally, "daughter of the commandments." Designation for a girl who reaches religious adulthood at the end of her 12th year. Bat mitzvah celebrations were first held in Reformed Jewish communities in the 19th century.

Berit milah (Brit): Literally, "alliance of circumcision." Circumcision is performed on the 8th day after the birth of a boy by a Mohel. The practice dates back to Abraham (Gen. 17:9–14) and is the outward sign of God's covenant with the Jewish people.

Bet Din: Literally, "house of the law." Rabbinical court that has at least three rabbinical judges.

Bet ha-Knesset: Literally, "House of Assembly." Hebrew designation for a synagogue (see below).

Bimah: Literally, "pulpit, podium." A podium in the synagogue from which the Torah lesson is read.

Challah: A braided white bread eaten on the Sabbath.

Day of Atonement: See Yom Kippur.

Dhimma, Dhimmi: The legal rights and status of Jews in Islamic countries were regulated in a pact called the Dhimma. Those covered by it were called Dhimmi. All non-Muslims were designated Dhimmi, the followers of monotheistic religions based on revelation, namely, Jews and Christians.

Diaspora: Literally, "exile." The communities of Jews dispersed in countries outside Palestine.

Frankists: Jewish sect founded by Jacob L. Frank that converted to Christianity in the 18th century.

Gemara: Literally, "teaching." The Gemara is the interpretation and discussion of the Mishnah, which was developed in the learning centers of Palestine and Babylon. The Mishnah and the Gemara together make up the Talmud.

Guide to the Perplexed: Principle work of religious philisophy by Maimonides (ca. 1190).

Haggadah: Literally, "the telling." In a narrow sense, the Haggadah is the narrative of the Israelites flight from Egypt and the liberation from Egyptian servitude. The Haggadah is read at the seder, the festive meal on the eve of Passover.

Hanukkah: Literally, "initiation." Eight-day Festival of Lights, beginning on the 25th day of Kislev (November/December), commemorating the rededication of the Temple in Jerusalem by Judas Maccabeus in 164 BCE. According to Talmudic legend, the lights in the temple burnt miraculously for eight days on only one flask of oil. In remembrance, a light is lit on the hanukkiyah (see below) on each of the eight days.

Hanukkiyah: During the eight days of Hanukkah, a special menorah that holds eight candles for each night of Hanukkah and a ninth candle called the shamash ("the servant") which is used to light the others.

Hasidim, Hasidism: Literally, "pious." As early as the time of the Maccabees, in the 2nd to 1st centuries

Glossary

BCE, there was a religious tradition within Judaism called "Hasidism." From this tradition, in the Middle Ages the movement of the *Hasidei Ashkenaz* (the "Pious Ashkenazi") emerged. In the 18th century, Hasidism was a religious reform movement that originated in eastern Europe and taught a traditional piety of common people.

Haskalah: Hebrew designation for "Enlightenment." The Haskalah movement of the late 18th century represented religious, cultural, and social emancipation for the Jews. Founded by Moses Mendelssohn in Germany, in the 19th century it spread into eastern Europe—after a considerable delay—and there had great influence.

Havdalah: Literally, "division." Term for the transitional ritual at the end of the Sabbath or a holiday, at the "separation" between the holy day and the regular workday. In the Havdalah, one recites a blessing over wine and aromatic spices. The spices are kept in a special box called the Bessamim box.

Herem: Banishment, or excommunication, from the Jewish religious community, usually for supposed heresy or sacrilegious teaching.

Holocaust: Literally, "burnt, or total, sacrifice." The word used in the Anglo-Saxon world for the ideologically grounded, systematic murder of 6 million Jews by the Germans under Nazi rule from 1933 to 1945.

Huppah: The canopy under which the Jewish wedding ceremony takes place.

Israel: In the pre-exile period, the biblical term for the entire Jewish community. Since the end of the empire after Solomon's death, the term Israel came to have a double meaning: On the one hand, it represents in a narrow political sense the Northern Kingdom, rival to the Southern Kingdom; on the other hand, Israel also remains the name for the entire people that formed a political and national entity under David and Solomon. This counts in a religious usage: the community, which stands in a particular relation to God, the people of God, are called Israel, independent of territory or government. So the choice of the name "Israel" for the modern Jewish state signals an ongoing political claim.

Kabbalah: Literally, "tradition." Moses de Leon, Jewish mystic and teacher of 12th-century Provence, who later moved to Spain, developed the first flowering of Jewish mysticism with his *Zohar* ("Book of Splendour"). From there the Kabbalah spread quickly through the Judaic world. In the 16th century, its center was the city of Zafed in Galilee. The Kabbalah had great influence on Hasidism.

Kaddish: Old Aramaic prayer in which God's holiness is praised. It is a part of the daily worship and the mourning prayer said at the grave and by the family during the period of mourning.

Kashrut: Literally, "ritual worthiness, suitability." The dietary laws that govern what may be eaten, how a kitchen may be kept "pure," and how foods may be prepared.

Ketubah: Marriage contract. The ketubah is written in Aramaic, the language of the Talmud.

Kibbutz, pl. kibbutzim: Literally, "collective." A settlement founded on socialist principles with communal living, production, and work. The kibbutz provides housing, food, clothing, child care, and for other personal needs of its members. The oldest kibbutz, in Deganya, was founded in 1909.

Kiddush: Literally, "consecration." Blessing spoken over a wine-filled goblet before meals on the Sabbath and holidays.

Klezmer, pl. klezmorim: From the Hebrew *Kle Semer* ("musical instruments"). East European Jewish folk music tradition (and a musician who plays it). A typical klezmer band includes cymbals, fiddles, flutes, clarinets, and bass.

Glossary

Knesset: Literally, "assembly." The Israeli parliament with its seat in Jerusalem.

Kosher: Literally, "pure, suitable, appropriate." The method of preparing food and following the *Kashrut*.

Ladino: Also known as "Spaniolish" or "Judeospanish." The language of the Iberian Jews and their descendants (see *Sephardim*). Ladino, like Yiddish, was written with Hebrew characters.

Lulav: A bouquet of palm branches, citrons, myrtle, and willow branches gathered for Sukkot (Feast of Tabernacles). Because the palm leaf is larger than the others, its name is given to the bouquet.

Mahzor: Literally, "cycle." Prayer book for the holidays.

Marrano: Originally a derogatory term (literally meaning "pig") for Spanish or Portuguese Jews who converted to Christianity to escape persecution, but were suspected of remaining loyal to their Jewish faith and customs.

Matzoh: Unleavened bread, eaten during the eight days of Passover to remember the flight from Egypt, when there was no time to let the bread rise.

Megillah, pl. Megillot: Literally, "scroll." The five biblical books, Ruth, Song of Solomon, Lamentations, Ecclesiastes, and Esther. The end of Megillah, specifically the book of Esther, is read on Purim.

Mikveh: Ritual bath.

Minyan: Literally, "number." Traditionally, ten men over the age of 13 form a minyan and are required for the formation of a community. A minyan is also traditionally necessary for holding a worship service.

Mishnah: Literally, "teaching." The Mishnah is a collection of writings on religious law, which were ordered around 200 CE by Rabbi Judah ha-Nasi and written down. The Mishnah and the Gemara together form the Talmud.

Mishneh Torah: Literally, "second to the Torah." The systematic codification of Maimonides of the whole Halakhah in 14 books (1180), also called *Yad Ha-Hazakah* ("Strong Hand"), because a "strong hand" had systematized the writings on the religious law.

Mitzvah, pl. Mitzvot: Literally, "commandment, good deed."

Mohel: One who performs circumcision (see *Berit milah*).

Moshav, pl. moshavim: Literally, "settlement." A cooperatively organized settlement in Israel. The settlers pledge themselves to mutual help, for example, in buying and supplying on a cooperative basis. In contrast to the kibbutz, each settler follows his or her own occupation and lives in his or her own home.

Pale of Settlement: see Settlement radius

Passover (Hebrew Pesach): Holiday commemorating when God "passed over" the houses of the Israelites when killing the first-born sons of the Egyptians. Eight-day celebration from the 14th to the 21st of Nisan (March-April) in memory of the liberation of the people of Israel from servitude in Egypt. The seder (festive meal at home) is characteristic of Passover, at which the Haggadah is read and symbolic foods (like matzoh) are prepared and served according to a prescribed ritual.

Pentateuch: Literally, "five-scroll book." Greek name for the five books of Moses (the first five books of the Old Testament), the Torah.

Pesach: See Passover.

Pilpul: From Hebrew *pilpel* ("pepper"). Sharp-witted Talmudic custom of debate to deepen understanding of the Halakhah, today often connoting nitpicking or hair-splitting.

Pogrom: Russian word for "devastation." Organized violence against Jews, often with understood support of authorities.

Purim: Joyful holiday on the 14th and 15th days of Adar to remember the rescue of the Persian Jews by Queen Esther.

Rabbi: Literally, "my master, my teacher." The title of teachers in Palestine in Talmudic times, whose

Glossary

interpretations of the Torah were binding for the community. (In Babylon, they had the title "Rav"). Used for modern Jewish "clergy" of all branches of Judaism.

Rosh Hashannah: Literally, "head of the year." Jewish New Year celebration, celebrated on the first two days of Tishri and encompassing the 10 days of atonement that culminate with Yom Kippur.

Seder: Literally, "order." A meal at home during Passover to commemorate the flight from Egypt. The ritual is described in the Haggadah.

Sephardic, Sephardim: Originally, a place name in the bible (Obad. 20). Became the Hebrew designation for the Iberian peninsula. Sephardic Jews came from Spain and Portugal, which marked their traditions. The descendants of the Spanish Jews driven out in 1492 are known around the world as Sephardim.

Settlement radius or Pale of Settlement: From 1791, the czarist government in Russia issued a series of decrees restricting the living rights of Jews to a certain area in western Russia. These restrictions remained in force with few changes until World War I. Within the Pale of Settlement, in the 19th century Jews made up one-ninth of the population.

Shabbat (Sabbath): From Hebrew shavot ("rest").

The seventh day of the week, on which Jews rest and are not supposed to work. The Sabbath commemorates the seventh day of creation on which God rested (Ex. 20:11) and the flight from Egypt (Deut. 12:15). It begins on Friday evening and ends at sunset on Saturday. The Sabbath is dedicated to prayers and rest.

Shavuot: Literally, "week." The "week holiday" celebrated seven weeks after Passover. Commemorates the revelation on Sinai with the reading of the Ten Commandments and is the holiday of the "First Fruits."

Shehitah: Slaughter of pure, healthy animals according to the Kashrut. Performed by a trained butcher, the shohet.

Shoah: Literally, "extermination." The Hebrew word for the Holocaust.

Shofar: A ram's horn that is blown at the close of Yom Kippur in the New Year celebration.

Shtetl: Yiddish word for a small Jewish town or village. Home in eastern Europe to the majority of Jews. The shtetl was the center of eastern Jewish culture, where the Jews, in relative isolation from the gentile world, maintained their identity, traditions, and laws. The everyday life consisted of hard work, threat of pogroms, and restrictive measures by the civil authorities. The Revolution in Russia

and the Holocaust virtually wiped out the culture of the shtetl.

Siddur: Literally, "arrangement." Prayer book.

Simhat Torah: Literally, "rejoicing of the law." Holiday on which the last excerpt of the Torah (Deut. 24) is read in the cycle of yearly worship, to begin again with Genesis 1. Characterized by festive Torah processions to express the delight the Torah brings.

Sukkot: Literally, "tabernacle." On Sukkot, every Jew is supposed to remember living in the tabernacle for seven days, as their ancestors once did on their way out of slavery into freedom.

Synagogue: After the destruction of the Temple, the synagogue (literally, "assembly house, community") became the real religious and business center of Jewish community life. The Greek word synagogue corresponds to the Hebrew word Bet ha-Knesset ("House of Assembly").

Tallit: Prayer shawl, which, from the day of his bar mitzvah, a man wears at morning prayers.

Talmud: Literally, "learning." The Talmud is the principal work of rabbinical Judaism, which has come down from oral tradition and remains today the authoritative source of religious learning and religious law for observant Jews. It consists of two

Glossary

parts, the Mishnah and the Gemara. The Talmud comes in two versions, corresponding to the two centers of rabbinical learning in Palestine and Babylon: the Palestinian or Jerusalem Talmud (ca. 425 BCE) and the Babylonian Talmud (completed in the 6th century CE). The voluminous Babylonian Talmud soon found canonical favor and supplanted the Palestinian.

Tefillin: Leather prayer straps worn by adult Jews for morning prayers on workdays, though not on the Sabbath and holidays. Given to a bar mitzvah on the morning of his 13th birthday so that he may say morning prayers for the first time with tefillin.

Tik: In countries of the Orient, the usual container for the Torah scrolls, like the Torah mantles of the Ashkenazim.

Torah scroll: For liturgical readings in the synagogue, the text of the Torah in Hebrew quadratical script is written on parchment; the parchment pieces fit together and are rolled on two wooden rods.

Torah shrine: Shrine or "ark" in which the Torah scrolls are kept. As a rule, it is kept on the wall that faces toward Jerusalem, which is the east wall in synagogues of the western Diaspora. The Torah scrolls are only removed for ritual readings.

Torah: Literally, "Teaching, instruction." The first five books of the bible—Genesis, Exodus, Leviticus, Numbers, and Deuteronomy—which according to Jewish tradition were given to Moses by God on Sinai. For use in worship services, these "Five Books of Moses" are written on a parchment scroll, the Torah scroll. In a wider sense, the Torah is the whole bible with the Prophets and historical books and ultimately the whole corpus of traditional Judaic literature. Thus, a scholar of the scripture is called a Torah scholar. The Torah, with the prophetic and historical books of the bible, constitutes the "written" teachings, while the Talmud and other rabbinical texts are the "oral" teachings.

Yeshiva, pl. yeshivot: Institution of higher learning in which the study of the Torah is pursued. Traditionally, there is no set course of study and no graduation, since study of the Torah is supposed to be a lifelong pursuit.

Yiddish: As a consequence of being driven out of Germany and western Europe into eastern Europe, the fleeing Ashkenazi brought to their new homelands their middle-high German language which—especially in religious and ritual circumstances—was mixed with Hebrew and Aramaic. Through the eastward migration of the Ashkenazim, Yiddish absorbed aspects of the Baltic and Slavic languages and developed new linguistic elements; it became the everyday language of the shtetls. Yiddish was, like Ladino of the Sephardim, written with Hebrew characters.

Yishuv: Literally, "living place, settlement." The Jewish population of Palestine before the founding of the State of Israel.

Yom Kippur: Literally, "Day of Atonement." The highest Jewish holiday, peak and ending of the ten days of repentance that began on Rosh Hashannah, spanning the 1st to the 10th day of Tishri. It is observed with fasting and prayer in the synagogue. In the final worship service, the shofar (ram's horn) is blown.

Overview of the History of Judaism

Overview of the History of Judaism

ca. 960–1028 (or 1040) Gershom ben-Judah, the "Light of the Exile"

1040–1105 Rabbi Shlomo ben-Isaac, called Rashi

1090 Emperor Henry IV grants privileges for the Jews in Speyer and Worms

November 27, 1095 Pope Urban II exhorts Christians to the first crusade at the Council of Clermont

1096–99 Destruction of many Jewish communities during the first crusade

11th century Jewish migration from West to East begins in response to the crusades

1135–1024 Rabbi Moses ben-Maimon, called Maimonides

1146 Forcible overthrow of the Almohads on the Iberian peninsula; beginning of mass Jewish emigration

ca. 1150–1217 Judah ben Samuel HeHasid, leading figure of the ethical-mystical piety (the Hasidim) movement in Germany

ca. 1165 Forced conversion to Islam, emergence of a false messiah in Yemen

1172 Letter of consolation from Maimonides to the Jews of Yemen

1194–1270 Rabbi Moses ben-Nachman, known as Nachmanides

13th–15th century Formation of large Jewish communities in northern and central Italy by refugees from southern Italy, Germany, France, Spain, Portugal, and the Levant

1215 Fourth Lateran Council under Pope Innocence III. Renewal and sharpening of anti-Jewish regulations by the Church.

1235 First accusations of ritual murder in Germany (Fulda)

1236 Emperor Frederick II designates Jews "servants of the chamber"

1240–42 Debate and Talmud burning in Paris

1263 Debate of Barcelona

1264 Boleslaus the Pious grants privileges to Polish Jews: Statute of Kalish

ca. 1280 The Book Zohar

1282–97 Sicily (1282) and Sardinia (1297) come under the rule of the Spanish kingdom of Aragon

1290 Jews driven out of England under Edward I

1348–50 Plague pogroms throughout Europe

1391 End of the Seville persecutions in Castile and Aragon

1391–1496/97 Immigration of Spanish and Portuguese refugees into the Magreb (northern Africa)

1394 Jews expelled from France

15th–16th century Jews driven out of most German cities; increase of rural Judaism in Germany; emigration to Poland, Lithuania, and northern Italy

1413–14 Debate of Tortosa

1438 In Fez, Morocco, the first obligatory Jewish quarter is established

1453 Conquest of Constantinople by Sultan Mehmet II

1475 Trient ritual murder incident

1484–1527 Italian Jewish publishers, the Soncinos, expand into different Italian cities

March 31, 1492 Spanish Edict forces all Jews to leave the Spain by July 31, 1492

1492–93 Expulsion of about 40,000 Jews from the Spanish-controlled islands of Sicily and Sardinia

1496–97 Expulsion of the Jews from Portugal

The Renaissance

16th–17th century After the expulsion of the Jews from Spain (1492) and Portugal (1496–97), the Inquisition threatens all "New Christians," or Marranos, especially if they adhere to Jewish customs. Many return to Judaism and emigrate, for example, to the Ottoman empire or to the Netherlands. Amsterdam becomes the "Jerusalem of the West"

Overview of the History of Judaism

ca. 1500–1648 Peak of immigration to eastern Europe and flourishing of Polish-Lithuanian Judaism

1516 Establishment of the first "ghetto" in Venice

1516–48 Daniel Bomberg, Venetian printer

1516–1917 The Holy Land under Ottoman rule

ca. 1525–72 Moses ben-Israel Isserles

1527–30 Gershom Soncino opens printing houses in Salonika and Constantinople

1553 Talmud burning in Rome and Venice

1555 The Church's anti-Jewish policies reach a peak with the bull *Cum nimis absurdum* of Pope Paul IV, which orders the beginning of the ghettoization of the Jews

1564 Sultan Sulayman leases Tiberias and its environs to Don Joseph Nassi to found a Jewish settlement

1568 Book burning in Venice

1578 First printing of the *Shulchan Aruch* with the comments of Moses Isserles in Kracow

1580–1764 Four-country synod organized as an organ of self-determination in Poland

17th–18th century The fall of the Ottoman empire damages conditions for Jews

1602 Founding of the first Sephardic community in Amsterdam

1604–57 Manasseh ben-Israel

to 1623 Self-governing Lithuanian synod

1626 Menasseh ben-Israel founds the first Hebrew printing shop in Amsterdam

1626–76 The "false messiah" Shabbetai Zevi

1635 Founding of Ashkenazi community in Amsterdam

from 1648 Rise of the "Court Jews" in the absolutist German principalities

1648–49 Chmielnicki pogroms in Ukraine, Belorus, Podolia, and Volhynia. Beginning of immigration back toward the west

1630–54 In Pernambuco, a flourishing Jewish community develops under Dutch rule

1654 The Portugese take back Pernambuco and enforce the Inquisition; 23 Jewish refugees from Pernambuco reach New Amsterdam (later New York)

1655–56 From Amsterdam, Manasseh ben-Israel negotiates with Oliver Cromwell for the resettlement of Jews in England

1656 Excommunication (*herem*) of the Dutch philospher Baruch De Spinoza

1671 50 Jewish families driven from Vienna are allowed into Berlin by Margrave of Brandenburg

1698–1738 Josef Süss Oppenheimer

1700–60 Rabbi Israel ben-Eliezer, called Baal Shem Tov ("Master of the Holy Name"), founder of east European Hasidism

1729–86 Moses Mendelssohn

1743/44–1812 Meyer Amschel Rothschild, founder of the world-famous banking house of Rothschild

1772, 1793, 1795 The three Polish divisions

1778 Founding of the Jewish Free School in Berlin

1780–83 Moses Mendelssohn's German translation of the bible is printed

1781 Christian Wilhelm von Dohm, "On the Civic Improvement of the Jews"

1782 "Tolerance Decree" of Emperor Joseph II for the Austrian Jews

1791 Equal civil rights granted French Jews; Catherine II of Russia establishes the Pale of Settlement

1796 Full equality as citizens for Dutch Jews

1796–99 In France, the call for equal civil rights brings about the abolition of ghettos

1801–75 Zacharias Frankel, theoretician of Conservative Judaism

1808–88 Samson Raphael Hirsch, founder of Neo-Orthodoxy

Overview of the History of Judaism

from 1810 First Reformed services in Seesen (1810), Berlin (1815), and Hamburg (1818)

1810–74 Abraham Geiger, advocate of Reform Judaism

1812 Prussian Emancipation Edict

1814–15 Congress of Vienna reinstates discriminatory ordinances against Jews

1819 Hepp-Hepp riots in Germany; founding of the Society for Culture and Knowledge of Judaism in Berlin

from 1820 Mass emigration to central Europe; from 1880 east European Jews emigrate to the United States

1827 Czar Nicholas I requires 25 years of military service from Jews

1840 Damascus affair: Accumulation of accusations of ritual murder in the Ottoman empire

1844–46 Assembly of Reform Rabbis in Braunschweig, Frankfurt, and Breslau

1848 Civil equality for Jews through the Frankfurt National Assembly, reversed after the 1848 Revolution

1851–1939 Publication of the *History and Knowledge of Judaism Monthly*

1854 Founding of the first modern rabbinical seminaries in Germany: the Conservative Jewish Theological Seminary in Breslau

1856 Jews in the Ottoman empire are granted full civil rights

1860 Founding of the Universal Israelite Alliance in France

1862 Moses Hess, *Rome and Jerusalem*

1869–71 Equal civil rights in the North German Alliance and then in the German empire

1872 Founding of the liberal College for the Study of Judaism in Berlin

1873 Founding of the Rabbinical Seminary for Orthodox Judaism in Berlin

1876 The Prussian "Withdrawal Law"

1878 Adolph Stoecker founds the anti-Semitic Christian Socialist Workers' Party; beginning of modern anti-Semitism

1881–82 Pogroms in Russia and the Ukraine, beginning of mass emigration

from 1881 Organizations formed in Russian cities to promote the colonization of Palestine

1882–1908 First immigration waves to Palestine

1882 Russian Jews found the first Jewish colony, Rishon Le-Zion ("First in Zion"), in Palestine

1893 Nathan Birnbaum coins the term "Zionism" for the Jewish nationalist movement.

1894–1906 The Dreyfus Affair in France

1896 Theodor Herzl, *The Jewish State*

1897 First Zionist Congress in Basel; founding of BUND in Poland, the first Socialist (non-Zionist) party in eastern Europe

1905 First publication of the *Protocols of the Elders of Zion*

1909 Founding of Tel Aviv

ca. 1910 The Lower East Side, the Jewish immigrants' quarter of New York City, is the second most thickly settled area in the world, second only to Bombay

1914 The Balfour Declaration

April 1920 The Conference of San Remo gives Great Britain the Mandate over Palestine

1929–48 The Imam Yahya prohibits Yemenite Jews from emigrating

January 1933 Adolf Hitler becomes chancellor of the German Reich, beginning the Nazi regime

April 1933 Boycott of Jewish businesses and practices; law to "Restore Civil Authorities"

September 1933 Founding of the Reich's Agency for German Jews

September 1935 The Nuremberg Race Laws strip Jews of their civil rights

March 1938 "Annexation" of Austria into the German Reich

Overview of the History of Judaism

August 1938 Jews required to add "Israel" or "Sarah" to their official names by January 1939

October 1938 20,000 Polish Jews from Germany are deported to the border station Zbaszyn

November 7, 1938 Polish-Jewish teenager Herschel Grynszpan assassinates Ambassador Ernst von Rath in Paris

May 17, 1939 The British government in a White Paper limits Jewish immigration into Palestine

September 1, 1939 World War II begins with the invasion of Poland

September 1941 Jews in German jurisdiction are forced to wear the yellow star

January 20, 1942 Wannsee Conference

1943 About 44,000 Jews from Salonika in Greece are deported to Auschwitz

April 19, 1943 The Warsaw Ghetto uprising

August 4, 1944 Anne Frank and her family are discovered in their hiding place in Amsterdam and sent to different concentration camps (Anne and her sister Margot perish in Bergen-Belsen barely a month before the camp is liberated by the British)

January 27, 1945 Soviet troops enter Auschwitz

May 7, 1945 Germany surrenders

November 1945–October 1946 War crime trials held at Nuremberg, Germany

November 29, 1947 U.N. General Assembly votes for the division of Palestine

May 14, 1948 David Ben Gurion proclaims the State of Israel; beginning of the War of Independence

1948–73 After the establishment of the State of Israel come mass immigrations of Jews from Islamic countries

1949–50 In the "Operation Flying Carpet," about 50,000 Yemenite Jews are flown into Israel

November 10, 1956 Suez Crisis

1965 Diplomatic relations established between Israel and West Germany

June 5–10, 1967 Six Day War

October 1973 Yom Kippur War

September 1978 Camp David Accord between Israel and Egypt reached through mediation of U.S. President Jimmy Carter

October 6, 1981 Egyptian President Anwar al-Sadat murdered by an Islamic fundamentalist

June 1982 Lebanon War

December 1987 Beginning of the "Intifada"

September 13, 1993 Washington Territory Agreement between Israel and the PLO for increased autonomy in Jericho and Gaza

1994 Establishment of a *Bet Din* (rabbinical court) in Germany

February 25, 1994 Jewish settler Baruch Goldstein murders 29 praying Muslims in the Ibrahim Mosque

May 4, 1994 Israeli Prime Minister Yitzhak Rabin and PLO leader Yasir Arafat sign the Gaza-Jericho Accord

October 26, 1994 Peace agreement between Israel and Jordan

November 4, 1995 Assassination of Prime Minister Yitzhak Rabin after a peace demonstration in Tel Aviv by Jewish student Yigal Amir

1996 Conservative leader Benjamin Netanyahu becomes Prime Minister after defeating Shimon Peres in parliamentary elections

Jewish Museums

Jewish Museums

Amsterdam
Joods Historisch Museum
Jonas Daniel Meijerplein
2–4
1001 RE Amsterdam
Netherlands
Tel. (20)26 99 45

Basel
Jüdisches Museum der
Schweiz
Kornhausgasse 8
4051 Basel
Switzerland
Tel. (61)261 95 14

Berkeley
Judah L. Magnes Memorial
Museum
2911 Russell Street
Berkeley, CA 94705
Tel. (510)84 92 710

Berlin
Jüdisches Museum
Lindenstraße 14
10117 Berlin
Germany
Tel. (30)25 86 28 39

Budapest
Zsidó Múzeum
Dohany utca 2
1075 Budapest
Hungary
Tel. (1)42 13 50

Cologne
Kölnisches Stadtmuseum
Jüdische Abteilung
Zeughausstraße 1-3
50667 Köln
Germany
Tel. (221)23 52

Eisenstadt
Österreichisches Jüdisches
Museum
Wertheimerhaus
Unterbergstraße 6
7000 Eisenstadt
Austria
Tel. (2682)51 45

Frankfurt
Jüdisches Museum
Untermainkai 14–15
60311 Frankfurt
Germany
Tel. (69)2 12–3 50 00

Museum Judengasse
Börneplatz
60311 Frankfurt
Germany
Tel. (69)297 74 19

Hamburg
Museum für Hamburgische
Geschichte
Jüdische Abteilung
Holstenwall 24
20355 Hamburg
Germany
Tel. (40)350 423 60

Hohenems
Jüdisches Museum
Villa Heimann-Rosenthal
Schweizer Straße 5
6845 Hohenems
Austria
Tel. (5576)39 89

Jerusalem
Israel Museum
Rechov Ruppin
P.O.B. 71117
Jerusalem 9170
Israel
Tel. (2)69 82 11

Kracow
Museum Judaistyczne
Stara Synagoga (Old
Synagogue)
ul. Szeroka 24
31–053 Kracow
Poland
Tel. (12)66 05 34

Ghetto Museum
Apteka Pod Orlem
pl. Bohaterów Getta 13
31–053 Kracow
Poland
Tel. (12)56 56 25

London
The Jewish Museum
129 Albert Street
London NW 1
Great Britain
Tel. (171)2 84 19 97

New York
The Jewish Museum
1109 Fifth Avenue
New York, NY 10128
Tel. (212)42 33 200

Paris
Musée d'Art Juif
42, Rue des Saules
75018 Paris
France
Tel. (1)42 57 84 15

Jewish Museums ... Selected Bibliography

Prague
Statni Zidovské muzeum
Jáchymova 3
11001 Prague
Czechia
Tel. (2)231 06 81

Tel Aviv
Beth Hatefutsoth Museum
of the Jewish Diaspora
Rehov Klausner, Ramat Aviv
P.O.B. 39359
Tel Aviv 61392
Israel
Tel. (3)6 46 20 20

Venice
Museo d'Arte Ebraica
Campo di Ghetto Nuovo
Venice
Italy
Tel. (41)71 53 59

Vienna
Jüdisches Museum der Stadt
Wien
Palais Eskeles
Dorotheergasse 11
1150 Vienna 1
Austria
Tel. (1)53 50 43 10

Washington, D.C.
United States Holocaust
Memorial Museum
2000 L Street, NW
Washington, D.C. 20036
Tel. (202)48 80 400
Fax (202)48 82 690

Selected Bibliography

The following bibliography is by no means an exhaustive list of sources for further reading. It is something of a cross-section that will introduce the interested reader to some of the events and topics covered in this book in greater depth.

Ainsztein, Reuben. *The Warsaw Ghetto Revolt.* New York: Holocaust Library, 1979.

Ausubel, Nathan. *Pictorial History of the Jewish People.* New York: Crown Publishers, 1989.

Bachrach, Susan D. *Tell Them We Remember: The Story of the Holocaust.* Boston: Little, Brown, 1994.

Bauer, Yehuda, and Nili Keren. *A History of the Holocaust.* New York: Franklin Watts, 1983.

Bellow, Saul, ed. *Great Jewish Short Stories.* New York: Dell, 1963.

Ben-Sasson, H.H., ed. *A History of the Jewish People.* Cambridge, MA: Harvard University Press, 1976.

Chicago, Judy, with Donald Woodman. *Holocaust Project: From Darkness into Light.* New York: Penguin Books, 1993.

Cohn-Sherbok, Lavinia, and Dan Cohn-Sherbok, eds. *A Short Reader in Judaism.* Oxford: Oneworld, 1996.

Cohn-Sherbok, Lavinia, and Dan Cohn-Sherbok. *A Short History of Judaism.* Oxford: Oneworld, 199?.

Comay, Joan. *Who's Who in Jewish History: After the Period of the Old Testament*, rev. ed. by Lavinia Cohn-Sherbok. New York: Oxford University Press, 1995.

De Vaux, R. *The Early History of Israel to the Period of the Judges.* London: Darton, Longman & Todd, 1978.

Ebban, Abba. *Heritage: Civilization and the Jews.* New York: Summit Books, 1984.

Fast, Howard. *The Jews: Story of a People.* New York: Laurel (Dell), 1968.

Frank, Anne. *The Diary of a Young Girl*, edited by Otto H. Frank and Mirjam Pressler. New York: Doubleday, 1991.

Freedman, Marcia. *Exile in the Promised Land.* New York: Firebrand Books, 1990.

Gilbert, Martin. *The Holocaust: A History of the Jews in Europe during the Second World War.* New York: Henry Holt, 1986.

Goldhagen, Daniel J. *Hitler's Willing Executioners: Ordinary Germans and the Holocaust.* New York: Alfred A. Knopf, 1996.

Harris, Lis. *Holy Days: The World of a Hasidic Family.* New York: Summit Books, 1985.

Hertzberg, Arthur. *The Zionist Idea.* New York: Atheneum, 1986.

Bibliography ... Abbreviations

Herzl, Theodor. *The Jewish State*, trans. by Sylvie d'Avigdor. London: Constable, 1955.

Howe, Irving, and Eliezer Greenberg, eds. *Voices from the Yiddish*. New York: Schocken Books, 1975.

Howe, Irving, ed. *Jewish American Stories*. New York: New American Library, 1977.

Howe, Irving. *World of Our Fathers: The Journey of the East European Jews to America and the Life They Found and Made*, revised ed. New York: Schocken Books, 1989.

Jacobs, Louis. *The Book of Jewish Belief*. New York: 1984.

Jacobs, Louis. *The Book of Jewish Practice*. New York: 1987.

Jacobs, Louis. *The Jewish Religion: A Companion*. Oxford: Oxford University Press, 1995.

Klepfisz, Herzel. *Culture of Compassion: The Spirit of Polish Jewry from Hasidism to the Holocaust*, trans. by Curt Leviant. New York: KTAV, 1983.

Krausz, Ernest, ed. *The Sociology of the Kibbutz*. New Brunswick, NJ: Transaction Books, 1983.

Mendelssohn, Moses. *Jerusalem and Other Jewish Writings*, trans. by A. Jospe. New York: Schocken Books, 1969.

Newman, Louis I., trans. *The Hasidic Anthology: Tales and Teachings of the Hasidim*. New York: Schocken Books, 1963.

Oz, Amos. *In the Land of Israel*. London: Fontana Paperbacks, 1983.

Potok, Chaim. *Wanderings: Chaim Potok's History of the Jews*. New York: Fawcett Crest, 1984.

Rapoport, Nessa. *Preparing for Sabbath*. Sunnyside, NY: Biblio Press, 1981.

Roskics, Diane K., and David G. Roskics. *The Shtetl Book*. New York: KTAV, 1979.

Roth, Cecil, and Geoffrey Wigoder, eds. *Encyclopedia Judaica*, 16 vols. Jerusalem: 1972.

Sachar, Howard M. *A History of Israel: From the Rise of Zionism to Our Time*. New York: Alfred A. Knopf, 1986.

Samuel, M. *The World of Sholom Aleichem*. New York: Alfred A. Knopf, 1944.

Scholem, G. *Major Trends in Jewish Mysticism*. New York: Schocken Books, 1995.

Silver, Jeremy, and Bernard Martin. *A History of Judaism*, 2 vols. New York: 1974.

Singer, Isaac Bashevis. *An Isaac Bashevis Singer Reader*. New York: Farrar, Straus and Giroux, 1981.

Waskow, Arthur I. *Seasons of Our Joy: A Handbook of Jewish Festivals*. New York: Summit Books, 1982.

Zborowski, Mark, and Elizabeth Herzog. *Life Is with People: The Culture of the Shtetl*. New York: Schocken Books, 1952.

Abbreviations

BC	Common, or Christian, era
BCE	Before the Common, or Christian, era
Deut	Deuteronomium
Ex	Exodus
Gen	Genesis
Lev	Leviticus
Num	Numeri
Ps	Book of Psalms
RaMBaM	Maimonides (Moses ben Maimon)
Sam	Book of Samuel

Subject Index

Subject Index

Subject Index

Index of Names

Index of Names

Index of Names

Index of Names ... Picture Credits

Picture credits

Picture Credits

Jewish Historical Museum, Amsterdam 65, 132, 133, 163, 165, 166, 167 (Photo: Han Singels), 168 (Photo: J. Nooter), 195

Jewish Museum, Prague 211 a–c

Jewish National and University Library, Jerusalem 60, 98

John Rylands University Library of Manchester 3

Judah L. Magnes Museum, Berkeley, California 138, 143, 154

Judaica Museum Wien, Sammlung Berger 19, 202, 206

Jüdisches Kulturmuseum Augsburg 204

Jüdisches Museum der Schweiz, Basel 159

Jüdisches Museum Frankfurt 199

Jüdisches Museum Westfalen, Dorsten 158 , 209, 235

Kaplan, Jewgenija, St. Petersburg 122

Kölnisches Stadtmuseum, Köln 160

Kralisch, Winfrid, Köln 78

Künzl, Hannelore 46, 74, 115, 117, 170, 174 (two illustrations)

Sarajevo Museum 4

Leo Baeck Institute, New York 214

Library of the Jewish theological Seminary of America, New York (Photos: Suzanne Kaufman) 81, 153, 196

Macht, Jiri, Prag 75

Marx & Co, Berlin 135

Moni Haramati-Air Photography, Tel Aviv 35, 36

Musée du Louvre, Paris 144

Musée National des Thermes et de l'Hotel de Cluny, Paris 155

Museum Boymans-van Beuningen, Rotterdam 173

Museum für Kunst und Gewerbe, Hamburg (Photo: Maria Thrun) 176

Nathans, Rhoda 124

Oronoz, Madrid 59

Österreichisches Staatsarchiv-Kriegsarchiv, Wien 101

Peitsch, Peter, Hamburg 180

Photographique de la Reunion des Musees Nationaux, Paris 27

Radovan, Zev, Jerusalem 34, 37

Reuter, Ursula , Köln 120, 193, 197

Rheinisches Bildarchiv, Köln 14, 67, 69, 83, 84, 227, 230

Sammlung William L. Gross, Ramat Aviv (Photo: Zev Radovan) 152

Schmitz, Heinz , Köln 39, 45

Schwarberg, Günther 234

Staatliches Ethnographisches Museum, St. Petersburg 17, 95, 105, 108, 110, 112, 114

Stadtarchiv Worms 72, 73, 80

Stichting Vrienden van het Mauritshuis, Den Haag 172

Stiftskirche St. Augustin, Austria, Klosterneuburg 10

The Nasser D. Khalili Collection of Islamic Art, London (Photo: Ch. Phillips) 61

The Sir Isaac Wolfson Museum, Hechal Shlomo, Jerusalem 106, 109

Ullstein Bilderdienst, Berlin 244, 246

Universität Köln, Martin-Buber-Institut für Judaistik 126

van der Meulen, Erika, Köln 212

Vishniac, Roman 102, 103

Vrienden Portugees-Israëlietische Synagoge, Amsterdam 169, 171

Yiro, New York 113

Zardoya, Barcelona 96, 239

Zoktowska-Huszoza, Teresa, Krakau 89

© VG Bild-Kunst, Bonn 1996: 8, 236

All rights for illustrations not mentioned here belong to the author, the publisher, or could not be located.